LOVE IS THE MESSAGE

In a psychic's footsteps

Published by: Love Publishing.
Suite 188, 16 Cotham Rd
Kew, Vic 3101
Fax: (03) 9853 7722
Email: kew@mbe.com.au

Copyright ©2002 Paula Armstrong

Designed by: Rhett Nacson
Printed and bound in Australia by: Griffin Press

ISBN: 0-646-41961-7

LOVE
IS THE
MESSAGE
In a psychic's footsteps

Paula Armstrong

DEDICATION

*So many people to be thanked
and blessed for holding the
dream for me, among them:
Four beloved children, their fathers,
my family, my beloved partner and
best friend Geoffrey, all my loving friends in
Malaysia, Singapore, New Zealand and Australia.
Most of all, Guruji,
I thank thee.*

ACKNOWLEDGMENTS

Grateful acknowledgements are due to the following persons who have inspired, supported and influenced me.

Dr. Deepak Chopra, Dr. Wayne Dyer, Dr. Leonard Laskow, His Holiness The Dalai Lama, Ms. Denise Linn, Mr. Stuart Wilde, Mr. Benjamin Creme, Ms. Marianne Williamson, Ms. Louise Hay, Dr. Jean Houston, Swamiji, The Sisters of Mercy Nuns, Mr. Martin Nowell, Mr. Gareth McSweeney and Matt Vella at MBE Business Service Centre Kew, Mr. Stephen Roache, Mr. Francis Zemljak, Ms. Inga Salins, Mr. Geoffrey Waite, Ms. Mary Lloyd, Mr. James Goulding, Mr. Hugh Crago, Mr. Leon Nacson, Mr. Rhett Nacson, Professor Christopher Chen, Ms. Stella Yfantidis Chen and to all my clients over the years who have taught me so much,

Thank you and God bless you.

PREFACE

Beloved reader,

I've been motivated and inspired to write this book describing an ordinary woman's extraordinary journey towards self-actualisation. During the writing of this book, I understood that the search for the Beloved, for love, for the awakening of the Divine nature inside myself, had always been the driving force in my life.

I started out on a journey of self-discovery and have finally found myself.

It's my feeling that as primitive man once turned his face in wonder to the Sun, which was his God, in the New Millennium the Divine nature in man and woman will turn their faces and their hearts towards God. God is Love and Love is God.

Above all things, each human being longs for love, to love and to be loved. Love is the purpose for living.

If you care to follow in my footsteps, walk through the pages of my life, holding my hand, it's my fervent prayer that we'll both walk towards the Divine and go home together, back to the Source of Love.

May Love be with you, my Beloved, as we walk this path together. May all the enlightened Beings who have ever walked this path before, bless us on our journey towards wholeness.

TABLE OF CONTENTS

CHAPTER I

A PSYCHIC CHILDHOOD

GENTLE GHOST: SURVIVAL EVIDENCE

My grandmother and her younger sister were close friends. Both girls were psychic and intuitive.

"The Downey girls are both 'fey' their old auntie and uncle said to their neighbours.

The girls' mother and father had died tragically in a motoring accident when the girls were small and had left auntie and uncle guardians and executors of their substantial estate.

My grandmother remembered her father's huge house in London, her mother's exquisite furs, the family silver, the army of servants, her father's booming laughter and tickling moustache.

When their parents died, the two little girls were taken to Ireland where their aunt and uncle lived.

The two small orphans clung to each other in their grief and vowed never to be parted.

They both promised each other that whoever married first would take the other sister to live in her home.

They made a sacred pact with each other that if one died, she would return to give her sister evidence of her survival after death.

The younger girl was married first and as she'd promised, took her sister, my grandmother, to live in her new house with her.

The new husband was delighted as he'd grown fond of his new sister-in-law and regarded her as a friend.

The two girls felt that now life would be good to them, and the loss of their Mama and Papa faded into the rich background of their new lives.

The young husband invested wisely with his wife's money and permission, and longed for adventure in a new land.

He decided to migrate to Australia, where several of his friends had moved and had written well of the country.

Auntie and uncle had both passed away within twelve months of each other, so the sisters had no more ties with England or Ireland. They both felt they were leaving all the sadness behind them when they sailed out of England.

The move was made and they settled in Sydney, having purchased a large and beautiful home, with the expectation of a large family and an Australian husband for my grandmother.

The time came not too long after they settled in to their new country, when the young bride joyfully announced the imminent arrival of an Australian baby. The sisters thanked God for their happiness.

The little boy was about three weeks of age when his mother took him for a quiet walk after lunch, one rainy wintry day in Sydney. She decided to cross the busy street to browse in front of the shop-windows on the other side of the road, a new hat for her sister's birthday on her mind.

Engrossed and pre-occupied, she stepped out behind a bus to cross the road, not seeing the large black car bearing down on her in the rain.

The driver saw her too late, braked, and the car skidded.

Upon seeing the car, with a mother's impulse, my grandmother's sister pushed the pram with the sleeping baby sharply to the opposite kerb, hard.

Providence stopped the pram so that the baby was not harmed, but his mother was struck by another car.

She died instantly.

At home, her sister staggered a little and grabbed her chest, struck by a chill. She knew that some disaster had struck, but did not know it was so close to home.

Witnesses to the tragedy cared for the crying new-born baby until police searched his mother's handbag and found her identification. My grandmother stayed calm upon being informed of the news that broke her heart, and focussed on supporting the young husband and trying to persuade the baby to drink from a bottle. All day, the young husband and his little son cried, and both slept an exhausted sleep that evening.

My grandmother slept on a folding bed in the baby's nursery, tossing and turning, her rosary-beads clutched in her hands, praying for the soul of her sister to ascend to Heaven.

The baby whimpered from time to time.

Deep shadows filled the corners of the room and the night-light wove strange, distorted shapes.

Something woke my grandmother instantly.

A shiver ran up her back and across her scalp. A dog howled somewhere in the still night.

"What was it?" She thought, frozen.

A white mist hovered around the baby's cradle and as she watched, it formed itself into her dead sister.

As she gasped, the ghostly form turned slowly in her direction and held out its shaking hand.

She stared long and hard at her dead sister.

The ghost was clad in a long white gown.

"Is it her shroud? Or is it a sheet that covers her?" She thought. The pathetic girl's fine blonde hair hung tangled down her back. My grandmother noticed that she looked cold. Her hands shook and her small feet were white and bare. Pity ran through the grieving sister.

My grandmother threw the bed-clothes back and stood up quickly, calling softly:

"Darling heart, is it really you?"

The ghost spoke in a whisper:

"It's me, Dolly. Remember our promise? I've come back."

My grandmother was astonished.

It was true! Her sister had managed to cross the bridge between life and death and had come back to prove that she had survived death.

It wasn't just all over. She had survived!

My grandmother had so many questions to ask and moved towards her sister, her arms outstretched, wanting to touch the quivering girl.

The ghost moved back sharply and said:

"No, Dolly! Stop! No further.

You must not touch me or come any closer.

My energy's not strong enough to maintain the materialisation for long. I've only got a moment to ask you to look after my son. Tell him how I loved him, that I'll always watch over him and protect him.

Please Dolly, pray for me. Offer Masses for me, I love you. It's all right. We must let go of each other now, sweetie. We'll meet again.

Tell Gill I'm all right. Tell him it didn't hurt me at all; dying doesn't hurt.

Remember always how much I love you."

After a long and loving look down at the small baby in his cradle, the gentle ghost began to de-materialise like smoke in a breeze. My grandmother fell to the floor and cried.

She told me that a sweet light went out of the world with her sister's passing, and she missed her physical presence and her loving personality very much, but she believed that her sister's soul lived on in the spiritual realm.

My grandmother looked after the new baby for a time, until the young husband married again.

His new wife and my grandmother became good friends and both were aware of the angelic mother who looked after the baby in spirit. In time, my grandmother found her own husband and had her own family to look after, but her gentle little sister always occupied a special place in her heart.

The gift of clairvoyance my grandmother and her sister shared, passed down to me and to my children in varying degrees.

My grandmother told me it was her belief that the gift had always been in our family, as her old aunt and uncle had told her:

"All the Downeys and their kith and kin have always had the gift."

It was normal and natural for us to see, to sense and to feel deeply, things that others could not.

It seemed so unnatural to us that others were blind and insensitive.

This sensitivity was at times a curse as well as a blessing.

THE ANGEL OF DEATH

After the death of her younger sister, and looking after the new baby until his father married again eighteen months later, my grandmother met an Englishman visiting Sydney on business who was twenty-one years older than herself.

She found herself completely overawed by his sophisticated and flattering attentions and after seeking her brother-in-law's advice, soon succumbed to his charm.

She made a beautiful bride, glowing and radiant in snowy white tulle and antique lace.

A world honeymoon followed, on an elegant ocean-liner.

My grandmother told me wryly that:

"Your grandpapa flirted with all the female passengers even on our honeymoon, the rascal."

Fortunately, she and her husband liked each other very much and their eccentric marriage endured for more than half a century. When my grandmother died, grandpapa followed her a scant twelve months later, declaring:

"Life has lost its lustre without my darling in it."

I remember as a young woman at a party, my grandpapa going down on one knee to my grandmother, before the guests, singing to her:

"If you were the only girl in the world…." and he kissed her hand.

Everyone agreed they were a handsome couple.

Within nine months of the marriage, upon their return from Europe, my grandmother was delivered of a small and weak baby boy.

The labour had been long and painful, and my grandmother's screams broke her husband's heart.

The baby was pale and exhausted by his ordeal.

My grandmother refused to allow the midwife and nurse to take the tiny scrap of humanity away from her, willing him to live.

She told me he was too weak to suckle, so she expressed a little milk into his mouth at every opportunity.

She prayed intently for the baby's life, between dozing and encouraging him to swallow her life-giving milk.

At about 2 am. on his third day of life, she awoke with a shiver, at once wide awake and aware of a spirit presence in the room. She held her son closer to her, protecting him from something she intuitively knew meant danger.

A tall, dark form with dark eyes, stepped out of a dim corner and approached the bed where the quivering mother and sleeping baby lay.

The tall, dark stranger spoke whisperingly in her mind:

"I am the Angel of Death.

I have come for the baby in your arms.

It is time for you to let go of your hold upon him."

She sat up, eyes wide and called out to her husband:

"Paddy, Paddy, come quickly. Help me!"

No-one in the house heard her call.

My grandmother watched helplessly in horror, as a dark shadow crossed the tiny infant's face and it gasped a tiny breath, then breathed no more.

Its mother cried out harshly:

"No! No! Don't take him. God! God help me! Mary, Mother of God! Not my baby. No! Please, not my baby!"

The little one lay limp and cold.

The sad, dark stranger stepped back into the shadows and was gone.

It was many months before my grandmother stopped crying, and only the birth of a strong, plump little girl made her smile again. Grandpapa said the little girl was a noble looking child. The little girl thrived on her mother's rich milk and was a model baby.

In time, my grandmother could relax and sleep at night, though she still kept the baby near to her at all times.

She refused to let anyone else care for the child until her second little daughter made her entry into the world.

My grandfather travelled often, supervising his extensive international business investments and was forced to leave his growing family alone for long periods of time. My grandmother was resigned to the fact that he wouldn't be lonely while he was travelling, and she continued to find joy, love and satisfaction in her two little girls.

She had a glorious singing voice. Her aunt and uncle had encouraged this natural talent by engaging various tutors as she'd grown up. She'd also learnt violin and piano.

During her husband's long absences, she continued to study voice and piano with a teacher in Sydney. We all grew up around the Steinway piano and later I too had singing lessons, as I'd inherited my grandmother's soprano voice.

MY MOTHER IS BORN

When her oldest girl was eight years of age and her second girl was six years of age, a third little girl was born.

This baby came easily and quickly into the world, causing her grateful mother little discomfort; a fact that made her even more lovable to her young mother.

This child was my mother.

The two older girls loved their baby sister and treated her like a little doll.

The three little girls were as intuitive as their mother. They made fairy-gardens and saw angels, devas and benevolent spirits all around them, as I later would.

They were brought up as devout Catholics and under their mother's guidance had a special devotion to Mary. They always burnt a lamp or votive candle beneath a Marian altar as they grew up.

My mother grew up almost without knowing her father, as his business interests kept him abroad for most of her childhood. She attended a Catholic girls' school with her sisters and was a sweet-natured and innocent girl.

When she was about sixteen years of age, a young English sailor in his twenties began talking to her on her way home from school, a friendship blossomed between them rapidly, unknown to her mother or older sisters.

Friendship kindled to love and the conception of a baby was the result. Suffice to say it was a scandal at the time.

The young sailor went back to England with his ship, vowing to return as soon as he could.

One Sunday in May 1949, my mother was dispatched to a convent to await the birth of her baby.

She told me how she found comfort and peace in the dim, quiet and serene chapel, in front of Mary's altar, where she felt that only Mary understood her plight.

As the birth date came closer, my mother was brought home to Sydney by her family.

Those quiet months surrounded by spirituality and prayer, no doubt had a deep influence on the developing baby in her womb.

The young man returned from England in late October with a letter from his parents, giving their blessings to the young couple.

The two young lovers appealed to my mother's family for their blessings and permission to marry.

My grandmother and grandfather gave in.

As my mother was almost ready to give birth, it was of necessity a private wedding in the sacristy of the Mary Chapel adjoining the local Church. The young lovers were married just in time.

I AM BORN

In November 1949, in a Catholic hospital near home, my mother's trial began.

After twenty-two hours of suffering, I was dragged, protesting loudly, into the world by doctors with steel instruments. My mother was too exhausted to be interested in me at first, so it was my grandmother's arms that first held me. She nursed my mother lovingly during those early weeks.

Upon her homecoming my grandmother insisted that my mother rest and stay with her until she'd recovered from the difficult birth.

My parents agreed to stay in my grandmother's large and beautiful home near the beach until my mother was strong enough to establish her own home.

When I became spiritually mature, I realised that this young woman who became my mother, had been my companion and my teacher in many lifetimes on Earth.

It's fascinating to note that as the Buddhists say, we drink from the river of forgetfulness when we take on birth, so we didn't recognise each other. This is no doubt the way it was supposed to be.

From my birth, my grandmother felt a bond with me. She believed she was destined to be my spiritual guardian and teacher until the next teacher came along in my maturity and took her responsibility towards me very seriously.

My mother was afraid her strong-willed mother would take her child away from her, and as it later turned out, her fears were justified.

During my second week of life while my mother slept, my grandmother took me to an astrologer to have my birth chart and horoscope drawn up. We went to a phrenologist to have the bones of my head and facial features studied.

Then we went to a palmist who read my small palms. All these findings verified the messages she'd been receiving from the spirit realm, that this infant had extraordinary gifts.

MY FIRST PARANORMAL EXPERIENCE

My grandmother told me my first paranormal experience occurred during my second week of life in her home by the sea.

Apparently, this house was well known to be haunted, which explains my mother's reluctance to stay there with a new baby.

Haunted houses held no fears for my grandmother.

The psychic phenomena began to intensify as soon as I was brought home from the hospital.

I was placed in a pram on the wide, wooden verandah for a sun-bath in the early morning.

Heavy footsteps were heard on the wooden steps going up to the verandah, then the footsteps encircled my pram. A loud, persistent knocking was heard on the front door.

I cried loudly at this intrusion, but no-one physical was to be seen.

This annoying spirit phenomenon persisted several times a day and I became increasingly distressed and unsettled the more it happened. My mother found that once my pram was taken inside the front hall, the footsteps and knocking ceased, and I was able to sleep peacefully.

My family moved house shortly after this experience, as my mother and grandmother felt the spirit was disturbing me too much and my grandmother wanted to keep my mother and I with her, as my father had returned to sea.

PSYCHIC MILESTONE

My first conscious memory of this lifetime is of an experience I had at about two years of age. This memory is very clear in my mind. I used to sleep in my grandmother's big bed with her. One night she was entertaining some friends, and I lay in her bed with the door ajar, listening quite peacefully to the adults' talking and laughing.

A very bright light above my head captured my attention. It appeared from nowhere.

When I sat up and curiously looked at the light, I saw the disembodied head of an elderly man with a long white beard. His beard was at that moment tickling my nose. I also noticed he was wearing a funny hat on his head.

I was frightened and yelled loudly for my grandmother. She rushed in immediately, accompanied by several of her guests and took in the scene with a glance. No-one else could see what she and I were seeing. She sent everyone out, sat on the bed, held me in her arms and rocked me while I cried.

The light soon faded and the vision of the elderly man disappeared. I told my grandmother between sobs what I'd seen.

She said to me:

"It's scary for you now, little girl.

One day you'll understand that what you saw was a good spirit from your future.

Pray now to baby Jesus and sleep, my darling."

She rocked and sang to me until I fell asleep, my pillow wet with tears.

This vision was a premonition of the Teacher I would meet in forty-three years time, who would totally transform my life.

When I met this Teacher in 1994, I told him about my childhood vision.

He smiled and said to me:

"I waited a very long time for you to grow up, little girl." It was only then I realised my Teacher had been watching over me all my life, blessing and protecting me, until the Divine finally brought us together when it was time.

How mysterious and wondrous are the workings of the Divine.

As I grew up, I became the darling of my aunts and their wide circle of friends, as well as of my grandmother's circle, including the actors, singers and musicians who frequented our house.

My grandmother held 'soirees' and Sydney celebrities often attended. As she was also practising as a clairvoyant spiritual healer during her husband's absence, our home was a busy place.

ANNE BANCROFT

When I was about three months of age, my grandmother and her three daughters were having a meal at a Sydney hotel, when an attractive American woman dining with a party of local celebrities, came up to the table and said:

"Pardon me, I can't help noticing the beautiful eyes of that baby. Could I hold her for a moment, please?"

My grandmother was amused that the elegant lady thought she was the mother of the little baby.

The lady who held me in early 1950 was Anne Bancroft, whom I later saw in the movie 'The Graduate' as Mrs. Robinson with Dustin Hoffman, and in '84 Charing Cross Road' with Anthony Hopkins.

During my early childhood years there were many unusual and strange incidents that were difficult for a small girl to deal with, but my beautiful wise and loving grandmother was always there to hold me in her arms, to pray with me, to explain things and to comfort me.

My mother was very unhappy that my grandmother wanted to bring me up in her house, according to her ways.

My sweet, young mother loved me dearly and knew well the suffering that lay ahead of me on the spiritual path. She so much wanted to spare me life's suffering. Those who walk this path, walk the 'razor's edge' and are often very lonely. She wanted me to have the chance to grow up as a normal child, to be allowed to enjoy a carefree life as any other little girl.

However, she didn't reckon with the iron will and sheer determination of her mother.

When I was about six years of age, my grandmother won custody of me in a court in Sydney, saying my mother was too young to raise me by herself as my father was away at sea a lot of the time.

She got her way, as she'd foreseen she would.

My English grandparents also sued for custody, but weren't successful. The battle between my mother and my grandmother did not end there.

After the court decision, my mother stayed in my grandmother's home to do what she could to normalise my life.

I have vivid and heart-breaking memories of feeling torn between the two women I loved most in the world. I loved both my mother and my grandmother and didn't want to be forced to choose one over the other.

I couldn't choose.

No doubt, this was the result of karma between them. I only knew it made me unhappy.

MY SISTER IS BORN

After one of my father's trips home, my mother was delivered of a second daughter whom I adored and carried about whenever no-one was watching.

My father bought a new house near my grandmother's house and my mother and the new baby went to live there. She wasn't going to let go of her second little girl. I remained with my grandmother.

My little sister and I, two years in age difference, grew up mostly apart. When my mother came to visit me, my sister and I played very happily together. We were close friends even though I grew up in comparative luxury and was quite spoiled.

I secretly envied my little sister for being able to live with our parents and for not being wanted by my grandmother. My grandmother wasn't very interested in my little sister. Apparently, my little sister didn't inherit the second sight, but was 'normal'.

When I was five, I attended a convent school and was educated by the nuns.

As I matured, I took extra classes in music, singing, languages, (Latin, French and German), elocution, the classics and art. These were all moves initiated by my grandmother as part of my education in preparation for the world.

I had private ballet lessons and grew to love physical movement. My spiritual education went along hand in hand with my scholastic studies. I later came to understand that my education, guided by my grandmother, was of body, mind, spirit, and truly wholistic. My grandmother was ahead of her time in the way she viewed education for a girl.

I was at this time in my younger years, also constantly experiencing visions and visitations by the angelic spirits. Several memories stand out in my mind.

GUARDIAN ANGEL

I was aware that I'd long had a Guardian Angel called Michael, who'd told me his name in a dream.

Michael watched over me while I slept and often finished my prayers for me when I fell asleep.

To me he was a shimmering, tall pillar of light who spoke to me in my heart. I have during my lifetime seen many angelic beings. They are accompanied by a feeling of deep peace and serenity, golden light and far away beautiful music.

I'd always been aware of my special angel in my auric-field and thought all children had a friend like Michael to talk to.

Having a guardian angel as friend and companion seemed normal and natural to me.

Every night, I said my prayer to my guardian angel before I slept:

"Angel of God, my guardian dear, to whom God's love commits me here. Ever this night, be at my side, to light and guard, to rule and guide. Amen."

When I slept with my grandmother in her big bed, I fell asleep to the gentle whispering of her prayers, feeling safe and comforted.

I was aware that God spoke to me through my dreams and was told by my grandmother very early in life, of the importance of dreams and how to understand the messages they contain.

Every morning at the breakfast table, she'd say:

"Tell me about your dreams," we would interpret them together until I was familiar with the process and understood their meaning for myself.

Dream recall and interpretation was a very powerful resource I grew to appreciate more as I grew up. I know that God speaks to us every night through the higher mind, giving us direction and guidance in all areas of our lives, through dreams and visions.

Whenever I had a problem I was instructed by my grandmother to:

"Ask God for a dream that will guide you, that will show you the solution in a simple way."

Sure enough, the dream would come. It still does.

THE SPIRIT PRIEST

One day, when I was about seven years of age, I arrived home from school and as I passed our lounge-room, I noticed an elderly priest dressed in black sitting on the couch. He smiled to me and waved. I nodded my head and smiled and went into the kitchen to greet my grandmother.

When I asked if the nice priest was having dinner with us as they often did, she asked me:

"What priest, darling? Did you see someone?"

I replied: "The nice old priest who's sitting in the front room. He smiled and waved at me."

She said in a puzzled voice:

"There's no-one here except you and I. He must be from the spirit realm. There'll be a meaning to this."

We both went into the front room and she was right.

He must have been a spirit. The room was empty.

A faint odour of incense lingered tantalisingly in the air. My grandmother said:

"He came to bless you, little one, don't be worried."

I was to see this elderly priest a few more times during my childhood and always felt he was a loving and benevolent spirit. My grandmother said he came to bless our house and to remove any negative vibrations brought by people who came for healing or for counselling. We all became used to our spirit priest.

MY FAIRY GARDEN

My grandmother helped me one summer to build a fairy garden of my own under a sprawling fig tree in our large backyard.

As we planted tiny violets and purple pansies, she told me:

"The fairies like purple best of all, my darling."

We made a miniature rockery and a fairy-sized pond for the fairies to play in.

I loved my fairy garden and spent many happy hours there with all my dolls around me, talking to myself quite happily until dusk.

I felt the light and gentle love of the little fairies all around me, and grew accustomed to the darting flashes of light that danced before my eyes.

Even as an adult, whenever I felt sad or troubled, I would sense the sweet subtle energies of the fairy spirits in roses and would feel comforted.

I felt sad that other children couldn't see what I saw, and felt as if my grandmother and I were the only people in the whole world who could see.

I've often felt like this as an adult, too!

As well as the good, kind and loving angelic spirits around me, I also sometimes sensed an ominous, dark, frightening presence that oppressed me.

THE DARK MAN WHO HAUNTED MY CHILDHOOD

For as long as I can remember, a vision of a tall, dark stranger dressed in black had haunted me.

When I was a child, he appeared in my dreams and I would feel a sense of creeping cold and paralysis, and wake up screaming.

At other times just after falling asleep, I would feel a dark heavy presence sitting on my chest suffocating me, and after what felt like an eternity I could scream and wake myself up.

I was very afraid of him and told my grandmother of my fear.

She listened intently and said:

"We'll pray for God's protection on your sleep, my darling. We'll sprinkle holy water on the bed every night. That may keep him away. Trust in God, little girl."

Sometimes, it'd be months before he came again and I'd begin to relax.

Then, there he was again.

As if the dreams weren't enough to disturb me, he began to appear in the daytime as well.

I became afraid to look in mirrors because I'd see him standing right behind me watching me, and if I spun around, he'd rapidly de-materialise.

Once I caught a glimpse of a sword at his side.

The dark man didn't touch me or approach me too closely, yet I disliked him intensely.

My grandmother and I couldn't work out why he came or what it meant.

When my next Teacher came into my life when I was forty-five years of age, he taught me how to deal with this troubling spirit menace, by banishing him to the spirit realm.

As a child, my grandmother told me often:

"You must have no fear of these things. Be strong. Have faith. You carry the sacred triangle of psychic protection in your palms. Nothing can hurt you! Fear's an illusion. Don't give any power to fear."

It's interesting and relevant to relate at this point that far off in my future, two other people would see my dark man.

When I was grown up and married, my daughter saw him, sword at his side, in a mirror and screamed. I'd never told any of my children about my own childhood or about any of the visions that had haunted me. Yet at age fourteen, my daughter saw him and described him in the same way I'd described him to my grandmother as a small child. I took the same measures of spiritual protection for her as were done for me.

Much later, overseas in Malaysia in 1996, a gifted Indian psychic had a dream about a dark man who meant harm and danger to me. It wasn't long after this that the man left me finally. I was free of the dark stranger looking over my shoulder for the first time in forty-five years. It took a few more years before I could believe I was truly free.

It's my feeling the dark man was symbolic of death.

It occurred to me that he may have been the same dark and handsome Angel of Death who took my grandmother's baby son such a long time ago.

SEEING COLOURS

As a small girl, I was accustomed to seeing the colours around people, that my grandmother told me were called 'auras'.

I used to be quite happy looking at people on the buses and trains, watching their auras pulsing, blending, shifting, merging, expanding and contracting.

Occasionally, I'd encounter a 'dark' person as I called them, and would bury my head in my grandmother's lap.

I intuitively knew whom to trust and whom to avoid.

"This is the gift of discernment," my grandmother told me.

CROSS-ROADS

As a child, I found it difficult not being able to explain to other people the things I was seeing. I hated funerals and grave-yards because I'd see disembodied spirits hovering around, trying to attract people's attention. I found this very distressing. I avoided cross-roads and traffic junctions as I often saw accidents and fatalities being re-enacted over and over.

The tragic images were superimposed on today's scene, and sometimes it became confusing to differentiate between yesterday and today. When accidents happen, the disembodied spirits gather at these energy points and remain trapped. They attempt to draw human lives towards themselves, so that they can continue to live through humans.

At cross-roads, if I see a tragic accident that's occurred somewhere in Time, I ask the Divine to send the spirits on.

TIME TRAVEL

One day when I was about six or seven years of age, I was happily playing in my bath when the bathroom wall appeared to open like a window in Time!

I was looking at a large strong-looking man in strange clothes hammering out a sword on an anvil. I stared at him, fascinated. I could feel the heat from the fire he was stoking. I could smell his sweat and other faintly unpleasant smells, and I could hear his loud rhythmic hammering.

I was watching all this like a movie until he saw me!

He dropped his hammer in shock and stared at me, at a small girl with long dark hair, sitting in her bath surrounded by plastic ducks and floaty toys in the twentieth century.

He yelled something at me in another language. I screamed in fright and my grandmother came running.

She always seemed to be close at hand when I needed her.

She snatched me up out of the water and took me out of the bathroom.

As she crooned to me and wrapped me in her fluffy dressing-gown, she explained that the man was from the past and that he got a bad fright too, seeing me appear in my bath from the twentieth century in his iron-monger's shop.

This sort of time travel happened occasionally for me and we'd always write down what I'd seen. It lost its fear for me after a while, and I was usually able to leave the scene before anyone saw me. I wondered if the blacksmith had been psychic, too.

FIRST HOLY COMMUNION

As a child, my spiritual training included attending Mass with my grandmother, praying before food to raise the vibrations, praying before sleep, religious instruction by the nuns, as well as having my visions and dreams explained to me by my grandmother. This was a full and busy schedule for a child.

Friendships with other children my age were not always easy, due to the fact that some parents thought I was a strange child. Nevertheless, I played with many nice girls and boys who were fascinated by my stories that they thought I made up.

The nuns thought I had a vivid and colourful imagination and some of them even encouraged its development, so I was a very fortunate girl in many ways.

I enjoyed a fairly happy childhood, though I missed my mother and father.

I spent most of my school holidays with my parents, or my mother and my sister came and stayed with me, so life went along very nicely, until I was about seven years of age.

It was traditional for Catholic children to make their first Holy Communion at seven years of age, and I was very excited and happy when my turn came.

I wore a new white lace party dress, white socks with white patent-leather shoes, and a wreath of white silk roses on a white veil on my hair. I felt very holy, very pretty and special. I loved Jesus very much.

The nuns fussed over us outside the little church, re-tying sashes, straightening veils, tucking in little escaping locks of hair, brushing shoes, determined that we looked our very best.

Finally, we filed quietly into the church, trying not to notice our families turning around to look at us, all of us suddenly self-conscious and shy.

One by one, little girls on one side and little boys on the other, we made our way quietly up to the communion-rail where father waited patiently to give each child the tiny round wafer of shiny bread that was, we were told, now miraculously transformed into God.

As my turn came to walk to the communion-rail, it was no longer Father I saw.

I saw a young boy, a little taller than me, about my age, wearing a shining white gown with long sleeves, with brown hair and beautiful eyes, smiling at me and reaching out to hug me.

I had such a wonderful feeling, such a burst of warmth and love inside my chest that I cried with the joy of it.

"It's Jesus!" I thought.

"It's Jesus, He's come to see me take my first Holy Communion!"

So it wasn't a priest who gave me my first Holy Communion at age seven, but Jesus Himself who so tenderly placed the little wafer on my tongue.

The nuns said to me at our celebration breakfast:

"Your dear little face was radiant, child. What happened? You stood so long and so still in the aisle that Mother Anne wanted to poke you."

I told them I'd seen Jesus and they were amazed.

Some of them believed me, some thought I might have imagined my vision or made it up, but they loved the idea of it anyway.

I was in no doubt. I never cared whether anyone believed me or not, and I still don't!

It was funny how Jesus seemed to grow up as I grew up, and was a dear and comforting presence in my dreams.

I remember being very sad to see my beloved friend in such a tortured pose on the crucifixes and paintings in the Church, and I got into a lot of trouble for prising the tiny contorted Jesus figure off my rosary-beads with a nail-file in school.

As I grew up, I came to realise that the only way for me to see Jesus in a meaningful way, was not as a tortured, blood-stained and mangled body, but as a shining radiant Being of Light who was triumphant over death.

My beloved Jesus is raised from the tomb.

FIRST NEAR DEATH EXPERIENCE

A few days after all the excitement of my first Holy Communion and seeing Jesus, I caught a bad cold.

From birth I'd been prone to coughs and colds and chest infections, so my grandmother always took special care to protect my health. In order to strengthen my immune-system, she used to give me castor oil and cod-liver oil, a spoonful of malt, various vitamins and all sorts of strange herbs and concoctions.

This time nothing worked. I became very ill suddenly.

My cold rapidly escalated into double pneumonia. Our family doctor was concerned and so was my mother. She was sleeping near my bed one night, as she'd come to help nurse me.

I awoke in the middle of the night feeling suffocated and very hot.

While my mother slept a deep and exhausted sleep, I climbed out of the window in my nightgown and walked around the garden in bare feet.

I felt very light-headed.

It was a bitterly cold winter yet I didn't seem to feel the cold at all.

Frost crunched on the icy grass under my bare feet and ice sparkled like diamonds in the shadows of the moonlit garden.

I lay down or fainted or slept, in my fairy garden.

At some stage, I vividly recall bursting out of my body through the top of my head, and rushing down a purple tunnel that was spinning so fast that I became dizzy.

I emerged into a beautifully coloured and vivid, warm place. It was a huge meeting place or hall, filled with beautiful young and glowing people, all smiling and gloriously clothed in colours and radiant light.

I felt very well and happy.

At the end of this hall, waited a glowing Being whom I knew was God, and I felt drawn to Him.

Without moving, I just thought of going to Him, and next thing I was right in front of Him. I was so happy! My heart was bursting with joy.

"Home at last with Him!" I thought.

I was gloriously, blissfully happy.

He spoke to me without words. His voice was like beautiful, vibrating music, like liquid warmth flowing through me and around me. I wanted to feel that heat and warmth forever.

I now know the feeling I felt was the energy of Divine Love.

This glorious feeling of warmth and radiance was my experience of the Divine.

My heart tells me what God feels like.

This was a true mystical experience that was to repeat itself later in my life. There is no mistaking this kind of personal experience because it transforms your life.

I know God exists because I've felt it.

The message He was communicating to me was:

"It's not time for you to be with Me, yet. It's too soon. You must go back to your body quickly. Just think it, and it will be so.

You have a very important job to do for Me on Earth when you grow up. I want you to be a good girl. Keep praying, keep talking to Me in your heart. I want you to be kind and loving to every person you meet. Do this because you love Me. When your work is done, come Home. I'll be right here, waiting for you."

I cried a lot, and had a terrible tantrum about going back, I so longed to be with Him. Earth was so hard.

He motioned to one of the shining Beings I'd not previously noticed, who were at His side, and said:

" This is Michael. You already know him. I have long ago appointed him as one of your guardians on the Earth plane. He serves you well. He's been watching over you since before you were born.

Go with him, now. Michael will wait for you and guide you back to Me when your work on Earth is done. Go now."

The next thing I remember is waking up in a hospital bed with the sound of my grandmother's voice calling my name, calling me back. My mother's arms were around me, her hot tears falling on my face. That was my first near death experience at seven years of age.

CHAPTER 2

PSYCHIC MILESTONES

POLTERGEISTS AND MALEVOLENT SPIRITS

My family often moved house when the spirits became extremely troublesome and malevolent.

My grandmother slept little as a result of ghosts on the loose and spiritual prowlers as she called them, and she prayed during the night hours.

She would say to me:
" All the spirits come to trouble me at dark, little one. I can get little sleep until dawn. After 4am, they disappear."

When I was about nine years of age, poltergeists and malevolent spirits came to really trouble our household.

One morning as I was dressing, I noticed a spot of blood on my underwear and I was alarmed.

It hadn't occurred to any of the women in my family to prepare me for menstruation as I was still a child.

When I told my grandmother, she decided to tell me about growing up, making it an exciting and positive experience.

LOVE IS THE MESSAGE

We didn't worry about school that day but took a shopping holiday buying new pretty undies, with a wonderfully expensive High Tea at a hotel afterwards.

I was thoroughly spoilt that day and I liked it.

My grandmother told my aunts and my mother what had happened to me and they gave me glamorous grown up presents over the next few days, making me feel pretty special.

How grateful I am to these wise and liberated women for preparing my developing mind for womanhood in such a positive way. Due to this, I've avoided much of the miseries that seem to trouble other women and have even enjoyed ageing, since I saw only positive female role models in my formative years.

When I grew up and had my own daughter, I passed on to her the positive gift of the celebration of womanhood that had been given to me.

One night just after the bleeding began, we were all woken by what sounded like bricks or rocks being thrown onto the roof of our house.

We all got out of bed and nervously went outside to see what was going on. We expected our neighbours' lights to be on and other people to be out in the street, as the noise had been almost deafening.

Silence. No-one else had stirred.

" How peculiar," we said to each other.

Unable to see or hear anything amiss, we were prepared to laugh it off.

" Must have been possums or something," my grand-mother said.

When we closed the front door, it whipped open again by itself and slammed hard!

We stood stock still, disbelieving what we saw.

" Oh no! Here we go again, it must be spirit interference," my grandmother said.

 Someone, then several 'someone's' began knocking on the door, then on the walls. I held my grandmother's hand, my other hand to my mouth, trembling.

" Whoever it is, it sounds angry," I thought.

We prayed together, saying the rosary together under my grandmother's direction. We asked the Divine to protect us from what we knew to be angry spirits.

The awful noise continued for an hour then stopped as suddenly as it started.

Apparently, it wasn't audible to anyone but us.

We suffered for a week or so with the noises of rocks being thrown on the roof, lights blinking on and off, doors opening and slamming, furniture moving around in the other rooms, taps turning on and off, knockings on walls and doors, in all a general cacophony of sound.

My aunts, my mother and I found this noise and spirit manifestation very frightening and upsetting. We were unable to sleep very much at all during the long nights.

In desperation, my grandmother finally contacted a priest who was a long-time friend, and had been trained in Rome as an exorcist.

She felt he'd show us how to remove this infestation, as all her efforts had been unsuccessful.

We called him Father Bon (Bon is French for good) as he was so good to us, and had freed us from the spirit infestation so many times in different houses.

He was short, plump and very Italian, even after many years in Australia.

Dear Father Bon had enormous faith in God and was totally unafraid of spirits.

He'd turn up in his suit, then go to another room to wash and change, eventually emerging in a long black gown with a white lace-edged shirt, a purple stole around his neck and a Bible in his hand.

He brought with him a special book containing the ritual and the prayers of exorcism.

He'd use the holy water he'd brought with him for the specific purpose of cleansing our house, a gold crucifix, and a tiny container in his pocket blessed by the Holy Father in Rome which contained a saint's relic.

These artifacts were all powerful talismans against evil, due no doubt to the belief that was attached to them.

THE RITUAL

Father Bon had instructed all of us to bathe before his arrival. We'd prepared a bowl of water for Father to wash in and a small white towel to dry his hands.

I thought to myself while my grandmother and aunts were cleaning the house prior to Father's arrival:

" This is exactly what we all do when the doctor's coming. This time our house is sick."

Father had instructed that after cleaning our house from top to bottom, we place fresh bowls of flowers in each room, and have new candles lit and ready.

Father Bon made his way through the house, from the front door, up the hallway, into each and every room, chanting in Latin the sacred prayers of exorcism, splashing holy water liberally all around the rooms.

We followed him chanting the rosary, carrying candles and incense censers to cleanse the rooms.

Father Bon commanded the evil spirits to leave our house and never to return. He spoke with the power and authority vested in him in the name of the Holy Father and the Divine.

I remember Father Bon performing this holy ritual many times during my childhood. After Father's visit all would be peaceful again, for a while.

SHOWING OFF

During the same time as the poltergeist activity, I discovered quite by accident one day, that if I focused on light bulbs hard enough they'd explode!

This was an activity that wasn't encouraged by my family when they caught me at it.

My aunts were very cross and made me clean up the mess.

My grandmother explained to me that the power of my electromagnetic energy field had increased due to emerging womanhood, which explained the poltergeist activity around our house.

From time to time over the next several months, playful and malevolent spirits troubled us less and less.

As a child, in idle moments, I used to love laying on my back on the lawn and making clouds disappear by focussing on them.

One day my grandmother found out what I was doing and told me:

" The people in the city need the rain in those clouds you just destroyed. You must learn to think. Stop showing off, darling." It was so unusual for my grandmother to reprimand me that I remembered this incident and didn't repeat the same mistake.

She also told me that because I was bored, I'd broken a natural law and there were always consequences for doing this.

SPIRITS OUT OF BODY

Many people are fascinated by hearing stories of hauntings, poltergeists, angelic beings, malevolent entities and visitations by deceased loved ones.

It's been my experience that people believe spirits can co-exist alongside human beings, without there being the need to send them on to another dimension or realm.

However, it's clear to me that disembodied spirits have no place on Earth. Earth is for the living.

Orgamisama, the great Japanese Master said:

"There are more disembodied spirits walking the Earth today than there are human beings in a physical body.

This is a terrible situation for mankind."

UNREDEEMED SOULS

Spirits are unable to co-exist in harmony with human beings because they are mainly negative, unredeemed souls trapped on the Earth plane, unable to continue with their souls' development.

Most are extremely childish.

They may not mean to harm human beings but harm inevitably comes about.

The negativity contained within these spirits who possess humans in order to live, results in quarrels, temper, aggression, violence, murder, suicide, catastrophe and war.

I believe unredeemed souls embody all the evils of mankind!

Once they become attached to humans, they're unable and unwilling to let go.

Many great Masters have given clear instructions on exorcising unclean and evil spirits, and freeing human beings from spirit possession.

SPIRIT TYPES

Psychics and sensitives are especially vulnerable to spirit possession.

We all need to be aware that opposing and negative forces exist. There are several gradations of spirits in different realms:

1. There are the malevolent spirits who fully possess human beings and enjoy causing disharmony and harm.

2. There are malevolent spirits who chiefly haunt human houses, trapped in a time or place of illusion, acting out old dramas from which they're unable to escape.

3. There are malevolent spirits who take delight in frightening human beings and driving them to madness and suicide through fear.

4. There are lost and wandering spirits who haunt and frequent graveyards, crossroads, places of death, hospitals and desolate places.

5. There are spirits of nature of the lower forces who haunt trees and natural landscapes. These can be of the lost, benevolent or malevolent nature as well as being ancestral spirits.

6. There are benevolent spirits who partly possess human beings and want to co-exist with them. These spirits do not have the intention to cause harm, yet still don't belong here.

It's my understanding and experience that human beings can be possessed by ancestral spirits, spirits on the loose, malevolent and benevolent spirits, nature spirits, and spirits sent for an evil purpose by other malicious human beings.

Wherever, whenever a human being is out of control, aggressive, violent, sexually abusive or suicidal, this is a sign that a malevolent spirit is possessing, using and manipulating the unfortunate individual.

An individual such as this is afflicted by the lower forces, and needs considerable assistance.

A lot of prayer has to be done for and around such an unfortunate human being.

Sometimes, people wonder why a good and loving person who's died can't stay around the Earth plane with their loved ones. This is simply because the Earth plane is designed for the existence of human beings.

The Earth experience is a physical experience.

After a person has ended life and left the physical body, the soul needs to progress towards its next stage of growth, learning, evolution and development on a higher plane.

It's selfish to hold back a deceased loved one from experiencing their evolution. This is the reason why it's important to let loved ones go.

FROM THE CITY TO THE COUNTRY

When I was about nine years of age, my family moved from Sydney to a city in the country in New South Wales.

My grandmother rented a house large enough for my mother and father, my sister and I to live with her.

I was very happy to be re-united with my family at last.

My sister, my cousin and I attended the local Catholic school and settled in.

It wasn't long though, before we had to call in our old friend Father Bon to exorcise our new house. Apparently, the previous owners of the house had taken all their furniture and their possessions with them and left us some annoying spirits.

Father came to bless, dedicate and cleanse our new house.

Despite all these spiritual precautions, my grandmother had her first heart attack in that house. What my grandmother called spiritual prowlers troubled her night after night, causing her anxiety and fear which culminated in a mild heart attack.

I found out years later that an incredible coincidence had brought my future Teacher and his fourteen year old son to the same town at the same time my family moved there.

From Malaysia, my Teacher decided on this small town in Australia as the best place for his oldest son to complete his education. This meant that my future Teacher was walking the same streets as my grandmother and I when I was a small girl.

The hand of God was bringing me closer to my Teacher.

SECOND NEAR DEATH EXPERIENCE

My second near death experience occurred when I was ten years of age.

My family and I had enjoyed a wonderful Christmas dinner and I decided to spend the night with my aunt and uncle who were very dear to me.

During the night, I had a stomach-ache and thought it was due to too much Christmas pudding.

My aunt sent for a doctor, poor man, being called out on Christmas Day, as she was receiving that it was something more than overeating. After the doctor had examined me, finding nothing amiss, he said:

" Call me if anything further develops."

Well, something sure did develop overnight!

I suffered terrifying visitations from playful spirits that escalated into malevolence.

I saw and felt what seemed like hundreds of birds flying around in my room, hitting me with their fluttering wings, nipping me with their beaks and scratching me with their tiny sharp claws.

It hurt!

There was an incredible rushing of air in the room as they flew and swooped and battered their wings against the walls and the windows.

I was distraught.

I called out for my aunt who carried me into her bed to sleep. She didn't see the birds, but she was also psychic and sensed there was negativity and some sort of a threat around me. She was worried and held me in her arms until I fell into a restless sleep. My aunt felt that the birds were a premonition, which they were.

In the early hours of the morning, my inflamed appendix burst and I almost left my body permanently this time!

During the emergency surgery to remove my appendix, I once again left my body.

To my delight, I ran down the tunnel once more and this time found myself in a beautiful garden, surrounded by laughing children and toddlers. This place of happy babies and children was like the Summerland the North American Indians describe.

It was a gloriously beautiful place.

I found myself standing in the middle of a vivid green meadow. There were brilliant flowers everywhere and many babies and children were being watched over by sweet and gentle angelic guardians.

A fun fair had a colourful ribboned merry-go-round and giggling toddlers riding it. I wanted to ride it too.

This place was a joyful transition between the Earth plane and the next plane of existence.

I remember very little of this second near death experience, but I do remember Michael appearing, letting me play with the happy children for a while, then taking me firmly by the hand and drawing me back to life.

I once more felt very sad about coming back and was depressed for some time. I was angry with Michael for bringing me back but as I grew up, I became more and more grateful for his loving presence in my life and thanked God for my dear and special Angel often.

The nuns who nursed me in hospital said:

"Your aunt believed you were going to die. You were terribly ill. We saw her fall to her knees outside the door of the operating room. She cried and promised God to give Him a year of her life in service, if He would only let you live. Your aunt said she regarded you as her own little girl, as her baby girl had died at birth." After I recovered from surgery and was allowed to go home, my aunt kept her promise to God and worked for a year in an Aboriginal mission in the Northern Territory desert area of Australia.

After a long period of recuperation in hospital, it was back to my grandmother's house for me.

A year of semi-invalidism followed.

This illness cost me almost a year of my life and kept me away from school and the company of other children. This isolation and suffering had a profound effect upon me.

This enforced period of rest gave me time at only ten years of age, to pray, to meditate and to contemplate. I became very introspective.

The priests visited often with Holy Communion and the nuns sent my school work to me to be completed under my grandmother's guidance.

I read voraciously and devoured all the books in the children's section of our local Library.

My grandmother brought me baskets of books from the adult library on many varied topics which were to serve me well as I grew.

I loved and understood Shakespeare and staged mini-plays from my room for my family, enlisting bit-players from anyone who would agree. I especially enjoyed Greek and Roman Mythology and craved any book that dealt with Egypt and lost civilisations.

During the year of my recovery, my creative imagination developed at a rapid pace.

An innate gift for languages also flourished at this young age and a French tutor guided me.

I found out when I grew up that intuition, creativity and imagination are all functions of the right hemisphere of the brain. The development of imagination is vital to psychic development.

It's my belief that God was using this opportunity to train my young brain to receive images. As I read about other lands I created images about what I was reading.

I began drawing, painting and writing poetry and short stories. Before I was eleven years of age, my poetry was published in a leading Sydney newspaper and I received a small cheque which I treasured.

My family was quite concerned about my state of health at this stage, as I'd had two serious illnesses and didn't seem very strong. Many doctors were consulted and many noxious concoctions were fed to me in a bid to build up my strength.

No doubt I enjoyed all this extra attention and care that was lavished upon me.

I remember that my beloved and devoted grandmother always called me 'darling' and 'love'. I discovered I was only called by my name when I did something really naughty. And sometimes I did!

My aunts told me I was always up to some mischief or other and was a high-spirited, charming child, despite the loneliness and health challenges.

I only know that Love surrounded me and carried me through all the adversities in my life.

I knew even at this young age that I was privileged to have experienced God and I knew with a deep certainty that death was not a thing to be feared.

The nuns at my school were also concerned about my health and prayed for me. They thought I was a little saint.

When my mother heard what the nuns thought of me, she smiled and told the Reverend Mother:

" Let me tell you Reverend Mother, it's not easy living with a little saint sometimes."

CONFIRMATION: SAINT MARIA GORETTI

After my protracted recovery period, I was given permission by the Archbishop of our Diocese to be confirmed at age eleven, which was three years before my peers would be confirmed.

I was eager to be confirmed as an adult member of our local church and to be anointed and blessed by the Bishop.

My grandmother, my family and our parish priest believed that the sacrament of confirmation would be of benefit to me and would strengthen me. An exception was made in my case due to the two major illnesses I'd suffered and the two near death experiences.

To this end, our parish priest had informed the Archbishop I was a devout and special little girl.

My grandmother told me that if I died, my soul would be empowered through the sacrament of Catholic confirmation.

When the confirmation day came, I stood before my family and the congregation in our local church, in my white dress and veil, renouncing Satan and all his wiles in the high clear voice of a little girl.

That day I felt a spiritual maturity beyond my years, as confirmation served to deepen my faith in God.

I clearly recall going to the church during one lunch time at school just after confirmation, prostrating myself on my stomach with arms outspread before the altar, surrendering my life to God and meaning it.

My role models during these years were the saints and martyrs who'd surrendered their lives to the Divine in ages past.

Catholics choose a spiritual name as a sign of spiritual awakening when they receive the sacrament of confirmation.

I chose the name of Saint Maria Goretti.

Saint Maria Goretti was a fourteen year old Italian girl who wished to devote her life to God as I longed to do, and who'd died rather than submit to rape by a young man called Alessandro.

After her death, Maria appeared to Alessandro in his prison cell and forgave him his crime.

This mystical saintly spirit visitation converted the young man and totally transformed his life.

This true life story of a little girl like me had a profound effect upon my consciousness at eleven years of age.

As a confirmation gift, my grandmother gave me a beautiful framed portrait of that dear little Italian teenage saint and martyr, Maria Goretti, who had long dark hair just like mine.

Much later in my adult years, another Teacher would give me another spiritual name to mark my further awakening.

I HAVE A VOCATION

In my senior years at school, I began to nurture a desire to join the convent.

I wanted to be a Carmelite nun, retiring from the

world, taking a vow of silence and praying for the world in seclusion until death. The Carmelite Order when I was a little girl, was a contemplative one, which appealed to my longing for peace and contemplation.

I later discovered, this desire to renounce the world was due to past life influences. I wasn't to know at this stage that a convent was not meant to be for me this lifetime.

All I knew was, I wanted to serve God!

I confided my longings to the nuns who were closest to me, who encouraged and supported my vocation.

In those days, it was considered a blessing in a family for a child to nurture a vocation to the convent or the priesthood, so the nuns believed my family would be very happy to give a child in service to the Divine.

When a girl or a boy professed the desire to enter religious life, everyone envied the fortunate parents, knowing that God's blessings and approval would fall upon the family who encouraged and motivated the child.

During this time, I began to withdraw more and more from my family, attaching more closely to the younger nuns and to the convent.

I kept my secret close to my heart.

My family felt this spiritual fervour was just a phase that many girls went through and it would pass.

I remember how the loving nuns allowed me to attend their private chapel, to sit in a pew behind them, where they meditated as a community and recited their private prayers.

I felt I was a little nun already, part of their loving sister-hood.

An elderly nun with whom I'd been very close, passed away.

When a nun died, her body would be tended lovingly by the sisters, dressed in white, placed in an open coffin, surrounded by roses and tall white candles in the nuns' private chapel. A three day prayer vigil would be held to elevate her soul.

The body of a deceased nun would never be left alone.

During the entire three days and nights that it lay in the chapel before the altar, a nun would sit beside the body, meditating and praying for the soul of her dead sister in Christ.

My special friend, sister Mary Michael, asked me if I'd like to sit beside the body of the dear elderly nun whom I'd loved so much.

I felt happy and privileged to do this act of love and service for a lady who'd been a spiritual teacher to me.

As I sat beside the body of my friend and teacher, I gazed for long hours at the beautiful face that was totally unlined and at peace. I felt I was in the presence of something wonderful.

I sensed that the soul of this dear teacher was no longer around her body.

I knew at this young age that when a soul leaves a body, is propelled upwards by faith in the Higher Power, supported in its journey by the prayers of the ones who knew it and loved it, it's a liberating experience.

There was no sadness, no negativity, no shivery feelings, no heavy heart, nothing in this experience to frighten me. My friend, the nun, had made it home.

At about thirteen or fourteen years of age, I went into a spiritual crisis and fasted to the extreme, losing a lot of weight in the process.

This spiritual fervour led to my attending daily mass and evening Benediction.

I prostrated myself for hours on the cold stone floor of the nun's private chapel and made Novenas (nine day prayer cycles) all the while looking forward to the day I'd be a bride of Christ.

Though I kept this secret in my heart, my grandmother looked at me oddly at times.

She was becoming concerned about all this religious activity and long absences from home, but kept silent and allowed me to continue.

THE FLYING GLASS

My grandmother had become increasingly concerned about the debilitating headaches my mother was suffering.

She decided to have a healing circle for my mother, and called several of her regular clients and friends to attend.

She asked me to sit in on the edge of the circle for added energy and as part of my experience and training.

I was reluctant to be part of this.

The nuns had long been advising me against being involved with "your dear grandmother's spiritual activities" as they called it. People in trouble or suffering from a disease always sought her counsel, including a few of the ones who warned me against being involved! For example, my grandmother regularly visited one of the nuns who had an advanced cancer. My grandmother was an extremely tolerant woman.

She knew intuitively that synergy was required for healing and would always call a group of sympathetic people together for healing. I was used to being in bed while they met as a child, but this was the first time I was asked to be in the room.

That night I felt a little apprehensive, hoping the nuns wouldn't find out.

The healing circle proceeded in its usual fashion. Prayers of protection were said, the group's energy of love was projected towards my mother though she was ignorant of the meeting, then the group meditated quietly.

This time, a spirit presence manifested!

This was not usual.

When the malevolent presence manifested as a freezing mist in the room, my grandmother immediately commanded it to leave the circle. Although she was brave, strong and commanding, she didn't have the power to remove such a powerful spirit.

Everyone became uncomfortable.

The temperature in the room dropped rapidly.

The evil energy was very real and could be felt.

My flesh prickled and I seemed to shrink into myself.

I was very afraid! I felt I had to do something before we all got affected and somebody got hurt, because I sensed the threat. Spontaneously, without thought, I leapt to my feet and yelled loudly:

" No! No! Go away! Get away from my family! In the name of God and all the Saints get back to where you came from! Now!"

As I did that, a glass of water that had been sitting on the table in front of my grandmother, flew - of its own volition - at my face!

The glass struck me with full force on my right eyebrow and shattered. When the glass cut me, I screamed.

As if it wasn't frightening enough to have a spirit hand dash a full glass of cold water into my face, now blood ran down from the deep cut in my brow.

The circle broke up in pandemonium.

I cried loudly as my grandmother sponged the blood away from my face to assess the damage.

The malevolent spirit attracted to the energy of the circle as a light attracts a passing moth, had gone back to where it came from.

My eyebrow needed stitching, so off we went to the local outpatient's department with a fabricated story.

I still bear the scar of that spirit's anger to this day.

I learnt that when a gateway is opened into the spirit world, real danger can result.

It was only as a mature adult that all these things were explained to me by someone who knew what he was talking about.

MY LAST HEALING CIRCLE

When I was fourteen, my grandmother decided it was time for me to sit in with her again on the healing circles. I said:

"No, I won't! I remember what happened to me the last time you asked me to sit in on a healing circle. I've still got the scar on my eyebrow to remind me. Don't ever ask me again."

The Reverend Mother at school had cautioned me against following in my grandmother's footsteps.

She didn't understand or approve of my grandmother's spiritual activities.

Reverend Mother made it quite clear to me it wasn't Christian to conduct healing circles.

One day, I tried to talk to Reverend Mother about the voices I heard, about my dreams and visions.

After listening with a worried look on her face, she said:
" My dear child, you must ask God for protection and guidance in these matters. It's my feeling these voices and visions of yours aren't good for you. You must ignore the voices and refuse to follow their directions. I'll pray for you."

I felt confused after speaking to Reverend Mother. When I'd been reading my little book 'The Lives of The Saints', I'd read about how Saint Joan of Arc had heard voices and seen visions just as I did.

I knew the Church had burned Joan at the stake as a heretic.

I wondered if Reverend Mother thought I was a heretic!

One night, my grandmother gently but firmly insisted that I sit in on the healing circle as part of my spiritual development. There was no arguing with her that night.

I remember so clearly what happened next because the event is burnt into my memory.

There were about ten men and women in our front room, seated around my grandmother in a large circle. It was quiet and still in the room. The gas heaters popped and spluttered. It was a chill winter's evening. Someone cleared his throat nervously.

All these small things stand out in my memory.

My grandmother motioned for me to sit on the chair beside her. Taking my right hand in hers, she softly explained:

" We're born to serve. We're not ordinary people. You, my child, are not an ordinary girl. The energy that's being directed through you is for the benefit of others. If you don't use that energy, you'll be unhappy. You must trust me in this matter."

She'd never said these things out loud to me before. I was suddenly overcome by the immensity and the responsibility of it all.

I was afraid of what the nuns and Reverend Mother would say if they found out I'd been part of my grand-mother's healing circle.

The nuns had told me many times that only God can heal suffering people. The nuns said it was my sacred duty to serve God in the convent. Reverend Mother had told me the healing circles were blasphemy.

Remembering this, I felt very upset and confused.

Everyone had joined hands and closed their eyes by now, unaware of the panic rising within me.

My grandmother held my hand firmly and quietly intoned:

" Our Father, which art in Heaven, hallowed be Thy Name," as she always did.

I just couldn't stand the inner conflict another moment.

I wrenched my hand out of hers, and as I pushed people aside roughly in my haste to get out of the room, my grandmother called out to me in a strong, clear voice:

" My darling girl, there's no place to go! You can't run away from God to a convent or anywhere else in the world. He's with you, inside of you, calling your name, wherever you go. Please stop! Don't run away, darling."

I recall the shocked faces of the people I'd pushed through in my haste to leave the room.

I recall the sight of my grandmother reaching out to me with such compassion on her face, but I had to run!

I half fell, half staggered down the stairs to the street, my heart pounding crazily and jumping wildly in my chest.

I ran out into the street into the rain and darkness of a winter's evening, coatless, walking the streets in a daze not knowing where to go, not having anywhere to go, until my grandmother's friends found me and gently led me home.

Once home, my grandmother tenderly helped me out of my wet clothes without saying a word.

She put me into a warm bed and blessed me.

I was conscious of the love that poured out of her and all around her. We never discussed that incident again and for that I was grateful.

I had my way. That was the last time I ever sat in on a healing circle.

A BROKEN HEART

Somehow, life went on for the next three years.

I remember though, every now and again I would become aware of my grandmother regarding me with a sad and troubled look.

I studied very hard, attended mass regularly, talked often with the younger nuns who'd become friends and tried to blend in with the other girls.

I got into the habit of physically exhausting myself so that I could fall into a deep sleep at night. I was a budding ballerina and had two formal classes per week as well as daily practice.

I made sure that I didn't have any time to think about the sadness and disappointment that was evident in the dear face of my grandmother. I knew I'd let her down.

At seventeen, I matriculated with honours as a result of study and the hard mental discipline I'd subjected myself to.

After finishing school, I approached my family with the support of the nuns from my school and the Parish priest, to request permission to join the convent as I was under the age of twenty-one.

My grandmother and my parents refused their permission.

I was devastated, heart-broken.

No amount of crying, begging, starving, praying or pleading would shift them. They all said a convent was no place for me. I'd felt confident my mother would support me, but she too remained adamant.

I was totally confused.

All my life I'd believed that my life was to be devoted to God. My family's refusal was a cruel blow.

I refused to accept scholarships to University or Teachers' College, and continued to attend the church at every opportunity, crying piteously during each service.

The nuns felt for me deeply, counselling trust in God and patience. They all prayed for me.

In anger and despair, I ran away from my grandmother's house, and sheltered in a sympathetic friend's house for a few weeks. My friend's father managed a bank and gave me a position. Eventually, I moved into a Girls' Hostel run by the Church and refused to communicate with my parents and my grandmother.

A few girls at the hostel befriended me and I soon began attending dances in the local church hall.

One night, I met a nice man who was very impressed with me and took me home the following week to meet his family.

We began seeing each other regularly and a friendship blossomed between us. He was older than I was, mature and quietly spoken with a deep faith in God. I liked him and I liked his family's faith and love for each other, and I was very lonely.

His grandmother was so like my grandmother, being a wise and loving woman.

My parents missed me very much and sent my grandmother as peacemaker.

Over afternoon tea in a restaurant, I allowed my grandmother to bless me and all was forgiven on both sides.

The time spent living apart from my family, the loneliness and sorrow I'd experienced had matured me, and no doubt this was all part of God's plan.

I later learnt that our souls are polished through suffering.

THE HAPPY FUNERAL

During the time spent apart from my family, I experienced a few amusing paranormal experiences.

A dear teacher I'd known at school passed away suddenly.

I attended her funeral, even though I usually avoided funerals because of the suffocating feelings of the mourners and the spirits attracted to the church.

When I entered the church and sat down in a pew up the back, I saw my friend and teacher stride up the aisle in her favourite canary yellow dress, looking so vibrant and alive!

As she walked past me, she smiled and waved, kept walking up the aisle looking at everyone in the church and winking cheekily at those who'd come to mourn her passing. Of course, no-one else could see her at all!

She looked thoroughly amused by the whole spectacle and not a bit ghostly at all. If you'd not known she was dead, you'd think she was a flesh and blood woman.

When she reached the front of the church, she knelt

briefly at the altar and walked out, her form fading as she neared the side door, then she was gone.

Outside the church after the funeral, some of her friends commented in my hearing:

" Wasn't it strange? It wasn't sad at all. Isn't that funny? What a lovely funeral.

It's almost as if she were determined not to let anyone be sad. So like her, she was always so cheerful."

I smiled to myself, wishing they'd seen what I saw.

I knew how happy my friend was to be freed from her suffering body.

I only told one person that I'd seen our friend at her own funeral, a girlfriend who'd also been her pupil and had loved her dearly. I told Sue:

" She looked so well, Sue.

I wish you could've seen her laughing and winking as she came down the aisle. She walked right through Father."

Poor Sue nearly fainted.

THE LAST ONE OUT

Another time, after finishing a seminar and being the last person to leave the building, as I turned out the lights a very large female ghost in an old-fashioned overcoat came straight out from the back of the room and pushed past me to get out.

I was shocked at the time because she felt so real that the wooden floor-boards trembled under her heavy footsteps.

I knew without a doubt she'd not been in the room when I walked out and everyone else had gone home except me.

She had a very negative aura and I felt 'slimed'.

I remember thinking:

" She didn't even say 'excuse me', rude ghost."

During these years, when I was seventeen to twenty-one, my sensitivity heightened quite dramatically, and I had to explain to my fiancé I couldn't go to movie theatres or football matches with him because I'd be upset and nervous.

He assumed I suffered from agrophobia and didn't ask me questions, for which I was grateful.

I managed to keep my gift a secret for most of the marriage. If he ever suspected anything, he didn't tell.

CHAPTER 3

THE VALLEY
OF THE SHADOW

MARRIAGE

In 1970, my fiancé and I married and set up home.

As he wasn't Catholic, my family wasn't happy about my marrying into a non-Catholic family. I soon found myself snubbed by the girls I'd gone to school with.

The nuns were sad for me and said they'd continue to pray for me as I'd been very dear to them.

I felt as if I'd let everyone down, yet I knew I was doing what was right for me. I asked my grandmother how to resolve the inner conflict brought about by my decision to marry outside the Catholic faith.

She advised me in the same words she always used whenever I had a problem or a challenge to be overcome:

"Follow your heart. Be true to yourself. At the end of the day, you'll be the one to live with the consequences of the decisions you make. I trust that your heart is leading you in this situation. I trust also that you've prayed and meditated on this decision."

In 1972, I became pregnant with my first child.

It had been a worrying pregnancy from the beginning, with pain and bleeding on and off.

On and off, I suffered recurring nightmares about some tragedy about to happen. I was unable to sleep many nights. I had only shadowy, troubled impressions of the disturbing dreams, and was unable to discern the dream's meaning and the messages my sub-conscious mind was trying to convey to my consciousness.

My good-hearted husband got into the habit of making a thermos of hot chocolate and putting it within handy reach for me to have during the long hours of the night, when I lay awake wide eyed and staring at the ceiling.

MY SISTER IS LOST TO ME

A few months later, my night-time fears of an impending tragedy became a reality with the news of the accidental death of my sister, who'd been only twenty years of age.

I was devastated at her loss and the loss of our childhood together.

She'd been such a sweet and playful child, and we'd hardly had a chance to know each other.

Of the twenty years of her young life, we'd only lived in the same house together since our parents had moved to the country.

Even though we had, for the most part, grown up in separate houses, we'd been very good friends and loved each other dearly.

When I was informed of my sister's death, the memories of our time together came flooding back. I remembered how I'd made paper dolls for her that she'd loved so much. There were happy memories of how we'd talked to each other and did concerts while we washed and dried the dishes, how she'd cheated shamelessly at Gin Rummy, how we'd planned to travel together and live together in the same house when we were old ladies, as my grand-mother and her little sister had planned.

All those plans and dreams were shattered with her passing.

It was much worse for my poor mother.

She'd been diagnosed with multiple sclerosis and she was only thirty-eight years of age.

Our doctor, a close friend of our family, told my grand-mother:

"It's such a tragedy to see someone young and vital struck down by such a debilitating disease as M.S. Unfortunately, it's advanced in her case. There's nothing we can do. We don't even know what causes it, let alone how to arrest its progress. We can only assume that the headaches, fatigue and dizziness she's been suffering for years were indications of the onset of M.S."

My grandmother's way of dealing with my sister's death and her daughter's diagnosis of M.S. was to surrender to God's Will and to pray for both her daughter and her grand-daughter.

My mother's way of dealing with the M.S. was to totally ignore it, not to give it any energy or attach fear to the sit-uation, to just get on with her life day by day. My mother was a very practical person.

However she couldn't ignore the death of her little girl.

My sister's funeral was very sad.

Everyone cried.

Her young husband tried to throw himself into her grave, maddened by grief.

My grandmother comforted, held up and supported everyone as only she could. She reminded all of us that:

"The Good Lord knows what's best for our little girl. She's now safe in the arms of the angelic beings who'll take her to the Lord."

We all knew she was right, yet we missed our little angel.

My grandmother reminded us that we humans are so selfish, crying and clinging to the memory of a deceased loved one.

She told us:

"The Buddhists believe that if we cry and mourn for the loss of our loved one, the soul will attach to our grief and sadness and will stay on the Earth plane to comfort us."

She also reminded us that Jesus said:

"Let the dead bury their dead."

Her point was, that where we are, death is not!

She added:

"The Earth is for the living. When the soul leaves the body, it goes on to another existence in the world beyond. We must let go of our dear little one."

She illustrated her point by telling us a story of a young woman going on a wonderful journey to a new land, whose family comes to farewell her ship.

As the ship leaves, they all cry out:

"There she goes."

At the end of the journey, a huge crowd of loved ones are waiting to meet her at her next destination, and they all cry out:

"Here she comes."

Great sorrow happened all around me over the next several years and only my faith in Divine Love kept me going.

My constant prayer and affirmation was:

"All things work for good for those who love the Lord." I loved the Lord and my faith was sorely tested.

My mother's health deteriorated rapidly after the death of her youngest daughter.

Her courage and determination didn't falter, but it just seemed to be her time.

I can still see a vivid picture in my mind, of my mother crawling on her hands and knees rather than get into a wheel-chair.

She said haltingly, as it was becoming difficult to speak:

"Leave the wheel-chair there, I'll be needing it soon enough. But, while I've still got the strength to move my body, I'll move it for myself. After that goes, you can push me around if you must."

It was painful to watch but we admired her courage.

Our doctor said he'd never seen anyone diagnosed with M.S. deteriorate so quickly.

Even my mother's capacity to speak disappeared.

She was unable to communicate with us by writing either, as she couldn't hold a pen any longer.

The incontinence of bowel and bladder was humiliating for her.

She became unable to move or to do anything for herself, completely dependent on her mother, her father, her sisters and myself. It was as if she had become a helpless infant again.

Still, in spite of all of this, her eyes shone with a light and a beauty that told me my mother was at peace with herself and with God.

Her luminous eyes remained fixed on pictures of Jesus and Mary for hours and she smiled.

THIRD NEAR DEATH EXPERIENCE

The time had come for me to give birth to my first child.

I was afraid.

The aunt who was closest to me, who'd given a year of her life to God, came into the hospital with my husband and I to help in birthing the child.

My grandmother stayed at home and prayed for me constantly during the entire ordeal.

The Mother Superior of the nursing nuns was a close friend of my family, and as I was admitted in early labour, she was just finishing her eight hour shift on duty.

When she was informed that I was admitted, she stayed to help me. As the labour was over twenty hours she had a real job staying on her feet, but she did it!

I experienced my third near death experience during the birth of my daughter and again went into the presence of the Divine.

The baby was in a posterior presentation and the labour slowed down.

Both baby and I were tired and weak and I began to give up.

I began bleeding.

I cried out for my grandmother and lost consciousness.

I suddenly became aware of the fact that the pain had stopped.

I seemed to be up on the ceiling of the hospital room looking down on the body of a pale young woman on a blood-stained bed below.

I thought:

"Oh, poor thing, she's so young."

Then, with a start, I realised that I was looking at my body from above. I realised that I was no longer inside my physical body! There was a state of emergency in the hospital room and I saw staff coming in from other wards to assist.

The curious thing about all this though, was the fact that there was no sound at all.

I felt no emotion.

There was just a calm, warm, cocooned feeling.

I felt completely detached from what was happening to my body. I was aware that I no longer had any connection or emotional attachment to the body I'd vacated. It was a strange feeling, this feeling of total detachment.

The drama unfolding below me didn't seem to concern me anymore. As I was thinking all of these things, I felt that same spinning, dizzying feeling I'd felt as a child and saw the same tunnel opening in front of me.

I found myself propelled down that tunnel once more and into the Light that was radiating at the end of the tunnel.

I was surrounded by, permeated with glorious, burning, radiant Light!

I felt so good I began to cry with relief.

"Lord God, at last you've let me come home," I cried out.

After I'd said those words, I experienced a sudden push - a rush of energy - an enormous tug of pressure and was suddenly back in my body again.

I became aware of searing pain, the chill of the air in the labour room, the loud directions of the doctor to the staff, of choking and vomiting.

My body was shivering and shaking with cold.

I felt so cold!

I noticed that my finger nails were blue.

I found myself wrapped in what looked like a foil blanket, with several hot water-bottles tucked in beside me. I was grateful for the warmth.

I realised with a sense of grief and crushing disappointment, that I was no longer in the Light, but back in the wretched vehicle of the physical body I thought I'd left behind me for ever.

The sharp cry of my new baby had brought me back to life.

I had a lingering sense of almost having been in the presence of God again.

I could still taste the closeness of Him.

I felt the unbearable longing to be with Him again and experienced a bitter disappointment at being in my body once more.

Not even the presence of a new baby in the nursery could lift my mood. It seemed to me that God still didn't want me and I was very sad.

When I was back in my room, the doctor came in to talk to me.

He said:

"We had quite a tough time with you. Your baby's sleeping peacefully in the nursery now. She's had a tough time too.

You gave me quite a scare, I thought I'd lost you. We'd nearly given up on you, delivered the baby and then all of a sudden, you were back with us. I don't mind telling you, you're a very lucky girl."

After a moment, I replied:

"You made a pin-cushion out of me doctor, I must have about ten holes in my arms. I heard you say to that dark-haired nurse 'we're losing her' just before I left my body."

The doctor frowned, leaned forward and said:

"I couldn't get a needle in your arm because all your veins went flat. That's when I got really worried. What do you mean by 'I left my body'?"

I told the doctor how I'd observed, from the ceiling, everything that had happened in the labour room.

He was at first surprised and then interested in my description of events. He said:

"You know I'm from Europe. Where I did my medical degree, I heard of another woman who had a similar experience to yours. I'm inclined to believe you, because I know you to be a sensible person. More than that, I know that something extraordinary happened today."

THE GREEDY GHOST

As the days passed, I grew to love my sweet little baby and looked forward to her feeds.

As the memory of my experience in the Light began to fade, its radiant intensity diminished over time.

My grandmother was aware of the fact that I'd endeavoured to leave my body permanently and advised me that the Divine needed me as mother to the new little girl.

She said:

"Your sister's soul has ascended to Heaven and your baby's soul has descended to the Earth. Your duty is to attend to your family for as long as the good Lord wishes this to be so. You will know when your duty is done."

One night, when I was taking the baby back to the nursery after a very late feed about 2 am, I passed a door to a private room that was always closed.

I felt a distinct chill as I passed this door and thought to myself:

"Please God, no! I don't want to know what's in that room. I don't want to see. I'm turning off my mind. Don't, don't do this to me. I don't want it anymore! I don't want to see anymore."

The chill I felt outside that closed door and the nausea that arose within me, told me there was a malevolent spirit entity trying to attract my attention.

I felt the negative energy of that disembodied entity tugging at the edges of my auric field.

I didn't feel strong enough to deal with an entity of this nature at this time, and certainly not with a vulnerable new born baby in my arms.

There was nothing I could do about what happened next.

'She' came through the closed door wailing and sobbing and reaching out for the sleeping baby in my arms!

I recoiled in horror from the sight of this terrifying vision.

She was a white faced, wild-haired, mad-looking ghost.

I ran down the hallway to the well lit nursery, seeking the company and comfort of warm blooded, living humans.

The night nurses looked up, startled from their books and cups of tea.

I somehow managed to calm myself and asked them about the woman in the room down the hall.

Somehow, I felt that I already knew the answer.

The older nurse told me the story.

It seems that the previous year a young woman had been brought in with her baby dead in utero due to the mother's diabetes. The mother became psychotic with grief upon being informed she was carrying a dead baby.

Until the diabetes had stabilised, an operation to remove the baby's body was impossible. So, three days after the baby's death, she had a caesarean section and unfortunately passed away during surgery.

Ever since then, the night-bell would ring periodically by itself in her former room.

Since then, the staff on night-duty would sense a creeping chill down the hallway and hear the bell ringing from time to time.

Other sensitive women had occasionally mentioned to staff they too had troubled dreams while in the hospital.

No one was able to sleep in that particular room any

more. It was difficult to get staff to work the late shift now and the room was no longer used.

I didn't tell them the shock I'd received on seeing the greedy ghost of a mother who'd lost her child, her mind and her soul.

I checked out of the hospital early the next day and went home.

I realised that hospitals are grave-yards.

The souls of the departed ones stay near their place of death and need to be sent on to the spirit realm.

MY MOTHER'S JOURNEY INTO LIGHT

When my new little baby was a few months old, my mother was admitted to a nursing home for the terminally ill as she was totally incapacitated by now.

I held the baby up for her to see during one of my visits and her eyes told me she was glad. It was dreadful to see her so wasted and so dependent upon others for the smallest service.

She was fed by nasal tubes which distressed her and her bodily wastes were removed by tubing and bags.

My mother and I were able to communicate our love for each other through our eyes, our feelings and our hearts.

In addition, my mother expressed her love for me in dreams.

In my dreams, we had long conversations with each other where she told me it was necessary for her soul growth that she suffer in this way.

It helped me to know there was meaning in what was happening to her.

MY GRANDMOTHER EXPLAINS KARMA

"I think it's time for me to explain to you, a deeper understanding of the law of karma.

The karmic concept embodies cause and effect, action and reaction." She went on:

"For each and every decision we make, for each and every choice we choose, there is a consequence.

Karma is the energetic, impersonal consequence of the choice we make from moment to moment.

The woman I call my daughter and the woman you call your mother, is a brave soul who's chosen to pay back karma in this lifetime. We support her in her decision. We don't grieve for her suffering, but we're joyful to see her grow towards sainthood.

Learn from your mother's example, welcome suffering as it will grow your soul."

The nuns who nursed her told us:

"Your mother is a saint. She suffers all her indignities with courage and grace. She smiles at us often and her eyes thank us. We all love her."

Her rosary beads were wrapped around her hands, and she wore the brown and green scapulars which are a sign of Catholic devotion to Mary, close to her heart.

It was a tradition that life long devotion to Mary and the wearing of the green scapular would assure a blessed death.

A blessed death comprised the sure knowledge that you were about to die, absolution of sins had been given by a priest, and you were surrounded by loving people who prayed for your soul's transition into Light.

This certainly was true in my mother's case.

Upon her death, the nuns who nursed her gave the green scapular to me, ensuring that I too would enjoy a peaceful transition, surrounded by the prayers of loved ones, when I died.

An aunt, my husband, my baby and I sat with my mother all night on the night she left her body.

During the long night, I was able to tell her how much I loved and admired her and that I was so glad she'd been my mother.

As she was in a coma, the nuns said:

"It's no use talking to her. Your dear mother's in a coma and she can't hear you."

Silent tears fell down my mother's face as I talked to her and I knew she'd heard me.

When the time came for us to let go of her, we all knew it. My grandmother didn't feel the need to say 'goodbye' to her youngest daughter as she felt intuitively they'd soon be together again.

The night staff and my family joined hands around her bed and prayed loudly so that she could hear us.

She breathed out once.

Then she was gone.

The scent of roses enveloped me as she passed by me.

I missed my gentle mother very much but was comforted by her love that I felt all around me.

I knew she was alive and well in the spirit realm because I felt it.

My grandmother felt the loss of her youngest, most rebellious child very much, in spite of her enlightened perspective around death. She said to me:

"No mother should outlive her child."

The dreams in which my mother held me in her arms and comforted me facilitated the grieving process.

It seemed to me that God was calling all my loved ones to Himself and had left me on my own.

AU REVOIR MY GRANDMOTHER

Twelve months after my mother's death, my aunt gave a party for my cousin's birthday.

We all felt we'd passed through the valley of the shadow and were glad to have a happy occasion to celebrate as a family.

My grandmother looked beautiful that night and quite stole the show in a floor-length silver evening dress.

Her pure white hair shone like a halo around her, and her blue eyes had their old zest and sparkle.

She loved to party!

I sat beside her with my baby and we laughed at the speeches together.

She asked me:

"Darling, will you be a pet and go fetch my shawl for me? I feel a chill."

I told myself later:

"I should've known! When she mentioned she felt a chill, it meant something was going to happen to her!"

But at the time, I rose from my chair, hoisted my little girl to my hip and turned away to do what my grandmother wanted.

As I did so, I heard a strange sound behind me.

I heard a strangled cry that made me spin around.

I staggered at what I saw, heart in my mouth, as in disbelief I saw my grandmother hanging from her chair, almost lying on the floor, lifeless.

She was gone!

In the space between heart-beats, a cerebral haemorrhage had taken her from me.

My beloved, my best friend, my guide and teacher, was gone.

I couldn't bear it.

I held her body and cried, and my little girl sat on the floor and cried too, to see her Mummy so distraught.

An ambulance arrived eventually, and the paramedics went through their drill, but we all knew she was gone.

She'd left us.

Her doctor told us the next day:

"This marvellous woman had diabetes, arthritis of the spine and advanced heart disease. She'd been very ill for several years. It's a blessing that she's gone."

MY GRANDMOTHER SPEAKS TO ME

My grandmother continued to communicate with me after she'd left her body.

The first time I felt her loving presence was a few days after her beautiful and moving Celebration of Life service.

My grandmother had been adamant that she wouldn't have a funeral service.

"I hate the dreary funeral word and all the carrying on and crying it implies," she used to say.

During her Celebration of Life service, I sang her favourite songs,

"When Irish eyes are smiling" and "I'll walk with God," feeling in my heart that this beautiful lady was indeed smiling and walking with God.

I was determined to be strong and cheerful, as I'd always promised her I would be when it came time for us to part.

We all had a glorious and expensive 'wake' in the Irish tradition she'd loved so.

Whenever she'd talked about her death, she used to say that she wished:

"Real pain to my sham friends and (champagne) sham pain to my real friends," so we had a lot of champagne on hand to toast her glorious life.

She directed in her will that her body be burned.

So, a few days after her death, on a hill-side, her close friends and her family were assembled to bury her ashes.

I felt her loving presence.

I sensed her laughter and I felt her speak to me in my heart:

"Scatter the remains of my physical body to the four winds, darling."

As we did so, everyone sensed her presence.

She'd loved the works of the mystic Omar Khayam and her little green book was dear and familiar to all of us.

I read aloud a few of her favourite passages, ending with:
"And the moving finger, having writ, moves on."

We knew she liked it.

I never found out why she loved Kahlil Gibran and Omar Khayam so much. These books had influenced my own thinking as well, because she'd so often read these to me as I lay in her big bed at night as a child.

She'd also never told me who had taught her to meditate.

In many ways, this woman who'd been my grandmother was a mystery to her family.

It would be many years before I myself would be led by an Eastern Teacher to read the works of the Sufi poets Rumi and Kabir, and to appreciate the rich symbolism and messages of Divine Love expressed by these Masters.

I suspect that somewhere along the way, along her spiritual journey, my grandmother also once walked the path of Eastern mysticism.

CHAPTER 4

SPIRITUAL INFLUENCES IN ADULTHOOD

NEW LIFE: A BABY IS BORN

God was kind to my husband, my family and I, and gave us another beautiful baby to cherish a few months after my grandmother's death.

He was a sweet little boy who gave me relatively little pain during his birth. For this alone I loved him.

I'd been admitted to hospital a few days before the baby's birth and had the same doctor who'd delivered my daughter when I'd experienced leaving my body. My doctor was confident all would go well with me this time.

I awaited the baby's birth impatiently, anxious to see this new child.

It had been a trouble-free, uneventful pregnancy and I felt confident and positive about the birth.

One night I woke up feeling I needed to go to the toilet urgently. Experience told me the labour had begun.

I remember, after pressing the bell for the night nurse, how I begged her in my mind to hurry, as the contractions brought back to my mind the memory of pain around my first child's birth. Fortunately, my caring doctor arrived at the scene promptly.

The gas he gave me didn't seem to touch the pain much at all, but somehow I was able to go above it.

I remember at one stage during the night feeling the touch of my grandmother's hand on my brow, smelling the scent of roses in the room, their sweet and heady scent cancelling out the antiseptic hospital odour.

This calmed and strengthened me.

She told me, in my heart:

"Your baby will be born at dawn's first light, my darling. Watch the window well, little girl, a blackbird will sit there and sing of your baby's birth and he will be born."

"A boy!" I thought, "I'm going to have a boy."

And so it happened.

A blackbird sang at the window as my son emerged into the world, just as my grandmother had said he would.

He was a serene and peaceful baby, so unlike his sister, who'd cried and fussed for months after her birth. His big sister had been born during a time of family grief and mourning. I loved her dearly and kept her close to me.

With this new little baby, I was reminded of an old saying: 'especially beloved is the baby who sleeps all night'.

This baby needed to be woken up for feeding! I used to creep into his room terrified he'd slipped away from me, to see if he were breathing because he didn't cry for his feeds.

I was fascinated to see him awake, lying in his cradle peacefully, looking around with curious aware eyes.

I began to relax over the next few months, a little lulled and almost anaesthetised by the hormones of breast-feeding, and the aura of peace and love that emanated from this baby.

Perhaps the good Lord realised I needed an oasis to prepare me for the next parting from a loved one.

PADDY JOINS HIS BELOVED

My grandfather left the Earth quickly and gladly, not wanting to live without his beloved wife.

His older daughter and I sat with him, while my new baby lay in a pram in the corner.

We prayed for grandpapa as he gradually let go of his grip on our hands and on life.

A look of peace and joy appeared on his face as he saw his darling wife awaiting him in the Light.

As we cried, his soul ascended, led upward by her gentle hands and shining spirit.

After his death, his family and friends all assembled for a glorious Celebration of Life Service.

This time, we laughed more than we cried! At ninety-six years of age, he'd had a good life.

MY FATHER'S TIME TO GO

Life moved on.

My new baby boy grew fat and rosy, and his big sister adored him, though she needed lots of extra cuddles to reassure her of her special place in her parents' hearts.

My little boy was about four and a half years of age and

his big sister was a school girl when my father had his first and last heart attack.

He joined my mother without a word of farewell.

I knew it wasn't a heart attack at all, but a broken heart that had taken him from me. He found it very lonely living without my mother.

Just after his death, I had a dream that my parents were walking hand in hand down the tunnel I'd seen for myself before, and I knew that they would also walk into the glorious meeting place in the Light as I had. This sure knowledge of the survival of love after death of the physical body comforted me.

But how I missed him.

It was such a grief that I gave in to it.

I no longer had my grandmother's physical presence to comfort and support me and felt very alone.

I went to my father's grave, next to my mother's and sister's graves, lay on the grass crying day after day, wishing I could join my family in the glowing hall where the beautiful Beings worshipped God.

Each day, I took my little boy to the cemetery with me, leaving him sitting in the car in sight of me. I knew it was dangerous and unwise to visit graves because of all the spirits, but I didn't seem to care anymore. All the tears I'd been wanting to cry for my loved ones seemed to come out of me and kept on coming.

One day, as I lay on the grass sobbing, I felt a little hand on my shoulder. Surprised, I sat up and saw my dear little boy with tears running down his face.

He said to me between sobs:

"Please, please Mummy. Please don't cry anymore. I can't stand it anymore. You're breaking my heart, Mummy."

Pity and love washed through me and I got up immediately. I scooped him up in my arms and told him:

"You're right, darling, Mummy has cried enough. We won't come here anymore."

I drove away from that peaceful hill-side and I've never been back.

This son of mine was a wise and aware person who often counselled and supported me as he grew up.

He had a past-life memory he once told me, of a time when I was a Queen and he was a huge black Nubian slave in a leopard-skin loin-cloth and his duty was to protect me.

He did his job well this lifetime, too.

In about 1975, of my family of origin, I only had two aunts left and two cousins, whom I loved dearly.

My husband's family, particularly his grandmother, was a pillar of strength during these trying years. Many times, I would run the short distance to Grandma's house to bury my head in her soft large bosom and cry my heart out.

My husband's aunts were as warm and loving as their mother, and I felt embraced by all the members of this large extended family. Death and tragedy surrounded me and yet love was always there to support me.

Love came from the physical realms, from living humans with good and open hearts, and it also came from the spirit realm, from loving beings who were now out of body.

I knew from my own experience that Love survived death.

THE JESUIT PRIEST

In 1975, I met a man who would be a father-figure and a powerful influence on the next ten years of my life.

He'd been a Jesuit Priest for most of his life and had been awarded a Masters degree in Social Work and Psychology in the USA, after his study for the priesthood.

He'd been posted to South America at some stage and became disillusioned by the way in which the poor were treated.

He had a real socialist point of view about sharing and reminded me of St. Francis of Assisi, in his great love and respect for all people and his generosity and simplicity. He gave away all of himself in love as St. Francis did, and was the richer for the giving.

He often said to people:

"Mi casa, su casa" meaning "my house is your house."

In late middle-age, after leaving the priesthood, he met a loving lady who had been a nun, and who had left the convent.

They married.

His wife was Mexican-American who shared his views on the way the poor were treated.

They were well past the child-bearing age, so in order to have a family they adopted two children, a girl from Mexico and a black American boy. These two special babies grew strong, whole and loving in the atmosphere of love he and his wife provided.

They established a Family Therapy practice in the 1970's and soon became busy with referrals from the local doctors, impressed by their international credentials and experience.

I first met this couple when I was about twenty-five years of age. Two things immediately impressed me about the retired priest.

He offered me a cup of coffee, taking me to the kitchen to make it. We chatted comfortably over coffee and biscuits in the kitchen for about twenty minutes before I realised I'd already told him a lot about myself.

I'd felt so disarmed by his natural, friendly, easy-going manner that I'd let my guard down.

I learnt to use this homely technique with people myself when I too became a counsellor.

The other thing that impressed me happened when I was leaving his office after our session.

He put his arms around me and hugged me warmly.

I was embarrassed, yet comforted and had a warm feeling inside of me. Over time, I realised that he expressed security and love in every part of himself and all his patients truly trusted him.

I learnt to regard him as a father and grew to love him dearly.

He was a big, round bear of a man, with a full beard and longish, thick hair.

He had a massive sense of fun and humour and a whole kit-bag of Irish jokes on hand for any emergency. He was such fun to be around.

He radiated love to everyone. He kept his counselling fees to a bare minimum and never asked for money from poor people.

He worked hard, long hours that never seemed to bother him at all. Prayer, faith and love always renewed his energy.

He was a wonderful teacher.

I consulted this man and his wife whenever I had a problem, and they both soon began to treat me like one of their family. They became surrogate parents to me.

They both inspired me to become a counsellor due to my natural gifts of empathy and sensitivity.

MY FIRST COUNSELLING EXPERIENCE

When I was breast-feeding my second child, I began studying to be a counsellor through the Nursing Mothers' Association of Australia (NMAA) by correspondence.

I nearly gave it all up after my first practical experience of counselling a bereaved young mother whose baby had just died from SIDS (Sudden Infant Death Syndrome).

I'd visited her to deliver a casserole that our local NMAA group leader had suggested was a good thing to do, as part of our support and my counselling training.
I tried to remember what I was supposed to say to a bereaved parent and instead told her what I'd just seen about her baby in a vision when I entered her house.

I said quickly, before I had a chance to change my mind:

"I see things in my mind, visions and images. I've always seen things, since I was a child.

I see your little baby, smiling, looking so happy, in a beautiful place with your little sister who died as a baby too, with shining angelic beings all around them. They're both receiving so much love and caring. You don't need to worry about him anymore.

I have to tell you these things.

Please don't cry anymore about your baby. He's with God and the Angels. You need to know that it's not your fault, you didn't do anything wrong. It was just his time to go. He only needed the experience of birth one more time. He's gone Home."

The young mother looked shocked. She just sat there, staring at me.

I burst into tears and sat down abruptly at her kitchen table with my head on my arms and cried. She made me a cup of tea and put her arms around me and cried too.

I left eventually, feeling pretty silly:

"What a great mess I made of that," I told myself.

"Call yourself a counsellor, do you? You jolly well acted like a nutter!" I thought.

It seems funny now, but it didn't then.

The young mother later sent me a note telling me how grateful she was for the lovely things I'd told her, and she now carried a vivid picture in her mind of her smiling baby.

She told me she'd rung her mother to say I'd seen her mother's baby girl in a vision. During the 'phone call, her mother's grief for a baby lost long ago was healed.

The young mother said what had helped her the most was crying with me. She'd felt very touched by my sharing her grief and thought I'd make a brilliant counsellor.

I felt very happy about what she said, and glad that she and her mother had accepted the deaths of their children.

I believe it was love that helped the bereaved mothers, more than a professional, experienced and clinical approach.

I saw this love in action many times and as I grew in confidence, I allowed myself to speak more of the things I received.

I was to learn that it was more important to allow my heart, rather than my head, to lead me.

Trusting myself to receive Truth for clients led to some pretty embarrassing, humorous situations at times.

Sometimes, I seemed to have little control over what I said and just blurted things out.

For example, a young man came to see me one day to talk about his conflict with his parents.

While boiling the kettle in the kitchen to make him a cup of tea, I stood idly looking out the window and received illuminating information about his situation, unaware of what I was receiving. When I went back to the office and handed him a cup of tea, I said: "Have you ever thought about telling your parents you're gay?" The surprised young man spluttered over his tea cup and said:

"How did you know? Does it show?"

"I just made a lucky guess," I said, crossing my fingers behind my back.

This story had a happy ending when the young man told his parents about his 'problem', why he didn't want to marry, and trusted in their love for him.

I've found when dealing with clients and their challenges, everything always seems to turn out right no matter how stupid, inept or helpless I feel.

Because I trust in love and keep on loving, it's my feeling that it's Love that heals people, not what I say or do, or forget to do.

After completing my counselling certificate, I was keen to learn more.

I began a three year Diploma in Early Childhood Development with a major in Child Psychology.

As well as looking after a husband and home, I was now well into the 'breeding and feeding' mode, so it was a real challenge to study and attend classes twice weekly.

We also had a huge organic garden, a few sheep, a few cows and lots of egg-producing chickens on half an acre to maintain.

Life was full.

THE DARK ANGEL RETURNS

Life became even fuller, and so did my body with the advent of a third child in 1979.

I was quite ill during this unexpected pregnancy.

When the little boy was born just before Easter, he rapidly became very ill, and on Good Friday, we almost lost him.

He was lying in my arms in the hospital after a brief feeding, and he just went to sleep. Something alerted me that all was not well. I had an instant vision of that tall, dark, terrible stranger standing silently watching my tiny baby and I, from a shadowy corner of my hospital room.

"My God! Dear Lord, please don't let it happen. Make him go away. I won't let him take this one away! I won't."

I flashed back in time for an instant and knew just how my grandmother must have felt when that same terrible Dark Angel came for her baby.

I screamed out loud: "Help! Help! My baby's dying! Help!"

The nurses, alarmed, came running.

They tried to rouse my baby, alerted by the look of him and his limp little body. They had no time to ask questions, just took him from my arms and ran down the corridor to I didn't know where.

One of the nurses came along to sit and pray with me and to tell me calmly and gently:

"We've got your doctor here dear. He's told me to tell you he's called the Paediatrician. Your little baby is very ill, but he's alive and fighting. We're all praying for him. I called your husband and he's on his way."

It was some time before I saw my baby again. Before I did, the doctor prepared me for a shock. He told me:

"He's in a humidicrib. He's got a drip in his arm. His eyes are bandaged because we're giving him the 'lights' to flush the bilirubin, that's the bile released by the liver out of his blood-stream, and he's got tubes coming out of him all over the place. He's strong. He'll make it, we feel. After another day or so, you can hold him and see if he'll come to the breast. For now, feel good that we're giving him your milk through a tube. We're all praying for him."

This little boy was strong and determined, and I kept the Dark Man away from him for twelve months by constant focus, prayer and diligent attention.

We were both back in hospital when he was three months old, and I was exhausted.

He suffered a great deal of pain with his liver and various infections and cried almost ceaselessly. He wouldn't allow anyone except me to hold him, as if sensing that I was protecting him.

He also developed a gastro-oesophagal reflux that meant he would throw up much of each feed and I'd have to start all over again. He was thin and pale and cried a lot, and I loved him deeply.

This little baby survived, through the grace of God and today he is a tall, strong, gentle loving giant of a man.

BACK TO SCHOOL

After my third child grew into a toddler, I went back to school. After the Diploma and a six month practical teaching unit, I decided I'd had enough of small children, having three of my own by now, and went on to a degree in liberal studies with two majors, Psychology and Sociology and two minors, History and Education. "A double-banger of a degree" one of my lecturers called it!

My degree turned out to be like Tolstoy's "War and Peace"; it was so huge and took so long to complete.

In about 1982, as if I didn't have enough to keep me out of mischief, I took a casual job in a department store as I badly needed the money to finance my education without disadvantaging my family.

My youngest child was four and a half and keen to attend pre-school and went happily to a Centre while I went to work.

I STUDY HYPNOSIS

In 1985, I saw an advertisement in the local paper for a diploma course in clinical hypnosis and felt immediately excited at the prospect of studying hypnosis.

I rang the retired priest and his wife who were both enthusiastic and supportive about it.

"Go for it," was their advice.

They suggested that after attaining a diploma, I could commence working with them in their practice as a clinical hypnotherapist and student psychologist.

One Friday afternoon I left work early with the store Manager's blessings, and sat resting for a while, having a coffee in the restaurant of the hotel where the course was to be conducted.

I noticed an elegant older man, with white hair, in a pale-blue silk shirt and cream trousers, sitting in a corner looking intently at me.

I flushed, and looked away.

To my embarrassment, he got up as if summoned and came over to my table, asking:

"May I sit with you? Would you like another coffee?"

I looked up at him, and found myself staring into piercing deep dark eyes.

"Oh, my God! It's him! It's the hypnosis man. I hope he's not hypnotising me."

He laughed and said:

"Don't worry. I can see you know me already. You have the advantage, young lady, because I don't know you. Have you come here to do my course?"

Relieved and disarmed by his frank and courteous manner, I smiled and said:

"Very nice to meet you. I'm quite early, I wanted to just sit for a while. I'm very excited about studying hypnosis. I've read a lot about you in the material you sent me and I'm fascinated by the whole thing. Do, please sit down, and let me buy you a coffee."

He sat down and we talked for some time.

He had an arresting and charismatic air about him.

I peeked at his aura as I always did with people I'd just met, and saw that it was a deep and rich royal blue, and golden around his head.

My understanding of these colours was that he was a warm and caring man with an intellect far above others.

He was a most charming man with a deep rich voice. He had a marvellous sense of humour and was very warm. All this I discovered during the first meeting.

Little did I know what a life-changing decision I'd made, by enrolling myself in a diploma course in clinical hypnosis.

The Hand of God was again leading me forward, along the Divine Path laid out in front of me.

That Friday evening during the seminar's introduction and case studies, I avidly devoured every word that was spoken. The subject matter was fascinating.

After each case study, we were left with a sense of tantalising anticipation, which I later learnt was pure hypnosis.

The next day, there I sat bright and early, ready and waiting to write down every word, utterly determined to be the best student they'd ever seen!

I was so motivated I'd hardly slept all night; my mind had raced along with the prospect of adding this interesting tool to my tool-kit for 'fixing' people.

It made sense to me that the cause of all ill-health is in the deep sub-conscious mind of man.

The lecturer said it's erroneous to say the 'unconscious' mind, as the brain is always conscious.

He said the brain records every moment of our existence and stores the information, ready to retrieve it at our will. The only truly 'unconscious' mind is a dead mind.

This made perfect sense.

When the lecturer for Psychopathology appeared, I was at once interested and alert.

The tall, powerful-looking bearded man who lectured in this subject, would later prove to be another major influence on my life and a catalyst for personal growth.

MY REGRESSION BACK THROUGH TIME

During the course, as a gift to the students, we were given a group session to uncover and explore our past lives.

After being instructed to sleep, we were directed to allow our minds to go back in Time to our first experience and memory of our Soul's creation.

I experienced a blinding explosion of Light!

I was back with the Source of all that is, one with creation, and I felt the shattering grief at the separation of higher mind into matter.

I felt it was the same Light I'd experienced during the three near death experiences.

This session under hypnosis had a profound effect upon me and I was very thoughtful for sometime afterwards.

I passed my Diploma of Hypnosis with flying colours.

Apparently, I was a 'natural'.

I was keen to know more about this intriguing subject and loved the easy and relaxed way it was taught.

I decided to take up the offer to students to undertake further studies via a post-graduate diploma in Melbourne on weekends. I wondered how my husband would feel about this idea.

He'd been unenthusiastic about my working outside of the home and of studying, because he was a traditional man.

He felt my role as wife, mother and homemaker ought to be enough to satisfy me.

However, I felt very lonely at home even with the noisy, loving children, and felt I needed more in life.

I had so much energy, vitality and a great curiosity about all sorts of things.

I wanted to learn!

After some discussion, he agreed to my travelling to Melbourne in the company of other students of hypnosis.

However, his family made it clear to me that they also disapproved of my ambitions to be a counsellor, psychologist and clinical hypnotherapist. They felt a woman's place was in the home.

I couldn't bear this feeling of being held back from the future I intuitively knew was beckoning me.

I had to, as my grandmother had taught me, be true to myself and follow my heart, no matter the cost.

A lecturer at the University understood very clearly the pain and conflict I was feeling in wanting to please others and yet wanting desperately to follow my heart. He inspired me, even at that stage in my life, to write, and to follow where my heart was leading me.

He told me:

"There's a prize awaiting you.

It has a price in our society, especially if you're a woman.

It may cost you dearly."

He was right.

My enthusiasm for knowledge, education, experience and my inner longing to follow my heart, eventually led to my husband divorcing me and to losing my three children, as well as to losing the friendship of every person I'd ever known.

Yet, knowing full well the price of my freedom, I had to pay it and I did it again several years later.

MY MOTHER AND THE ROSES

In 1986, I was still studying towards the post-graduate diploma in clinical hypnosis, attending classes in Melbourne on weekends.

A friend had a friend who owned a charming Victorian terrace house in Melbourne, so several students decided to travel together and stay at our friend's house.

We agreed to share the cost involved, collected the key and off we went.

One of the students was a charming elderly gentleman, who'd been studying the powers of the mind for decades and who drove four of us to Melbourne in his four-wheel drive vehicle.

After our classes on the Saturday were over, we shared pizza and gelati in Carlton and went back to the house to sleep.

We'd dropped our bags inside earlier, but hadn't stayed for long.

When we walked in the front door, one of the girls exclaimed:

"What a beautiful fragrance. Roses! It's so strong. It's all over the place."

We could all smell it. It seemed to be strongest on the stairs.

I wondered: "Mummy, is it you, darling? Have you come to see me?" The sweet, soft, sighing answer came in my heart:

"Darling love, it's Mummy. Clean out your room. A nasty spirit haunts this place. I've done my best. I can't stay. I love you."

The house was on two floors, and had four bedrooms upstairs.

Up I went, deciding to check the house for spirits, following the heady scent of roses.

It became quickly apparent that the front bedroom with the bay window had a problem.

As I approached, I felt the cold immediately and shivered.

I began feeling nervous. I went into the darkened room.

Very old antique mahogany furniture dominated the room and appeared to absorb the light.

I crossed the room quickly and opened the windows. I put on all the lights and brought another lamp into the room.

I could definitely sense a depressive atmosphere in this room.

As well as the sensation of penetrating, aching cold, I experienced a heaviness in my neck, chest and back. I knew there was a malevolent Earth-bound entity haunting the building.

I also felt a tingling, hair-raising feeling across my scalp. My hair actually moved and my skin prickled uncomfortably all over. The atmosphere was very heavy with menace.

I had a feeling in my legs, of wanting to run away.

I had a sense of an angry old male presence, disturbed by the light, not a bit attracted to it, just cross and spiteful.

This was a malevolent spirit, trapped in time, haunting this house.

" Probably not a nice person even when he was alive," I thought. My colleagues were blissfully unaware downstairs, laughing and talking.

"Lucky them," I grumbled to myself.

I filled an empty hair-spray atomiser with water, that I had in my bag, blessed it after making an intention and saying 'The Lord's Prayer' three times, and sprayed the room and the ugly furniture liberally.

I walked around the room praying out loud, holding my hands out as I walked, sensing the cold spots, and radiating energy and light. After about twenty minutes, I'd done all I could to dispel the negativity and decided to look at the other bedrooms.

I could find no evidence of negativity in the other rooms, just in the front bedroom.

The bedroom at the back of the building was small and only had a single bed, yet the 'roses' were there, so obviously this was safe for me to sleep in.

Much later, we all settled down and the night passed uneventfully, except that one of the girls in our group crept in at some time and slept on the floor in my room.

Apparently, she kept having bad dreams and felt afraid to sleep by herself.

It's interesting to note that no-one felt inclined to sleep in the front room, though it was by far the most comfortable-looking room with the best furniture. All the members of our little band said it was 'cold'.

By the way, I hadn't said a word about my cleansing of the house, or the nasty old spirit in the front room.

As we left the house the next day, I whispered "thank you, Mummy."

LOVING VISITS IN SPIRIT

After they'd left their bodies, both my grandmother and my mother's visits to me in spirit were presaged by the overwhelming scent of roses, by light and vibrant colours.

I saw the colours with my inner eyes. My mother's colour was a cyclamen-pink.

My grandmother's colour was a deep magenta-purple.

Each had her own subtle feeling too.

My mother felt gentle and tender, while my grandmother felt majestic and regal.

I always knew intuitively when it was my mother or grandmother who whispered to me in my heart, or sent me a message through someone or something else.

For example, I was driving far too fast, anxious to get home to my baby one late wintry afternoon in 1979, when a voice inside of me yelled at me:

"Slow down now! Be aware of what you're doing! You're driving too fast."

I immediately slowed down and realised with wonder and gratitude it had been my grandmother's voice calling to me.

I was grateful for this warning and felt she'd saved me from an impending accident.

These two beloved souls, my mother and grandmother, comforted and guided me until 1994, when they were released from their bonds of love and sent on to higher service by my new Teacher.

He taught me that no matter how loving or beloved souls may be, the Earth Realm is not for them. They need to go on to the next realm of their existence, or they may become lost.

I VISIT MY FAMILY IN HEAVEN

I had a dream I was walking along a golden road that went right up to the sky.

I walked along a so-familiar street, entered a dearly loved, so-familiar front yard, went up the steps, opened the door and entered the front room of my childhood home.

My favourite uncle was reading the racing news in his singlet in his comfortable chair.

My grandpapa was snoozing in front of the TV.

My beloved mother was in the kitchen laughing and talking with my darling grandmother.

At that moment, my grandmother came into the room. Upon seeing me, she greeted me with joy and love.

She called out: "Look everyone, our darling girl is Home! How wonderful! Put the kettle on, we'll have some tea."

All my loved ones gathered around, hugging me all at once, laughing and crying.

My heart was bursting with happiness.

Then with a shock, I realised all these people were no longer living. I was the only living person there!

I was sorry I had that thought because it woke me up from my dream and brought me back to the Earth Plane.

I know my family is waiting somewhere for me.

The place I created in my dream is waiting for me too.

I know my dream was the fulfilment of a wish to be re-united with my family. God was kind to me and granted my wish.

PLANES OF EXISTENCE

After having experienced this dream, I realised my deceased loved ones had been able to ascend above the Earth Plane to a plane of transition.

I began to understand that when we leave the physical body, our souls exist in other dimensions. I have experienced several Planes in dreams and visions.

THE EARTH PLANE

This is the Plane of the physical experience of being in a body. There are two lessons to be learnt on this plane.

1. To communicate and reconnect with our Creator.
2. To serve mankind.

LOVE IS THE PRIMARY
LESSON OF THE EARTH PLANE

When a person dies without belief in the Creator, or the Creator's representative on Earth, such as a Teacher or Guru, or without any spiritual belief, their souls are unable to leave the Earth Plane. Here they stay. What are commonly called ghosts and spirits are indeed earth-bound souls unable to ascend.

THE PLANE OF LOWER FORCES

This is a negative plane, sometimes referred to as the Astral Plane. All negative thoughts and fears deeply held in the mind create negative manifestations.

This could indeed be the vision of 'Hell' experienced by drunkards, drug addicts and the diabolically possessed.

Malevolent entities exist on the lower plane.

THE PLANE OF JUDGEMENT: AKASHA

This is the Plane where we sit in counsel with wise elders, counsellors and guardians and review our life's work.

This is the place where we choose another life, other partners, other lessons.

All the resources we need are provided here to complete our mission.

I once had a dream where Divine beings handed me a book, upon whose pages were recorded details of all my past lives.

THE PLANE OF REST:
THE WORLD BETWEEN WORLDS

I once counselled a lady whose husband had died while jogging along a beach one morning. He was strong and healthy and totally unprepared for death.

In a vision, I saw him in this Plane of Rest, cushioned and cocooned, curled up on his side, sleeping as deeply and peacefully as a baby.

I saw shining creatures of Light tenderly watching over him. They told me he was in a state of denial and shock.

After twelve months, the lady's husband awoke and I was able to communicate with him and persuade him to let go of his attachment to life on Earth and to allow himself to be guided to a higher Plane.

THE PLANE OF BABIES AND CHILDREN

This seems to be the Summerland that North American Indians describe.

A woman and her husband lost a small baby and shared the same dream.

They dreamt they were watching their baby being cared for by loving beings in a gloriously beautiful place.

Many babies and small children were playing in a beautiful garden in sparkling sunshine. The parents experienced upon awakening and sharing their dream with each other, a deep sense of joy and peace.

It seems that small babies and children enjoy a peaceful transition between the Earth Plane and the next.

THE ANGELIC PLANE

This is the realm of the devata and angelic beings. These are wondrous benevolent beings, who watch over humans.

These beings long to be part of the Earth experience.

When an angelic being fulfils its mission as guardian of a human, it earns the right to incarnate as a human being and is able to ascend towards the Divine Plane.

It seems it is only by living a life on the Earth Plane, learning the lessons of Love and overcoming the ego, that a soul earns the right to ascend to the higher realms.

I had an uplifting experience in New Zealand in 1995, of meeting an angel, who touched me and showered heavenly love on me, and on everyone else to whom I told her story.

THE PLANE OF THE ASCENDED MASTERS

This is a higher Plane than the Angelic Plane.

This Plane is where great souls work together for the worlds of all creation, directed and commissioned by the Divine.

They are able to deliver messages from the Divine to human beings. These Masters are the Divinely inspired authors of the Scriptures of the world.

They have achieved mastery over the lower human nature or satanic influence of man in themselves.

Ascended Masters are more evolved beings who incarnate at a time in history where the Divine energy is sorely needed, whose souls only require one more lifetime to ascend to their goal - the Divine Realm.

THE DIVINE PLANE

This is where the Divine Creator resides.

This is the place to which we all aspire to return, known as Heaven to Christians.

Like reflections of the sun belong to the sun, like droplets of water join the sea, so human beings have the potential to return to the Divine plane.

GABRIELLE THE ARTIST

When I was working with the retired priest and his wife, as a clinical hypnotherapist in the family therapy practice in 1986, a brilliant young artist was referred by her psychiatrist.

The local doctors referred to us because the Practice seemed to work 'miracles'.

My friend the priest often said:

"Even though I've left the priesthood, the clients still come to me for absolution of their sins."

Gabrielle was unable and unwilling to forgive herself so we forgave her and loved her, until she was able to forgive and love herself.

Gabrielle was a gifted artist who had a drug problem.

In order to finance the addiction, she had resorted to selling her beautiful body from time to time.

I noticed how dead and flat her eyes were when she told me about this.

She bared her arms to show me the 'rail-road tracks' from the drug abuse to which she was subjecting her body.

I was initially at a loss as to how I could help this tragic young woman, yet the referring psychiatrist had such faith in me that I decided to meet with her and give it a try.

We began with progressive muscle relaxation and went on to hypnotic induction.

I felt that the deep sub-conscious mind would be able to tell us where the problem lay. Gabrielle liked and trusted me, so it was easy for her to go into trance.

She had been referred to us because she suffered from insomnia due to dreadful nightmares, and was unable to sleep which had resulted in ongoing health difficulties, depression, mental and physical exhaustion.

She also found it difficult to trust men and her male psychiatrist felt that if I could help her to make sense of the nightmares, then she would be able to sleep and look at her life.

During our first session, Gabrielle quickly and easily fell asleep. I felt it was important and necessary for her to rest, so just put a soft rug over her where she lay back in the big recliner chair, and left her to it.

I saw my other patients in the kitchen that day.

Gabrielle slept six hours and woke up feeling better than she had felt for a long time.

The next session, she brought a painting she had done to illustrate the 'demon' that possessed her, as she expressed it to me. I had been aware of the darkness around her from our first meeting.

The painting was in the surrealist mode and hinted of an influence of Van Gogh's tortured work.

It depicted a young woman resembling Gabrielle, being pursued by a shapeless monster along a darkened beach. This was the recurring nightmare that had plagued her periodically for as long as she could remember, she told me, but had recently come nightly.

It was the nightmare that was making her more and more afraid of sleep.

"If I sleep, the monster will get me. I'll die," she told me, eyes filled with fear.

Over the next few weeks, we continued to pray for Gabrielle.

In the course of therapy with Gabrielle, over several months, I incorporated hypnotherapeutic suggestions that the meaning of the dream would become clear to her in the conscious state, the fear would dissipate, Divine Love and protection were all around her, the drug addiction would let go of her, she loved herself, and she was already healed.

One day, after her session, she asked if my friend the retired priest would hear her confession.

She was too afraid to go into a church and talk to a priest, she said, because she couldn't trust men.

She told me:

"I can't even trust priests, but he's different. I know he could never hurt me."

He agreed, feeling intuitively that confession of her 'sins' would help Gabrielle.

Gabrielle asked that I be present while my friend heard her confession.

I sat in the corner of our tiny office with my back to her for privacy.

I cried quietly as her tragic life-story unfolded.

How humble I felt.

How awe-inspiring the experience was.

At the end of her catharsis, my friend solemnly pronounced the Latin words of absolution, and Gabrielle emerged from our office a new person.

All her heavy make-up was washed away by her tears, and she walked with quiet dignity down the drive-way.

Her therapy was rapid after that day.

She told me proudly soon after:

"Last night, I changed the outcome of the nightmare as you always promised I would.

I stopped on the beach.

I turned around and confronted the monster.

The monster was me! I was chasing and scaring myself.

I got such a shock when I saw my own face that I woke right up. I cried a lot, got up and had some Milo.

I understand everything now. I'm going to tell myself some really important things next time I have that dream."

Gabrielle didn't have the nightmare anymore.

Her dreams contained colourful symbols and images of castles in the clouds, aeroplanes, birds, clear pools of sparkling water and so many other beautiful spiritual images of cleansing and enlightenment.

The Divine Soul in her was now counselling and guiding her at night through dreams. She actually began to look forward to going to sleep.

Gabrielle's healing continued over many years, and is a true miracle.

She went on to a methadone treatment program and was no longer able to regard her body as a commodity to be bought and sold.

Her paintings began reflecting more of the light that was beginning to grow inside of herself.

Last I knew of Gabrielle, she was married and at peace with herself.

CHAPTER 5

THE QUICKENING

MELBOURNE - NEW BEGINNINGS

One weekend in May 1986 as part of the post-graduate diploma in clinical hypnosis, a counselling course was being conducted Saturdays and Sundays in Melbourne.

I was looking forward to this one.

One student came in late and sat around the corner from me. I took no notice until he spoke, and then something about his rich voice arrested my attention.

"Who's that?" I thought.

It was one of those moments when I knew something very important was going to happen.

Intuition told me that this man and I were destined to be together in some way.

One of our first role-plays that day was scheduled for after lunch and I found myself paired off with the owner of that voice.

I'll make a long story short. He ended up being my second husband within two years.

He also became the father of my fourth child.

After the parting from my first husband, not without its share of grief, emotional pain and regret, I'd moved to

Melbourne and had begun seeing clients in a Psychotherapy Practice in the south-eastern suburbs.

I'd finished my post-graduate diploma with honours and been awarded a scholarship for my studies in hypnosis.

I'd started out wanting to be the best I could be and ended up being it.

In 1988, I married the man with the beautiful voice.

Eighty people attended the wedding, but of all my family and friends in the country town where I'd grown up, only two people attended.

I gathered that I was persona non gratis in my old town. Married again! And another non-Catholic too!

In late 1988, I realised that at thirty-nine years of age, I was going to have another child.

My new husband and I felt concerned about the pregnancy and were both worried about my capacity to have a child at thirty-nine, after the difficulties I'd had with my son ten years before.

A GIFT FROM THE DIVINE

One morning we attended Church together to ask for guidance about continuing with the pregnancy and a truly miraculous event occurred.

A young, dynamic, visiting minister was conducting the service that day.

There was a large box on the altar tied up with a huge yellow bow. The minister talked about the many gifts a loving God gives to His children, and that we needed to be able to receive these gifts joyfully.

As he said this, I was thinking about my gift of clairvoyance and was totally unprepared for what happened next.

The young minister undid the bow with a flourish, whipped off the lid of the box and lifted out a small boy who'd been sitting patiently in the box waiting for this moment.

At the same time I heard a voice speak to me in my heart which said:

"Your child is a gift. Accept the gift."

I looked at my husband in wonder and told him quietly:

"We asked for guidance, and I've just received a message in my heart from the Divine. The child is a gift from God. We must accept the gift."

Neither of us ever regretted accepting that beautiful gift.

The child is the best thing we ever did together.

During the pregnancy, I continued to see a few clients, but this time from our home, as I did not feel up to travelling to and from work.

I'd received my degree in Psychology and was under supervision as part of the requirements for registration as a Psychologist.

My dream was about to come true - a Psychologist at last!

I had a few interesting clients referred to me during this time.

PENNY: THE HEALING OF ENDOMETRIOSIS

A sweet and attractive young woman called 'Penny', was referred to me by her doctor.

Penny longed to have a baby.

She was in a committed relationship and felt that she and her partner were ready to become parents.

She brought with her some x-rays that were provided by a specialist Gynaecologist some twelve months ago, showing a severe case of endometriosis. She'd already undergone surgery, but the condition recurred.

Endometriosis occurs when the lining of the womb, meant to nurture a developing foetus, grows outside the womb and attaches itself to the abdomen and internal organs.

The specialist felt it was unlikely that Penny would conceive.

Penny and I spent the next several months together, working on her childhood and family conditioning and patterns of behaviour, as well as using visualisation of a healthy abdomen and strong immune system.

She also began to pray again and to renew the faith she'd had as a small girl.

We examined previous intimate relationships and Penny let go of the pain involved in each relationship and recognised the lessons that each man had come to teach her.

"If we don't learn the lesson in a particular relationship, the lesson returns wearing a different pair of trousers, same lesson," I told Penny.

During hypnosis, Penny regressed to several past-lives and let go of several traumatic past-life experiences of sexual abuse and rape.

Her sub-conscious mind had brought these experiences to the foreground in our hypnotherapy sessions.

I'd told Penny under hypnosis:

"Your mind knows the source of the problem. Allow the mind to travel back in time to locate the original sensitising event."

After about two years of psychotherapy, Penny became the proud and loving mother of a little boy, as I also did in 1989.

After my return from overseas in 1996, I was delighted to hear that Penny had given birth to a second boy and her x-rays showed a complete healing of the former troubling condition.

It was amusing for Penny and I to note that she now needed contraception, for the first time in her adult life.

"It looks like I can't stop breeding now I've started," Penny told me laughingly.

A miracle of love, patience, hard personal growth work, utter commitment to life and health and a little dose of Divine magic, had made Penny's dreams come true.

THE YOUNG CHEF

A young woman was referred to me by a friend for what she called a 'peculiar problem'.

She was tall and thin, about twenty-five years of age and was enjoying a challenging apprenticeship as a chef in a leading Melbourne restaurant.

The problem was that she'd begun to be afraid of knives.

She'd been required to purchase her own set of knives and had started having frightening experiences.

One particular incident terrified her concerning a knife falling from a bench and imbedding itself right near her foot, narrowly missing her. Apparently, there was no-one near the knife except herself, and she'd not touched it.

"It's as if it suddenly just flew into the air," she told me.

A second incident a few days later, involved a serious cut to her hand, which she said had no possible rational explanation.

She began to have nightmares about a dark shadow in the corners of the kitchen, and felt that:

"Someone or something is out to get me."

As a psychologist, it seemed that my young client was suffering from phobic anxiety. A phobia is described by the text books as 'fear that is out of all proportion to the danger posed'. I also realised that perhaps another psychologist would add that my client had possible paranoic delusions.

As a psychic, I wondered if my client's 'dark shadow' was the same dark angel I knew so well!

It was clear to me that if she could not overcome the growing 'phobic anxiety' around knives, she would have to abandon her chosen career which she loved very much.

She didn't act or sound at all neurotic or psychotic, just frightened, puzzled and embarrassed about her feelings.

As she was speaking to me about a third incident that had occurred that day, a noise erupted from my kitchen.

We both jumped.

Where we sat, on a brown velvet couch, I could push open a sliding door to the kitchen without even moving.

I did so, and was not too surprised to see that my son's battery-operated robot had toppled off the bookcase and was standing upright on the kitchen floor, little motor ticking over. I say 'not surprised' because it had happened once before when he'd left it turned on and it had been too near the edge of the shelf.

"It must have happened again. Funny thing," I thought.

As we both laughed at our fears, the little robot's lights came on and he ambled across the kitchen floor to me, motor whirring, robot-voice activated saying:

"Danger! Danger!" And then it stopped.

I stopped smiling when I remembered with a chill that I'd become used to removing the robot's batteries at night and I saw the batteries on the shelf where I'd left the robot.

"The robot's empty. I took the batteries out! My God, that's not possible, unless... a spirit. She's brought a spirit with her," went rapidly through my mind.

I got up, closed the sliding-door and said:

"Let me top up your coffee, won't be a moment," and went into the kitchen humming cheerfully, trying to calm myself and my nervous client.

Unseen by my client, I picked up the robot, and yes, it was empty and silent now. No batteries!

I put the robot in the cupboard under the sink and blessed it.

When I went back to my client, I told her that her 'problem' was probably due to stress, anxiety and the long working hours related to her occupation.

I also advised her that she needed to be more relaxed, focussed and aware when she was working in a kitchen with knives.

Underneath the conversation, I prayed for the young woman to be cleared and protected, and for the restaurant's kitchen to be cleared of any negative, satanic influence.

My young client had faith in me and came to see me for about three months to learn meditation to dispel the stress that she suffered.

She didn't have any more 'near-misses' with knives at work, but I did!

One day, not so long after our session, I cut my finger badly when my vegetable knife slipped and I immediately thought of her.

Anyway, no more problems of the 'peculiar' kind for the young chef.

In gratitude, she delivered many delightful meals, complete with entree, main course, dessert and hand-made chocolates, to my home just in time for dinner.

As I had my three children from my first marriage staying with me for their school holidays, and I was pregnant, it was wonderful to receive these beautifully pre-prepared meals from my chef.

THE ASTROLOGER'S HUSBAND: DEATH ISN'T THE END

Just after the young chef, a doctor sent me a lady who was depressed. The new client told me she'd been depressed for about three years, following the death of her husband.

She was an astrologer, and had continued to maintain herself financially by her small practice. However, she could gain no understanding or insight into her own situation by astrology.

She had for a while recently contemplated suicide, she told me tearfully.

She said she'd feel much better if she could only know for sure that death wasn't the end, that her husband somehow lived on in some form somewhere else.

It was as a psychologist that she'd been referred to me, and it began to look like she was seeking a psychic's help.

"Here we go again," I thought, wondering if she'd tell her doctor about our session.

After a silent prayer, during which I surrendered myself to the Divine, I let go of any expectations around this session and waited for information that would assist my client.

No images. No visions. No feelings.

Nothing seemed to happen.

"This is a bit strange," I thought, "it doesn't usually feel like this. Oh, well, I'll just ask the Divine to give her some evidence via a dream or an experience as assurance that her husband has survived the death experience."

And that was that. Or, so it seemed.

'Dorothy' said she felt much more peaceful and accepting after our talk and meditative prayer and left smiling.

Sometimes, that's how it is and I'm left wondering what's happened to my client. If I don't hear from them again, I can only wonder.

About two weeks later, Dorothy rang to make another appointment, sounding quite cheerful. She said:

"Something wonderful and miraculous has happened. I want to tell you face to face."

We met a few days later and this is what she told me:

"That night, after I saw you, I went to bed and said my own little prayer.

I asked God or whatever it is, to give me three things as evidence that 'John' didn't stop existing.

The first thing I got was a dream. I haven't dreamt since I was a child, and I remembered it all. It was in colour and so real, as if it were really happening.

John held my hand, he looked so gorgeous, I just cried all the time."

Dorothy went on, with a beautiful smile on her face:

"He told me that he was only dead to his body and to the physical experience, that his soul had survived and his love for me was stronger than ever.

That's all I remember, but the feeling is still in me when I talk about it. I just know that John's all right and I'll go and meet him one day.

I'm not scared of dying anymore.

The next amazing thing happened a few days after the dream. John's photo on the piano was lying down on its face when I got up the next morning.

I thought: 'John did that to let me know the dream was real. One more sign and I'll really believe it'.

Well, the next thing happened when I got up the next morning. There was a pair of John's favourite 'Mr. Happy' socks, lying on the kitchen bench. I didn't put them there; they'd been in a suitcase in the back-room for three years. I'd never been able to bring myself to throw any of his things out.

The third thing, the socks, did it for me.

I was so excited that I just had to tell you all about it and to thank you."

I was delighted that God had heard both of us and had given us what we'd both asked for....survival evidence.

DAVID WON!

One night, the 'phone rang late.

I felt a chill run through me and knew that something was very wrong.

I sat quietly waiting while my husband spoke to whomever it was who'd called so late.

I quickly raced names through my mind:

"Who's hurt? Surely not a death? Is it the children? One of my aunts? Who is it? Please God, not the children!"

My husband came in and said:

"That was your friend, the Priest from the country Practice. His son David is dead, it was an accident.

They're all devastated.

They've got a full book of clients and they need you to fly tomorrow first thing to see the clients for them, to help them get through this terrible thing.

Can you do it? I told him you would."

I was happy to do anything I could to help.

"Their son! Oh, dear God, help them," I thought.

I prayed for their son's soul to ascend to Heaven.

During the next few days, my dear friends taught me, and taught everyone else who came to share in their grief, so much about love and acceptance of the Divine Will.

They were both able to cry and to express their grief whenever it arose within them.

The boy's mother was intuitive and she told me that she felt her son's presence all around her.

The sure knowledge that her 'little rose still grew beyond the wall', was a comfort to her.

One thousand young people attended their son's funeral and many hearts opened to Love.

My friends rang me a few weeks after their son's death with an incredible story.

They'd been driving to attend a conference and during the journey, they'd been talking about their son's death and praying for him as they drove.

The boy's father had looked in the rear-vision mirror and had seen a golden-yellow sports car coming up very fast behind him.

As he moved over to let it pass, his wife cried out as she saw the number plate on the gleaming car.

It read: "David 1."

When the car disappeared around a bend in the road, they pulled over, cried a little and prayed joyfully, thanking God for manifesting the evidence that their son had 'won'.

The manifestation of a golden car was their sure knowledge that their son had triumphed over death.

THE MIRACLE BIRTH

In 1989, on the anniversary of the first meeting between my husband and I two years earlier, a new baby boy was born to me at forty years of age.

His birth was a miracle.

There was no pain, no fear at all.

I'd decided not to go to a hospital to give birth this time, as I had so much fear around the hospital birthing experience, so chose a Birthing Centre this time.

I chose my own birth attendants at the beginning of the pregnancy and they became close and dear friends.

I felt it was important that the people who would attend this child's birth be supportive, spiritually aware and loving.

The labour began in the early hours of the morning.

Shortly after, our son was born under water.

He emerged from the water like a tiny dolphin, looking first into his father's eyes and breaking his heart with love, and then into my eyes and into my waiting arms, still connected with me by his umbilical cord.

He was born aware.

I was grateful to God for this wonderful and gentle birth experience and now felt I knew what it was like to 'give' birth, not to have the experience taken away from me in a hospital-setting by strangers.

No Near Death Experience this time.

At home once again, our little boy slept, fed, thrived and grew. Such a joy he was.

His big brothers and sister came to see him as soon as possible and they all fell in love with him, as quickly as he did with them.

IS THERE A SPIRIT IN THE HOUSE

My fourth baby brought me peace and tranquillity.

He was a robust and healthy little boy and I had no reason to worry about his health.

For some time I'd been aware of various benevolent spirit presences in our home.

When I'd first moved into the house, I'd prayed daily for the house to be protected by the Divine, who'd sent angelic spirits.

I had a sense of a loving spirit in the kitchen and on the stairs leading up to the first floor.

Whenever my husband and I began to disagree about anything, I would persuade him to sit on the stairs with me or have a cup of tea in the kitchen under the window, as all conflict would soon quickly disappear in these locations.

I intuitively sensed a warmth and a feeling of peace and love there and was quick to take advantage of it.

I soon found it was no use getting into a discussion anywhere upstairs at all, or there would soon be World War three!

One of the mid-wives who'd attended my son's birth was a spiritual counsellor and rebirther.

When she first visited the house, she told me:

"It's really important to generate harmony in your relationship with your husband in this house as negative vibrations such as those generated by disagreement, argument and conflict will attract negative disembodied entities," and I had to agree with her.

Sometimes as he grew, my little boy would stand up in his cot during the night and cry for me, as if he were frightened of something or had experienced a nightmare.

I would hold him and sing him prayers my grandmother had sung to me during the night.

I also wrote a special prayer of protection for my little boy and my husband would read it to him if I were away at his bed-time. My son soon memorised the prayer for himself.

The retired priest and his wife came to Melbourne to meet the baby and brought a wooden crucifix for his room, that had come from Rome and had been blessed by the Pope himself.

They also gave him a picture for his wall. In this picture was a young and smiling Jesus, surrounded by five children.

My friends pointed them out to me and named them one by one. Each child represented one of my own children.

There were the three from my first marriage, there was a plump baby boy on Jesus' lap and there was a shy little dark-skinned boy standing behind Jesus:

"That's David," his mother said.

I had given my little boy 'David' as one of his names, which made my friends very happy.

TRANSFORMED BY THE LIGHTS

Over the next five years, my spiritual growth accelerated at quite an alarming rate.

One night in 1990, I was awoken at about 3am. by a very bright light shining in my face.

As I forced my eyes to open, I saw to my amazement a band of luminous colours radiating down from the ceiling onto me.

The bright white light was followed by a golden yellow, then a vivid green, then a deep pink, then purple, then blue, then a piercing silver.

When the lights reached me, they seemed to penetrate my head through my eyes and a deep heat burned inside my chest.

I knew I could look at the coloured lights but somehow I knew intuitively I couldn't look at the silver light as it was too intense.

One night the temptation to look into the silver light became irresistible. I looked. I lost consciousness.

I slept deeply after the silver light completed the transmission and a profound transformation came over me, that stayed with me during the day.

Every night until 1994, these Lights would visit me, awakening me at precisely 3am.

This puzzled me a lot. I had no-one whom I could ask for an explanation.

As time went on, I grew to look forward to the Lights. Sometimes, it would happen to me in the day-time too, and I would feel dizzy and faint and would have to lean on something.

A friend gave me the name of a well-known Christian psychic one day whom she felt may be able to advise me.

I decided to take the risk and call her, to ask her if she knew anything about the Lights that I saw.

She was lovely, very clean in energy and wise.

At once, without asking questions, she was guided to tell me:

"I find that you are in a state of adrenal exhaustion. Apparently, you are receiving energy of a very high quality and frequency from a source I cannot identify.

Don't be afraid. It's for your good. I sense protection all around you.

I am guided to tell you to imagine a triangle in your mind when you pray. I want you to see me at one edge of the triangle, yourself at the other edge and Jesus the Christ at the top of the triangle.

We will all look after you while all this growth is happening. Don't hesitate to call me whenever you need to talk to someone."

I wrote her words down and found them comforting to read.

This lady worked without payment and truly lived to serve.

I was mystified by the Lights and wondered often what was happening to me.

I was becoming unwell. I'd gained too much weight, had high blood pressure, as well as spinal and skeletal pain.

I was having too many headaches and felt tired all the time. I tended to put it down to having a new baby at forty.

Later I would discover I'd been picking up negative energies for years with no system of removing them from myself, just like my grandmother before me.

I needed another psychologist to supervise me for registration, as my first supervisor had left Melbourne.

I remembered the psychologist I'd liked in 1986 who'd lectured for the diploma of clinical hypnosis and decided to ring him.

When I rang him and asked about supervision, he said he'd be delighted, so my new period of supervised practice began. During this period of ill-health, my faith in God, prayer and meditation kept me going.

During the time my new supervisor and I spent together once a week, he suggested books to me and began opening my mind to concepts I'd not experienced before.

I began to read voraciously on Neuro-Linguistic Programming (NLP), Psycho-Neuro-Immunology, and anything by Dr. Jean Houston.

I eventually discovered 'The Search For The Beloved' and 'The Possible Human' by Dr. Houston who had a doctorate in psychology, and found her books exciting and stimulating.

These books suggested a group concept of meditation as an accelerated growth potential and I began to consider running a group myself.

I suggested the idea of regular group meditation to two colleagues who quickly expressed their enthusiasm.

After hearing my plans, my supervisor also expressed his willingness to participate.

This group met regularly for two years.

We took turns reading the meditations to each other and leading visualisation exercises. I very quickly began having images and vivid visions. Two visions stand out above the others.

THE IMAM

During one of our meditation exercises, I had a vision of a tall, brown-skinned man in long white robes, wearing a small white cap on his head.

The man was standing at a cross-roads between two trees in some tropical country.

In my vision, I was guided to ask the man who he was.

He replied:

"I am the Imam.

I have come from your future.

Soon you will know me.

There is much I have to teach you."

I found this vision intriguing.

I had never heard of an Imam and didn't know what it meant.

My supervisor said an Imam was a Muslim holy man who intoned the prayers and guided the people. He explained that an Imam is an Islamic priest.

This meant nothing to me at the time.

"How strange and curious," I thought. Time would tell.

THE YOUNG KNIGHT
AND THE SWORD OF DESTINY

During a meditation with my professional group, I had a vision of a young female knight in shining armour, coming towards me out of the mists of Time.

I watched this female warrior in fascination and wonder as she seemed so real.

I saw her vivid life in rich colour and detail flash before my inner eyes.

She rode a horse at battle, carrying a king's standard.

I saw her wounded, rising from the battle field triumphant.

I saw her, weary and grimy, on her knees in a small chapel, golden light falling on her upturned face.

When I opened my eyes, I was amazed to see the young knight's image still reflected in the long glass french-doors of my lounge-room! She was no longer a vision, she appeared to be in this physical reality, though no one else in the room could see her.

I told the group members what I was experiencing. My supervisor asked me to describe the young woman and what she was doing.

I said: "She's bowing to me.

She's got a long sword at her side and she's holding it out to me, hilt first. She wants me to take it. I don't know what to do with it.

Why would I need a sword?"

As I spoke, she showed me what to do.

She took the sword back and put it at her side.

Smiling, she again handed the sword to me. I accepted it this time. She nodded approvingly.

I could feel no sword, but I saw that it was gone from her hand.

I put the vision sword by my side as she'd done and she appeared to be satisfied.

As I tried to make sense of the vision and the young knight, she bowed deeply and disappeared.

I understood she'd handed to me a gift of power and I felt stronger for it.

I liked her. She was a symbol of myself.

I never used the sword to draw blood, but I liked knowing I could, if I needed to.

Some mystics see the giving of a symbolic sword as the 'sword of destiny', a sign that something Divine is about to happen to its recipient.

A psychic in 1996, saw what he called 'The Sword of Shiva'.

He said:

"You carry the sword that is used to cut through the veil of illusion."

As a group, we also studied Joseph Campbell's work on mythology, Carl Jung's research on Symbols and Esoteric Psychology.

As well as meditating as a group, we shared a weekend together in a mountain retreat, and all experienced the same dream.

My dreams became more vivid at this time too and I kept a record and interpretation of each of my dreams.

My growing interest in dream interpretation led to reading Denise Linn's books.

Denise Linn was a Reincarnationist and Dream Therapist who came to Australia in 1992 and 1994 as a guest of the Body, Mind and Spirit Festival.

Two colleagues and I from the Australian Society of

Clinical Hypnotherapists, went to Denise's Sydney and Melbourne Seminar and enjoyed it very much.

I admired her warmth and authority.

Not long after this, I had some unusual experiences that stand out in my memory very clearly.

CURSE OR BLESSING

For me, clairvoyance has been both a curse and a blessing.

There have been many times I wished I was not clairvoyant. There have been many things I've seen I wished I'd not seen.

One morning, I was chairing a meeting of a women's group that was lobbying the Government on women's issues.

There were about fifteen women present.

As I was speaking, I glanced at each woman's face in turn, gauging her interest.

Around some of the women, I saw one or two shadows beginning to emerge.

As I gazed, I became aware of all the light in the room dimming and going to a focal point directly in front of me. The fan on the gas heater slowed, the pressure in my ears changed, it was as if everything slowed down.

Spirits began to emerge.

They seemed to absorb the light in some way, so that they became clearer and more distinct and the background began to blur.

I gazed at the scene in front of me in horror.

I saw that one or two women had several spirits attached to her aura.

Some of these spirits were small, child-like, pathetic creatures. Some were burly bearded men.

Some were ancient-looking entities.

These spirits appeared to be feeding on the auras of the women in front of my eyes like diabolic vampires.

All at once the spirits became aware of the fact that I could see them!

They began to laugh, sneer, and gesticulate in my direction in an obscene manner that was shocking.

Two of the women sitting beside me appeared to have the souls of little babies around their auric field.

These little unborn beings were innocent and gentle and non-threatening. I felt that these beings were potential children for these two women.

It was a totally bizarre and shocking experience.

I managed to conduct the meeting with all this happening in front of me. The poor women who were being preyed upon by these beasts from the astral plane were totally unaware of what was happening to them.

Unable to go on, I asked my deputy to chair the meeting and excused myself.

In the bathroom, I fell to my knees and prayed fervently.

When I went back to the meeting, the apparitions had faded and were almost gone.

ODOUR OF DEATH

Sometimes I receive intuitive information that a person will shortly die.

I feel very unhappy about having this knowledge.

A young woman accompanied her father to my house to deliver some documents for my signature and I offered them both a cup a tea while they waited.

As I reached over to hand a cup to the young woman, I noticed an odour that caused my hair to rise. My subtle senses alerted me to the fact that death was all around the young woman.

I have long been able to sense the subtle odours that are not discernible to others.

I don't smell the odour with the usual sense of smell, as in smelling a rose or onions frying, which is the coarse sense of smell.

The subtle sense is a deep and inner sense, higher than the olfactory sense and seems to resonate up towards the bridge of the nose. The odour is received, not sniffed or smelled. It is more of a 'knowing'.

I felt very sad when I caught the sense of Death in that odour.

I knew I was not allowed to inform the young woman of what seemed to be her impending death, and I silently sent her messages of love, comfort and courage.

Each time I've experienced this odour, I've agonised over whether to tell a person what I've received, but each time this happens, a feeling inside of me tells me to be silent.

I've sometimes felt that the gift of second sight is a curse.

I'd rather not know the things I know.

I wondered over the next few months if the young woman was all right. I hoped I'd got it wrong.

One morning, a friend of her father's rang me to say she'd passed away.

Two strange and wonderful things happened a few days later.

I had a dream about the young woman who'd died.

It was as if we were re-playing her visit to my house when she was still alive.

When I handed her a cup of tea, she looked up at me and smiled sweetly.

In exchange for the cup of tea, she handed me a small and exquisite crystal angel!

The next morning, I pondered the meaning of this dream after saying a prayer for the young woman's soul.

When the dead appear in our dreams, it's an indication that we need to pray for them, so they may be elevated to a higher level in that other dimension. Prayers and thoughts are vibrations. The dead receive our positive vibrations of love.

A few days after the dream, I received an impromptu visit from the young woman's father.

Deeply moved, he gave me a small box wrapped in blue paper. He said to me:

"The strangest thing happened to my wife a few nights ago.

She had a dream about our daughter. She was very happy to see our girl looking alive and happy and just like herself, as she always looked.

In this dream, she gave my wife what had been her favourite twenty-first birthday present, that her best friend had given to her.

The amazing thing is, she asked my wife to give it to you."

I didn't know what to say to him so I remained silent. We just stood looking at each other, at my front door.

He spoke again:

"When my wife woke up, she was pretty upset. She woke me up and we both had a good cry. She was too embarrassed and felt too silly to come to see you herself, as she's never met you before. I had a very strong feeling that I wouldn't get any rest until I did what our daughter wanted."

After saying this, he said 'goodbye' and left.

With a sense of wonder, knowing what I'd find in that little box, I opened it with trembling fingers.

It was the little crystal angel she'd given me in my dream!

Seeing this, I knew, that the young woman was now in Heaven.

MY EXPERIENCE

When I sit with a person who asks for my help as a clairvoyant, I see a window open in Time in front of me.

This experience is much more vivid and more exciting to me than a movie could ever be. The vision is a multi-sensorial experience. The colours I see in a vision are alive and multi-dimensional. These colours are more vivid than any colours I see with my Earth eyes or coarse sense of sight. The vision colours are luminous and vibrate with a penetrating intensity. I have no name for these colours.

During a vision, I become an observer, a silent witness in the drama that unfolds in front of me.

I smell the odours, I sense the atmosphere, I hear people talking, I hear all the sounds of existence in that other dimension, that has existed once or is yet to come.

It is all incredibly vivid and alive.

In the spiritual world, there is no time or space. There are no limitations or boundaries, all is known to me.

I see the past, no matter how distant. And I see the future, with all its pregnant possibilities.

AKASHIC RECORD

One night while I slept deeply, I had a dream.

I was sitting in a beautiful sacred place, surrounded by shining, singing, angelic beings of Light and Wisdom, when a beautiful, gold-embossed, red-velvet covered book was placed on my lap by a white-robed figure.

He opened the first page for me and smiling at me with a look of incredible love and sweetness said:

"Observe your lifetimes, my child.

Observe your soul.

All your life experiences are encoded, written, recorded upon your soul.

Read your soul and remember."

I looked down at the book in awe and wonder and saw that the pages were pictures filled with people enacting various dramas and events. There were no words or text on any of these pages.

As I looked more deeply into the pages, I saw the tiny figures come to life.

Fascinated, I turned back to the first page which was filled with great white light.

As I looked, the light burst out of the page and blinded me!

I knew that in my beginnings I was once a tiny bright spark of light.

I remembered and re-experienced the joy and excitement I had once felt when I first began the Earth journey.

As I continued to turn the pages, I saw myself as the tiniest atoms of existence: as water, animal, vegetable, mineral, Man.

All this happened instantly and spontaneously.

I saw myself in a Chinese Emperor's Palace as a small Chinese girl in a golden dress.

I saw myself giving birth, being born many, many times, as all races, colours, creeds. I saw myself existing in every civilisation at some time in history as man or woman.

The last page in this living book was blank...yet to be written on.

I asked the white-robed figure if he knew what would be written on the final page. He smiled and said:

"It is already written. It will be revealed to you soon."

After the dream, I woke up excited and gloriously alert, pulsating and vibrating with energy.

I got up, walked outside and looked up at the night sky...wondering.

I later learnt that the feelings of joy and euphoria I felt, were an indication of the dream's Divine inspiration.

WHITE EAGLE

In 1993, I was working one day per week as a lecturer in Psychology.

I enjoyed working with students and many came to me for counselling. One of the mature-age students became a friend and asked me to attend a White Eagle lodge with her one night, to experience the way they meditated as she knew I was a keen meditator. I agreed and we went together.

The meditation group was clean and clear in energy and no negative energy or disturbances occurred while I was there that night, which was a great relief to me.

I had a glorious vision during the meditation.

I saw a tall North-American Indian man come walking up the aisle of the little Chapel where we were sitting.

He was dressed in pure white buck-skins, wearing a white feathered head-dress.

His long black hair was plaited with leather thongs beaded with turquoise stones.

To my surprise, when he looked deeply at me, I realised that his eyes were a deep blue.

He stopped right in front of me and smiled, then joined his hands and bowed.

I had never seen anyone like this before and over supper told my friend what I'd seen. She went very quiet.

She told me:

"You're a very lucky woman.

I'd give anything to see what you just saw. That was White Eagle. He's an Ascended Master and the Master of our Lodge. How incredible. Would you mind if I tell the others?"

I said: "Please don't tell them now. Would you mind telling them when I'm not around?" She agreed.

This lady was interested in nurturing my gift of clairvoyance. She taught me much I needed to know and lent me books on many subjects.

I was leading a women's group and a small meditation group for clients by now and sometimes she came to add her warmth and energy to the group.

THE DALAI LAMA

One day, she asked me if I'd like to go and see the Dalai Lama when he was in Melbourne.

She told me a little about his life and background, as I was rather ignorant about him.

We agreed to go to the Tennis Centre together on the night Melbourne expected him.

The night before his Melbourne visit, a curious thing happened to me.

The Dalai Lama came to visit me!

I awoke during the night abruptly and got a terrible shock to see what looked like the Dalai Lama standing in my bedroom!

He didn't speak at all, just smilingly handed me a photo of himself.

I took it carefully and turned it over, as he'd indicated.

The photo had some words written on the back in another language. At the time, I felt this was a prayer and understood intuitively it was a blessing for me.

When I looked up from reading the prayer, the vision of the Dalai Lama was gone.

The photo I'd been holding in my hand just a moment ago, was also gone. I was quite shaken by this experience.

When I told my friend about my wonderful vision the next day, she said:

"His Holiness the Dalai Lama arrived in Perth last night.

I've heard that several of his Australian disciples and various intuitive people saw him in spirit last night, just as you did."

When we went to the Tennis Centre to see him, all I remember is how happy he looked and how much love and warmth poured out of him and all over the area.

Thousands of people watched him on a television screen outside because the Tennis Centre was packed to capacity that night. Melbourne had given the Dalai Lama a beautiful welcome.

BENJAMIN CREME

Over the next few months, two more interesting things happened to me.

My friend took me to listen to an English gentleman called Benjamin Creme one night.

She told me:

"Mr. Creme is the leading disciple of an ascended Master called Lord Maitreya. Mr. Creme's written many books and teaches Transmission Meditation around the world."

As Mr. Creme spoke, I saw a huge white cross of light across his body where he stood on the stage of the lecture hall. I wondered if anyone else could see it.

My friend was grateful that I could describe the vision to her. Apparently, she said, many psychics could see the cross of light that was superimposed on Mr. Creme's body, when he spoke about the Lord Maitreya.

Many members of Mr. Creme's audience went back the next day to the lecture hall for a meditation.

I found this experience quite distressing because we were asked to form a circle and hold hands for the transmission practice.

Mr. Creme asks people to meditate with him wherever he travels in the world, and he dedicates the synergy of the meditation to World Peace.

During the meditation, I 'read' the person on each side of me and had to leave the group as it was too upsetting.

I found the lady on my right had been raped and hurt by someone she'd trusted, and the young man on my left had a very negative aura that told me his soul was damaged.

I also found I was unable to focus on the brow area for too long in meditation, as it gave me a headache.

AN INDIAN HOLY MAN

Not too long after this experience, a meditation Master from India came to Melbourne and my friend suggested we experience his system of meditation.

However, on the night of the first meditation, my friend was ill and unable to attend, so I went on my own.

The Master was accompanied by some of his disciples, who were all dressed in white. He bowed and smiled at us, he looked very nice.

After an explanation, he led us in the first meditation and a strange thing happened to me.

I felt as if a train were rumbling under my feet and I felt the ground shaking.

I then saw a very bright light in front of me.

I opened my eyes in surprise and saw the meditation Master standing directly in front of me. I got a fright.

I rubbed my eyes, looked again and he was standing on the stage at the front of the room, as he'd been when I'd first closed my eyes. "What's going on?" I thought.

I felt shaken up inside. I was shaken by the experience, by the vibration under me and through me, and by the bright light.

I looked around, but no-one else seemed to be experiencing anything.

I found that if I lifted my feet up off the floor, the feeling stopped, and it started again when I put my feet down.

Just as I was doing that, the shaking feeling began inside my body and didn't seem to have anything to do with the floor anymore.

I just shook and vibrated all over.

Then in the next moment, the shaking was gone.

After my meditation experience, I asked the others sitting near me if they'd felt anything at all. Each of them said they hadn't experienced anything and looked at me curiously.

I had a lot to think about and went home early.

I decided I'd go again tomorrow to see if anything else would happen.

IN TWO PLACES AT ONCE

When I arrived at the hotel the next day, no-one seemed to want to talk to me.

The helpers who'd been so charming and helpful the day before, seemed to avoid me. I thought perhaps it was my imagination or perhaps they were busy.

At the first tea break after a lecture, I felt a bit uncomfortable as people seemed to move away from me, they appeared to be giving me 'the cold shoulder'.

"That's funny," I thought.

After the meditation, we were asked:

"Who seeks initiation?"

I knew I wouldn't be looking for that.

Something inside of me told me I didn't need to be initiated this life time.

Just as I was thinking this, a young disciple of the meditation Master leaned over to me and said:

"You might be mistaken about not needing initiation. You could be making a mistake by missing out on this."

I said, surprised: "I beg your pardon?" Wondering if he could read my mind.

He explained: "Last night at dinner, you were very vocal about not needing initiation.

Did you really need to express your feelings so strongly?"

I'd gone home early last night for dinner with my family!

I'd certainly not had dinner with this young man and his friends. I thought: "He's cracked. What's he up to?"

I said: "I don't know what you're talking about. I think you've got me mixed up with someone else. I didn't talk to you or anyone else about initiation."

I left the hotel after this conversation and went home.

Apparently, according to him, I'd been present at dinner the previous night, and argued hotly about not needing initiation. What a mystery!

I knew I hadn't been there.

It occurred to me much later it could have been a case of bi-location, a case of being in two places at once.

I hoped I'd had a good dinner!

In spite of these interesting experiences and interesting people I was meeting, I knew that I was still searching for someone or something, yet I still hadn't found it, and I didn't even know what I was searching for.

I just knew that I'd know it when it came.

In late 1994, that which I had been so desperately seeking came and found me.

CHAPTER 6

THE AWAKENING

THE AWAKENING

In late November 1994, one warm and sunny afternoon, just before I was due to collect my son from Pre-school, I was sitting at the desk in my office upstairs, finishing a report for a client.

I'd bought a couple of new magazines for the waiting-room and noticed a movement on my desk as a breeze blew the curtains into my face and turned the pages of the magazines.

I thought: "What was that?"

Shivers ran up my spine and my hair tingled.

It was one of those moments I've experienced before. There was a feeling of anticipation and excitement, and I knew that something very important was about to happen.

A photograph of an elderly, white-bearded Indian man smiled up at me from the pages of one of the magazines I'd bought on impulse that day.

Time stood still.

It was his face!

It wasn't possible! Yet, when I looked again, it was the face of the man who had frightened me so at two years of age and made me scream in the night for my grandmother!

He was here in Melbourne and apparently he was a meditation Master, so the advertisement said.

As I stared at his photo, it was as if it came alive at that moment and he smiled at me with such sweetness and love that my very being melted.

I cried, unable to accept what was happening to me.

I wiped my eyes, took hold of myself, noticed that it was time to go and collect my son and gave myself a good mental talking-to.

I went downstairs for the car keys, then stood still in the kitchen, unable to move.

A voice spoke inside of me:

"Ring the number in the magazine."

I fought the voice and said out loud:

"Not now, no time."

"Ring now!" The voice commanded again.

I was helpless to resist.

I went upstairs and rang the Pre-school to explain that I'd be a little late today. It was as if I were standing outside of myself, watching what was happening, without emotion.

I picked up the 'phone and rang the information number from the advertisement.

A man's voice answered.

I explained that I'd seen the advertisement for the meditation seminar in a magazine, I was a professional psychologist with an interest in meditation and the emphasis on the vibrational aspect of this technique intrigued me.

He said: "I'll tell you what, I'm only about ten minutes from you. Come over now and we'll talk some more.

I'd like to meet you.

In fact, if you're the person I think you are, we'd better meet."

I said: "Excuse me, but, who are you? And how do you know where I live? I didn't tell you."

He laughed and said: "I'm the Teacher of this method we're talking about. I just happened to be passing the 'phone when you rang and something made me pick it up. Usually, someone else answers the 'phone. Come on over, I'm free now."

I told him: "I can't come now. I've got another appointment shortly and I'm booked for clients tonight."

He refused to take 'no' for an answer.

He said: "Come now. Ring your husband. He'll collect the child." I hadn't told him I had a child or a husband!

To my utter amazement, I did as he'd suggested, as if I were in a dream.

All the time I was thinking:

"In the photo he looks just as he did over forty years ago when I first saw him in my childhood vision.

I know it's the same man. This can't be happening.

Who is he? How does he know about me?"

When I rang my husband at work, he was warm and supportive and not at all surprised that I needed him to come home.

He said: "Funny that you rang. I was just thinking that I'd call it a day and come home early. I'll pick the boy up now and see you at home soon. Put the kettle on."

My husband came home with our son and I told him I was going to meet a strange man to talk about meditation.

I'd never told my husband about the vision of the man I'd seen when I was two years of age, and I didn't tell him now.

He sipped his tea, and said:

"I'll drive you over. Just out of curiosity, I'd like to meet this fellow, too."

MY TEACHER AND I MEET

When we drove to the address the man had given me, I tentatively knocked on the front door, wanting, hoping to run away, wanting to be anywhere else at that moment.

I kept nervously looking back at my husband waiting in the car, and he waved at me, calling:

"Try again. Knock again."

At that moment, the door opened.

He stood there.

It was as if my heart stopped.

I stared and stared. Utterly speechless. Totally incapable of movement.

We stared into each other's eyes it seemed, for all of eternity. An unspoken communication passed between us.

I had a feeling of deep serenity and I knew somehow that everything was all right.

He smiled an indescribable smile and took my two hands in his. He was tall, over six feet.

He was wearing a gleaming, snowy white suit.

His skin was golden-brown. He was thin to the point of emaciation, to my eyes. He later told me I was too fat, to his eyes.

His eyes were deep-set, very black and twinkled at me, laughingly. I was at once aware of his warmth and friendliness.

He had a long white beard and a long curled moustache. Though he was obviously elderly, he gave off an aura of youth, strange though this may sound.

He was the first to break the enchanted silence.

I'd forgotten where I was, who I was, what I was doing there.

I felt as if I'd faint, or fall asleep at any moment. I had never felt like this before. He said:

"Dear lady, so very pleased to see you. I don't think it's a good idea for your little son to come in the house, they all have the chicken pox here. Tell your husband to take him home and I'll send you home later after our talk."

I did as he suggested. He waited at the door while I went to the car and told my husband I'd get a taxi home later.

He came outside into the bright sunshine, carrying a folder and a bag of paperwork and pamphlets.

I walked down that quiet, tree-lined suburban street with my mind in turmoil, unable to speak, unable to think clearly.

I wanted to cry, to laugh, to run, to sleep. I didn't know what to do next. I couldn't seem to get enough air into my lungs.

I kept sneaking glances at him, walking beside me, all the time feeling as if I were in a movie.

Nothing seemed real.

He just smiled at me and patted my hand, as if he knew my fears and said:

"All will be revealed to you my dear, be patient."

I understood all of this later as he'd promised.

He had some photocopying to finish for his seminar that weekend, and assumed that I wouldn't mind assisting him with the photocopying and carrying.

In the photocopying shop, I stood there wondering what I was doing. I'd cancelled my clients this evening to be doing this? He was supposed to be talking to me, not just giving me those funny smiles, as if he could read my thoughts.

He took his time; took forever it seemed, to complete his instructions to the photocopying staff.

I wasn't good at waiting. He acted as if he had all the time in the world.

I got annoyed.

Eventually, we left the store and he led the way to a small coffee-shop.

He'd still not spoken one word to me, and by this stage I was carrying all the photocopying!

I wondered: "What will he want to drink? Do I order a coffee?"

I was hanging out for a coffee!

"Isn't he a guru or something? Maybe he'll just have water. What does he eat? Is he a vegan?"

In the coffee shop, I noticed everyone was staring at us.

He looked so exotic, like a rare gem in that ordinary setting.

I ordered a hot chocolate and he promptly settled the drinks matter by ignoring me and ordering two strong coffees with milk, and two slices of cake.

"Thank God," I thought, though annoyed that he'd ordered for me. He later told me he'd been very amused by my efforts to deny the coffee addiction I had and he'd taken pity on me. During the brief time I knew him, he never gave up on his efforts to get me to give up coffee.

Finally, we sat opposite each other under the curious eyes of the girl behind the counter.

He said:"I facilitate a simple and natural system of meditation that I call Sahej Yoge, the Yoga of Surrender. Come to my meditation seminar this weekend."

I said: "Not this weekend unfortunately.

I've already paid a lot of money to attend a seminar in Sydney with Denise Linn on Reincarnation.

How long will you be in Melbourne?"

He said:

"This is my only basic seminar in Melbourne this year. Don't miss this."

I repeated:

"I can't come. I've got a prior commitment."

Patiently, he said:

"Then fly to Tasmania next weekend. I've got a seminar there."

No matter how I tried, he would discuss it no further.

I thought:"He's ordering me about! I will not go," yet knowing I would.

"Who does this man think he is? Who is he anyway?"

In total silence, we walked back to the house where he was staying. At the door he handed me some brochures outlining his history and the meditation system he taught, and gave me an audio-tape with firm instructions to listen to it every day until we met again.

I promised to attend his seminar, just to get away from him. Before I left, he took my hands in his again, gave me a piercing look from his dark eyes and said:

"We'll be meeting again soon, my dear. God be with you."

He went inside and closed the door.

I stood on the steps of that house bewildered, for a few minutes. I called a taxi from the local 7'11 'phone, and went home, shaken and confused.

At home, I wanted to convey to my husband what had happened, but I could find no words that were appropriate. Neither of us felt like speaking.

It was more of a feeling inside of me that disturbed me.

I slept badly, tossed all night, had strange and troubled dreams. I wanted to go back to how I'd been before I'd seen his photo.

This was too weird.

I suspected I'd never be the same again.

Something irrevocable had happened to me.

I felt like a child again.

PUSHING THROUGH THE RESISTANCE

After Denise Linn's Sydney seminar, I rang a friend at RACV Travel, not expecting to get on a plane to Hobart at such short notice. Almost immediately, the RACV rang back and had a cancellation for me.

I was going! By this stage, nothing surprised me, I surrendered to it.

After discussion, my husband agreed to come home early for me to catch the early evening flight to Hobart.

He tried his best to get home but everything conspired to make him late. Peak hour traffic was about an hour early, a car broke down on the freeway and he had to wait. Eventually, he got home an hour and a half later than he'd anticipated.

He suggested it would be faster to catch the tram at the end of our street.

When I reached the airport bus terminal at Spencer street, I found that the bus was running late.

Time was running out.

I'd waited thirty minutes for the bus, when a girl approached me and asked if I'd share a taxi to the airport with her, as she was running late for her flight too.

I agreed and we hailed a taxi together.

We offered the driver a lot of money to get us to the airport fast. Of course he agreed.

In the taxi, I told her about the strange man I was going to meet in Hobart and she was fascinated.

When we got to the airport with only five minutes to spare, she said:

"You run, get your flight, the taxi's on me."

It was about a thirty dollar fare. God bless her wherever she is.

I ran as fast as I could but it was too late for a boarding pass. All the passengers were already on the plane which was ready for take-off.

Something inside of me said:

"You've got to get on that 'plane."

Miraculously, the 'plane was kept waiting for me.

I felt such an aura of pure love from all the staff and passengers on the plane and I knew that they supported me to reach Hobart.

I also knew that it was somehow important for all those people that I make it.

TASMANIA

The flight passed in a daze.

I barely remember arriving at Hobart. People helped me.

Someone got me a taxi.

I was completely in the dream now, in other people's gentle hands. Somehow, I found myself standing in the hotel lobby and everyone seemed to know who I was.

There was a message at the desk that read:

"Dear lady, our meditation will have started before you arrive. We'll meet later."

I was suddenly afraid that I might be doing the wrong thing.

I realised I'd flown all the way to Tasmania because a stranger had told me to do this.

Shakily, I went up in the ancient, tiny lift.

When I reached my room, I heard faint singing coming from a room down the hall.

I was drawn to it. The door was ajar and I peeped in.

About eight people were standing, meditating, with eyes closed, so I tiptoed away, deciding I'd better come back later.

After about thirty minutes, I went back to his room.

He motioned for me to come in, not a bit surprised to see me and introduced me to two gentleman who'd stayed back and said:

"We'll now do another meditation practice with this lady. It's her first time."

I was used to sitting to meditate, and looked around for a chair, he read my intention and said:

"We begin our meditation standing up, my dear. Let the meditation move you freely."

I found this surprising, as I'd never heard of standing up to meditate before.

I SEE THE LIGHT

Without further ado, he began to sing the hauntingly beautiful song he'd sung on the tape he'd given to me in Melbourne.

I was very familiar with that song and his voice by now.

I closed my eyes.

I cried a lot.

I laughed at things that weren't even funny, not even knowing why I was laughing.

I cried even more. I didn't even know what I was crying

about. Then I fell heavily to my knees, feeling no pain, only a rushing, searing joy.

All the while, he sang as sweetly and tenderly as a mother lulls her fearful babe.

I remember opening my eyes at some stage and seeing rays of piercing light filling the room. It was ten o'clock at night! The light was as bright as the sun.

He later told me I had seen the Naam, which is a word meaning the primordial Life Force, the Divine energy that permeates and maintains the Universe.

After I opened my eyes at the end of the meditation, I knew I would never be the same again.

Something that had been hurting me all my life was gone and a great hole in my chest was filled up.

My heart was full.

All the pain and loneliness I had always felt, since the death of my beloved grandmother, was gone.

All I could do was cry. All the sorrows I had ever known were gone, all washed away by his voice, by my tears, by the golden light.

He said to me after it was all over:

"Good girl," genuinely pleased with me, for me.

I said:"Good night, and thank you."

At the door, he touched my head briefly and said:

"Sleep well, my dear," and I did.

LET'S BUY SHOES

After breakfast, he asked me to help him with his photocopying and collation of material for his seminar that day.

We walked to the shops together.

As we walked, I told him I felt shy about saying his name as it was difficult to pronounce. I asked him how I should address him.

After some thought, he smiled and said:

"I'm your new Teacher.

If you were an Indian or Malaysian student, you'd call me 'Guru'. If you were a Jewish student, you would call me 'Rabbi'.

Since you're a Western lady, you may call me your Teacher."

I noticed as we walked down the main street of Hobart, how people stared at him.

I also noticed, with mild surprise, it was an unseasonably hot day for Hobart.

As we heard people complaining to each other in the shops about the weather, he told me:

"It's a funny thing about the weather.

Strange things happen to the weather, it seems, wherever I go."

After he'd left precise instructions with the photocopying staff to have the finished product delivered as soon as possible, we proceeded on our way.

He said to me:

"Now we go to buy shoes."

I was bemused.

"Buy shoes?" I thought.

"We've got a seminar in forty-five minutes and the photocopying isn't even done."

When I reminded him of the time, while almost skipping to keep up with him, all he could do was laugh.

We turned into a corner shop to buy shoes and a young man came forward immediately to assist.

Again, I had that feeling, associated with him, of being carried along too fast, in something that my mind could not cope with. He told the young man he wanted a pair of grey shoes. He said he needed comfort, value-for-money and durability.

The young man offered a pair of shoes that fitted the description. As he knelt down to remove his shoes, the young man looked up startled, and began to cry.

I was amazed to see the young man crying.

"How extraordinary," I thought.

"What's wrong with him?"

The Teacher smiled.

Warmth poured out of him in a wave.

He gently leaned down and touched the young man's head.

When he did this, my heart seemed to swell and burst inside of me, and hot tears filled my eyes too, and spilled down my face.

I couldn't make any sense at all of what had happened to the young man and I.

Then he stood up, offered his hand to the young man and raised him to his feet.

He said: "Perfect. Just perfect. The shoes fit. Put them in a box for me, good fellow."

I noticed that the young man's hands trembled, and he watched us as we left the store.

INSTANT FLU

On our way back to the hotel, I began to cough.

A cough had been more and more troubling me since the meditation the night before. During the meditation, I had quite spontaneously begun breathing very deeply for about five minutes and had coughed a lot.

I thought:

"I must be getting flu or something. I feel awful."

I'd had a long history of childhood illness and my grandmother had long fussed and worried over my chest.

I'd had several bouts of pneumonia, bronchitis, asthma, and the double-pneumonia that had led to my first near death experience at seven years of age.

X-rays had shown scars on my lungs from pleurisy and pneumonia that could almost be mistaken for TB. When I got a cough or a heavy cold, it was serious. This cough worried me.

Walking beside him on that too-hot Hobart morning, I coughed heavily again and gasped at a sharp pain in my side, fear gripping me.

He stopped, took my shoulders in a strong grip, looked into my eyes and said:

"Spit it out now."

I flushed and said:

"No. I can't spit in public. It's just not done."

He ignored me and repeated:

"You must spit out all the sickness. All the dirt. All the fear. All the evil. All the death that's choking you. Do it now. If you won't spit on the ground, spit in the bin."

He led me to a bin on the pavement.

I was becoming quite alarmed by now as the mucous appeared to be choking me.

He took out a handkerchief, handed it to me and said:

"Cough it up, dear. It's all right. Trust me."

I turned to the bin and coughed and coughed until I could breathe again.

This coughing which led to vomiting, continued the entire weekend. It was as if I had instant flu.

INNER CONFLICT

Over the weekend, I found that random irrational thoughts filled my head, yet I, the essential and authentic I behind and beyond all this, was exultant and joyful.

I knew that everything that was happening to me was meant to be, but at the time I had no words to express what I was experiencing. It was as if there were two voices, two personalities, two beings seeking expression within me. Two warring parts of what I called myself were doing battle.

The Divine, eternal, immortal self was awakening. The battle was hard-fought and was to continue for several years.

I also became troubled by burning pain and tenderness on the bottoms of my feet.

This started as an irritating sensitivity on the Saturday morning and had become so painful Saturday night that I asked him if he knew how to alleviate it.

He smiled as if he knew all about it and said:

"Wash the feet every hour or so.

The tenderness of the feet is normal at this stage, dear. All the etheric dross is being moved through the body.

The feet are in touch with the Earth and your magnetic field is being charged with a new frequency. Washing the feet often in a salt bath will remove the uncomfortable effects until you are used to the new frequency.

Try to walk barefoot inside and put your feet up when you can."

I kept washing the feet as he'd suggested and it helped wonderfully.

At the same time, I experienced a stiff neck.

I'd been seeing an osteopath and a chiropractor for several years for alleviation of pain in the neck and spine.

My most recent x-rays showed osteo-arthritis in the neck. The chiropractor had explained there was not a lot that could be done for this.

Along with the chest trouble, the neck and spinal pain, I also suffered with high blood pressure. The high blood pressure was of real concern, as I had a family maternal history of heart-disease. My doctor had suggested medication for the blood pressure. I'd told him:

"Let me try meditation and see how we go."

I'd been able to control it by meditation but it was still a source of anxiety.

A specialist had told me recently:

"We all want you to see your little boy grow up. You'll need to be careful with your health."

To add insult to injury, the sedentary counselling and psychology practice had contributed to an overweight condition, a recipe for disaster.

When we walked back to the hotel, the photocopying was awaiting us, and the two gentlemen from last night were waiting to help in collating the seminar material.

When we finished, he left us to change for the seminar.

He reappeared looking fresh and glowing in a dove-grey suit and sent the two gentlemen to greet early participants.

He'd already instructed the hotel staff to set up his material and prepare refreshments.

He appeared to be in control and relaxed at the same time.

I was an experienced seminar presenter and lecturer myself, and was impressed by his relaxed and confident manner. Nothing seemed to worry him or distract him. He just seemed to flow. He didn't consult a watch or clock and seemed to have a different awareness around time.

I found that when I was in his presence, I seemed to be enveloped in his calmness too.

All fears, all worries seemed somehow unimportant and far away.

It felt like the pre-medication I'd had before surgery, a warm, cocooned feeling; a feeling that nothing could possibly go wrong. He had this effect upon everyone he met.

THE SEMINAR

He said to me:

"I've decided that you're going to introduce me before the seminar. This is what I want you to say."

He then proceeded rapidly to tell me about his background and experience.

I was overwhelmed. Only five minutes to go and now
he tells me! How could I possibly remember all this?

He wouldn't let me take notes. He just took my arm
and walked us both to the lift, talking in that rapid way
all the time, his voice smooth and gentle.

Many of the words he used were unfamiliar to me
because they were Hindu words.

I felt rushed and unprepared.

I didn't like to be rushed. I took pride in doing everything
well. One of my childhood maxims was:

"If it's worth doing, it's worth doing well."

Somehow, I found myself agreeing to introduce him.

When we entered the room, a sea of faces and a murmur
of voices greeted us.

Curious faces stared at us.

He told everyone to be seated and went straight to the
front row and sat down, arms folded, legs crossed, looking at me expectantly. I felt nervous.

I realised, with a pang, that I'd have to climb up the
steps to the stage, to the microphone.

"I can't even pronounce his name," I thought.

"I'm going to look like a real idiot."

I did my best.

I made up what I'd forgotten about him and he laughed
at me like a small child.

I sat down, face flushed, feeling silly.

We began our seminar on a note of gentle warmth and humour and what a miraculous, life-changing day it was to be for me.

Little did I know that I was to die and be re-born that day in a ballroom in Hobart.

Nothing would ever be the same again.

My old life was about to end and a new life was about to begin.

TRANSFORMATION

The seminar began with a lecture on The Mind of Man.

He used diagrams and overheads to explain the three levels of the mind.

He told us there is a conscious mind, a sub-conscious and a super-conscious mind.

"This is basically a short course in introductory psychology," I thought.

He used a chart to illustrate the brain-wave frequencies of alpha, beta, theta and delta.

It was interesting to note that his chart used Hindu names for these brain-wave frequencies as well as the English names I was familiar with.

He said we can become trapped in a beta-conscious mind-state by chanting mantras, making repetitive meaningless sounds and by doing concentration-type meditative practices.

I wriggled a bit at this stage, as I'd spent several years learning TM and Vipassana Buddhist meditation and had focussed on mantras, postures, my third-eye, candles and whatever else I'd been told to focus on, in a futile attempt to control my thought processes.

As I was thinking about this, he said:

"It's useless to try to stop thoughts.

It's as useless as throwing coconuts at a treeful of quarrelling monkeys; they'll throw them back at you and you will have a war on your hands.

Let go of trying to control thoughts. Be a witness, be a detached observer of the mind thinking."

His logic made a lot of sense to me, as I'd often suffered a headache from focussing on the 'ajna' centre or third eye.

I realised I'd spent most of my life trying to focus, now he was saying 'let go of focus'!

I got a bit more interested at this stage.

He then went on to draw a diagram explaining what he called the easy way and the hard way towards enlightenment.

On his chart, self-realisation and enlightenment were called nirvana and satori.

He explained that when we were chanting or focusing, we were actually trapped in a conscious mind state. I was fascinated.

He talked about his meditation system of surrender, describing it as 'Sahej Yoge' which literally meant the Yoga of surrender.

He mentioned that this system was totally vibrational and he detailed the proof or evidence of a change of state once the process was embarked upon.

Apparently there was extensive, authentic and ancient documentation that detailed at least two-hundred and fifty responses and reactions as proof of the soul's awakening!

He described some of these responses.

When he described stiffness in the nape of the neck, burning feet, headaches, warmth, heat, tingling all over, crying, laughing, a feeling as of being in a dream, chills, goose-bumps, euphoria, blissful feelings, coughing, onset of sudden fevers, I became even more attentive.

As if he knew my thoughts, he smiled at me and nodded.

I thought: "Is this what's happening to me? Incredible! Is my soul awakening? Is this what it feels like when you really wake up? Is it possible?"

I started to really pay attention now.

It was as if a veil was lifted from my eyes.

He said this meditation was responsive, vibrational, experiential, in short it was a feeling.

During my first meditation the previous night, I certainly had experienced an incredible range of feelings.

He looked directly at me and said:

"If your Divine immortal soul awakens from its long sleep, won't you feel it?"

I had felt it!

That day, I felt as if he were speaking only to me. I felt excited, nervous, shaky and most of all happy.

Later, another woman told me she felt that he was just talking to her too.

He had a way of making each person feel that he or she was the only person in the world.

THE MEDITATION OF LOVE

After a brief tea-break, a quiet thoughtful silence came over all of us.

A feeling of excitement and anticipation began to build. It was with trepidation that we awaited the meditation.

He stood at the front of the room and told us:

"Let go of your fears.

Let go of your thoughts. Let go of all judgment.

Allow yourself to be surrounded by pure Divine Love.

Let go of all hate and hurt feelings. We begin our meditation with love in our hearts, brotherly sisterly love.

The seat of the soul is between the eye-brows. I want you to look at each other, at the soul in each other, the Divine in each other, with the look of love. Do this for a few moments."

We all felt a bit shy and self-conscious, then we began one by one, to turn and look at each other.

A deep, warm feeling began to build in the room and inside of us as we looked at each other, former strangers now feeling like friends. One or two people began to smile, then giggled, then all of us were laughing.

He addressed the group:

"Let's close our eyes, stand relaxed, not like sumo wrestlers but just relaxed, with our knees slightly bent and our feet slightly apart."

He began to sing again in that hauntingly sweet voice of his, that heavenly melodious song.

I AM REBORN

I don't know what happened to anyone else.

I only know that my heart broke, the hot tears flowed, I coughed and cried a lot and all my inhibitions fell away.

I fell heavily to my knees, no longer able to hold myself up.

I was still conscious but I was no longer in control.

I lay with my face on the carpet, observing as if from a distance a deep chill that was growing within me, from my feet slowly to my head.

I felt a gripping pain in my chest around my left breast area.

I was totally unable to move.

The pain was enormous. I felt as if a very heavy weight was sitting on my left side, slowly crushing me.

I felt a spinning feeling that was familiar to me.

I began to leave my body from the feet up and knew I was dying.

As I felt myself about to leave through the top of my head, he spoke quietly into my ear:

"Wake up now dear, wake up, it's all over. You're all right, I'm here. Wake up now dear."

Hearing his voice, I opened my eyes to find a circle of people standing around me, looking worried.

He asked them to take a break and he helped me to a chair.

"What happened to me?" I asked.

"I feel as if I died. I was so cold and then it felt like it was all over for me. The next thing I knew was that you were waking me up."

He said:"Yes, dear. You did die. You died the death by heart attack you would have died sometime this year.

You are born again.

No more physical suffering now, that's all over for you. No more talking. Just rest. We'll talk more about it later."

I was shocked and speechless.

As it happened, he was right. My next blood pressure test showed a normal healthy thirty year old BP....I was forty-five years of age! The weight disappeared little by little; the new x-rays I requested showed no osteo-arthritis; there were no scars visible on the lungs; there was no more pain or stiffness in the body; I suffered no more migraines.

I felt and looked ten years younger from that day.

The main difference that I noticed was in my state of mind.

I felt positive and optimistic.

I spent the lunch break by myself, thinking about the extraordinary experience I'd just had.

I felt changed in a way that I couldn't explain, even to myself.

I knew I'd just had a transformative, existential experience.

THE EMPOWERMENT AND THE VISIONS

The afternoon session began with a talk about food.

We were told about the five 'killer whites' as he called them, i.e. sugar, salt, rice, flour and milk. He explained that these 'whites' were dangerous due to the chemicals involved in bleaching natural products white and in refining rice and flour, stripping them of their essential fibre.

We began to understand the dangers inherent in eating genetically modified food, in particular chemicals and hormones in beef, chicken and pork. His approach to this subject was entertaining and humorous.

He said that as meat was already dead, to cook a carcass was to render it 'double dead'. We all laughed.

As far as food was concerned, natural and organic seemed to be the best option.

After the talk on food, he said:

"Now we'll have a deeper experience of meditation.

We'll ask the Divine to give you all an empowerment, a kick-start for those of you who've been unable or unwilling to surrender as yet."

He explained:

"You'll each receive the amount of energy that you can contain and sustain.

According to this capacity, your bodies, minds and spirits will be attuned to a higher frequency."

I'd been rapidly taking notes at the time and was completely astounded by what he said and the simple, matter-of-fact way he said it, as if this 'empowerment' were an every-day occurrence.

I had felt and experienced deeply the burning and thrilling feelings of an energy that seemed to overpower me, and now he said there would be more experiences.

I looked around the room into the faces of the other participants. No-one else seemed to be impressed by his words.

I wondered what was happening to them.

Were they as shaken, moved and transformed as I was?

EXTRAORDINARY VISION

The meditation began with all of us standing a little apart from each other.

"Friends and couples need to be at different ends of the room, because their intimate relationship may interfere with the energy being manifested here, now" he said.

I had never thought about it that way before.

As directed, with arms loosely at our sides, feet apart, eyes closed, as relaxed as we could be, we joined him in his sweet singing.

I opened my eyes and looked at him standing on the stage in front of me.

I gasped and staggered a little in shock as he was not himself anymore.

I saw a shorter, fatter, older Chinese man, wearing a conical red cap, a red and gold embroidered silk robe with huge sleeves that hung to the floor and a long, swirling white moustache and beard. As I looked at him, I realised he was looking at me!

As I gazed in disbelief, the Chinese man faded away, to be replaced in the same spot, by dozens of other people, all as solid-looking and as real as himself.

I saw many men of many races. Some were brown skinned, some were yellow skinned, all were Eastern.

I saw a man dressed all in white, wearing a white turban, white robes and holding a long curved sword.

I saw men wearing vividly coloured robes and turbans and hats and loose desert-looking robes.

Each manifestation looked at me as I witnessed their appearance and disappearance.

The visions ended with the appearance of an elderly Indian-looking lady, wearing a white dress, long white pants with a white veil covering her long greying hair, smiling at me with great love and tenderness.

During the appearances and disappearances of these persons, my heart raced and I trembled and shook on wobbly legs.

It was too fascinating to take my eyes for a moment from this incredible scene.

My eyes burned from my efforts not to blink, I didn't want to miss one second of this. At last, the spell broke and I could see him again as he was now.

The most extraordinary thing happened next.

He was standing now in a ray of golden-green. The colour that I saw was unlike any other colour I have ever seen before.

It was luminous and it glowed like the golden-green of new grass. As he raised his hand in blessing, I noticed that even his hand was golden-green.

After that, I don't know if I fainted or slept, but the next thing I remember is clambering to my feet from the floor.

He knew I had seen something during the meditation. During the next tea-break, he took me aside and said:

"You had a wondering amazed look on your face during the meditation. What did you see?"

I described the images that had come and gone.

He was curious and not at all surprised.

He gave me no explanation for these visions, just took out his wallet, handed to me a faded, creased photograph and said:

" Is this the lady who appeared in your vision?"

"Yes, that's the lady. Who is she?" I said.

"The lady is my mother. She's been dead for thirty years."

The rest of the afternoon passed in a blur.

A few of the seminar participants and I had dinner with him that night.

Everyone chatted and asked many questions.

I could find no words and was introverted and affected by what had happened to me.

I tried hard to be pleasant during the meal that I couldn't enjoy. He kept smiling gently at me.

I felt he was reading my thoughts.

I felt him saying to me beneath the conversation:

"It's all right, don't be afraid. All is well."

THE HOLY LIFE FORCE

After dinner, I went back to the hotel by myself. My head was spinning from so many thoughts and I needed to be alone.

When I got into bed and lay down, I noticed a strange golden-green glow manifesting on the ceiling of my hotel room.

It appeared to be the same golden-green I'd seen manifesting around him earlier that day.

I pulled the blankets up around my face and peeped out. "Now what's going on?" I thought.

The golden-green glow began to fall down on me like snow, soundlessly, and where it fell, I burned and trembled until I was hot inside and outside. I began to feel afraid and started praying. A deep sleep overcame me.

The next morning I awoke, feeling so good!

No aches, no pains, no headache.

I felt healthy and strong.

I remembered the golden-green light and wondered if this was why I felt so good.

There was no doubt in my mind that something miraculous had happened during my long and peaceful sleep.

I asked him the next morning what had happened, feeling that he would be able to give me an explanation.

He said I'd experienced what the Christians call 'manna from Heaven', what he called 'the Holy Life Force'.

He added: "You're a very fortunate lady to be so blessed. How fortunate you are to see what others cannot."

The second day of the seminar was not as outwardly dramatic as the first day.

During the meditations, I cried, I slept deeply on the carpet at times.

I felt and experienced many emotions passing through me.

I noticed that other people also had meaningful experiences.

During the day, I asked him if he knew anything about my grandmother and if she had ascended to Heaven. He assured me, after a deep and piercing look from his dark eyes:

"Your grandmother was a noble lady, she was a good Teacher to you. She is in a good place now. Pray for her soul to ascend even higher."

He told me he would teach me later how to guide a soul to the Higher Planes.

"Everything is a matter of vibration," he said.

"Our souls vibrate at a particular frequency.

Everything on Earth vibrates and resonates to its own harmonic frequency. When we take on the heaviness of the coarse carnal emotions, such as anger, fear, and sorrow, we actually alter our frequency and it is lowered to a disharmonious level.

This attracts other disharmony and unchecked, disaster can and will result. You see the evidence in the world around you of the result of man's Ego and disharmony rampaging unchecked.

War, disease and suffering result.

Man doesn't know how to climb up out of the pit he's dug for himself and his children's children.

It's only through surrendered prayer for your grandmother that her soul can go higher. Prayers are vibrations, as love for your grandmother is a powerful vibration.

I've shown you how to meditate in a surrendered, spontaneous way. Tonight, do a private meditation for your grandmother's soul. This will give her the assistance she needs to graduate to a higher Plane."

ATTRIBUTES OF A TRUE TEACHER

After the seminar ended that day, I stayed back to ask him some questions.

I was curious about whom had been his Teachers and the influences in his life.

I told him I'd met some interesting people and had experienced visions of several Ascended Masters.

I asked him:

"How do I know if a Teacher or a method is good for me or not? How do I know if this is a good person, or just a person wanting to make money out of inexperienced and gullible seekers?"

He said:

"Many Teachers have been sent to guide mankind to the Divine.

Not all people who call themselves Guru or Teacher or Master are necessarily to be trusted.

You'll need to use the gift of discernment to test those who claim they speak for God.

Jesus Christ told us 'By their works, you shall know them'.

It's my feeling that genuine Divine-sent and divinely inspired Masters all share the same attributes. A very important attribute is Divine Love. How loving is the Master? Your heart will guide you here.

Is he or she an arrogant person? Your Teacher must be humble and simple.

It's a natural and inevitable consequence of Godliness that a Teacher is sweet tempered, and lacks irritability.

A true Teacher is rational, peaceful and serene. Harmony goes hand in hand with higher spiritual development.

An awakened Teacher is able to teach you discernment; this means you are able to test situations and people and receive an answer from your awakened soul.

It's useful to have a sense of humour and to be wise.

He or she will also have an understanding of all the Scriptures of the world, and be able to interpret and convey this to his or her students.

We expect a good spiritual Teacher to have very little satanic influence or ego.

Above all of these qualities, the true Teacher possesses the ability to awaken your soul.

Have I answered your question, my dear child?" He said with a smile.

"You've answered my question very fully, thank you," I said.

This had been a most illuminating conversation.

After dinner that night, he told me he was planning to do a further day in Hobart, due to the intense interest his meditation system had generated in the seminar participants who begged for more.

I agreed to stay.

RE-LIVING PAST LIVES

On the third day, he shared more information and meditative experiences with us.

We had a further empowerment meditation. During this meditation on the third day, I had an interesting experience.

I went down on my knees again and slept for awhile. During this sleep, I saw visions of a person I knew was myself, in different bodies, wearing different clothes, having every human experience. I experienced being born, growing up in different countries, dying many times.

All these visions were experienced in a detached and passionless way, as if from a distance.

The visions came and went rapidly, and I only had a fleeting impression of each life that I'd lived.

After the meditation was over, I felt clean and fresh, as if I'd just had an invigorating shower.

The next morning, I said:

"Good-bye and thank you so much," to my Teacher, wondering if I would ever see him again. It was unlikely we would meet as he had seminars in Sydney to complete, a seminar tour in New Zealand and then he planned to fly home to Malaysia.

After I said goodbye, he gave me a long look and said:

"Only the Divine knows if we'll meet again, dear lady. God be with you."

He blessed me, touched the top of my head lightly, turned and walked briskly away to a waiting taxi.

When I reached home, I felt strange about seeing my husband again, after such a transformative weekend.

He asked no questions, just looked at me curiously, somehow sensing a change in me.

During my time away, he too had changed and undergone his own transformation.

CHAPTER 7

OVERCOMING FEAR

CHAOTIC MEDITATION AT HOME

After my Tasmanian experience, a surprise came the following Monday night.

The members of the meditation group arrived at my house as usual, and were curious to know why I'd stayed an extra day in Hobart and what it had been like.

I gave them a synopsis of the lecture content as well as I could, keeping to myself my personal transformative experiences.

Our meditation group didn't usually have a mantra or a mental focus. I'd always encouraged just sitting comfortably on couches, chairs or cushions on the floor, listening to ambient music and affirming progressive muscle relaxation.

The meditation usually began as a guided visualisation, with the members of the group being guided by my voice, then meditating in silence.

People enjoyed this peaceful experience very much and reported feeling much more relaxed in all areas of their lives.

Not so this night!

As soon as we began our meditation that night, it was as if a bomb went off in my lounge-room!

As soon as I'd stopped leading the visualisation, instead of the usual silence, one or two people began experiencing reactions and responses similar to the responses received by the Hobart group! One woman cried silently. One woman cried noisily.

One man laughed aloud.

Several people coughed.

One woman got up and walked around the room! No-one had ever moved in my meditation group before.

One man went to sleep despite all the coughing and movement around him and it seemed that there were bodies moving and jerking all over the place.

I was very shocked by the behaviour of the meditation group.

I thought: " They didn't do the surrendered meditation seminar. What's happening to everybody?"

At the time, there seemed to be no explanation for this incredible behaviour except for an even more incredible thought:

" Something happened to me during that Hobart seminar and now that 'something' is happening to them."

After a while, things quietened down a bit, but still some people cried.

Eventually, they all seemed to fall into a restful sleep; one or two lay actually full-length on the floor; most curled up in their chairs with their heads dropped onto their chests or resting on the wall nearest to them, or resting on their neighbour's shoulder.

It was most extraordinary.

I turned off the music and turned up the lighting. Most people yawned and stretched looking sleepy and puzzled.

Without any chatting, without any supper, two ladies went home immediately.

The ones who were awake talked about their experience while standing in the kitchen, where I made coffee and tea.

One young man slept on, and had to be woken gently after everyone left, so that I could go to bed!

Several people expressed the desire to meet my new Teacher, to learn about this surrendered, experiential meditation.

One woman expressed what they were all feeling, by saying:

"This is fun!"

After everyone had gone home, I lay awake for a long time that night, thinking over what had happened in Hobart and wondering what had happened in my lounge room that night.

To my surprise, the Teacher rang me the next day, to say:

"Hello, dear lady, I'm in Melbourne.

I've decided to offer one advanced seminar to an experienced group of people here, and thought you might like to come and learn some more.

We usually like people to wait a year or so to do the advanced, but we don't need to bother about that in your case."

I felt a bit curious about the advanced seminar, and I had

a lot of questions to ask him about what had happened to my meditation group.

THE DARK NIGHT OF THE SOUL

This second seminar was a totally different matter.

He was somehow different.

He seemed distant and detached.

I felt he'd changed his attitude towards me.

I understood later that the change was in me, not in him.

Ego had begun to arise within me.

Resistance had begun to awaken within myself. This resistance was directed towards him, the meditation experience and towards the other participants.

I found fault with almost every word he spoke.

The most descriptive word for the feeling I felt was anger. A real roaring fury was building within me and I was beginning to reflect my darkness, to project my anger and fear about letting go, onto him.

He told me later:

" The true Guru or Teacher is a mirror for his student."

During that advanced seminar, I suffered terribly.

The mental suffering occupied my time during this seminar. In Hobart, the suffering had been more physical in nature, as traumas and disease had been removed during the process of attunement.

He told me:

" This surrendered technique of meditation, which is literally an exercise for cleansing the soul, has cleansed the physical aspect of your body.

It's time for the mental aspect to be cleansed and the traumas to be removed from your mind.

Life is suffering, my dear child. It is only the ego that suffers as the soul is being polished.

Soul growth occurs only through suffering."

The philosophy of soul growth through suffering was familiar to me.

As long as I could remember, my grandmother had told me, suffering was necessary for character growth and spiritual development.

At school, the nuns had spoken of St. John of the Cross and his writings on 'The Dark Night of the Soul' and the emotional suffering of his dear friend St. Theresa of Avila, to explain to us the mental and psychological suffering endured by the Saints as they strove to overcome the dictates of the ego and to rise above their physical limitations.

As a child, I'd understood the path to sainthood was painful and narrow.

I'd loved reading the 'Lives of the Saints' as a child and was better able than most to understand what my new Teacher was talking about.

From this point on, it seemed that he never ceased from reminding me of my faults, my stubbornness, my egocentric nature and my disobedience.

This hurt me a lot and I cried often over his attitude towards me as time went on. I was destined to have a crash-course in soul growth.

" In order for me to get a breakthrough, I have to break your ego down," he said.

During the second day, all resistance seemed to leave me. I had several trauma releases and felt cleaner and lighter.

DISCERNMENT

During the second day, we learnt about discernment.

He explained:

" Man relies only on his five coarse senses to make sense of the world around him. By using only these coarse senses, man is using only about seven to ten percent of his mind's potential.

There are at least fourteen subtle senses accessible to man, which are lying dormant and sleeping.

By awakening these subtle senses the remaining ninety-three percent of your mind's potential is able to be used.

By being attuned to the highest vibration, which is beyond the speed of sound, light or thought, these subtle etheric senses can awaken.

The highest vibration is Divine Love.

You have the potential, through exercising discernment, to know anything, anywhere, anytime.

You all have the potential to be supermen and super-women," he concluded.

When the seminar ended, I said a warm and grateful goodbye to my Teacher.

He laughed and said:

" You are always saying 'goodbye' to me, dear lady. Perhaps, we shall meet again."

Early in the New Year, I received a 'phone call from my Teacher. He said:

"Your meditation group people may be interested in meeting me. I've decided to come back to Melbourne. I would like you to assist me in the seminar presentation."

I was surprised that he was coming back.

THE GESTALT MAN

Several of my clients attended the seminar, curious to meet the man I'd told them about.

One woman said, when I introduced her to him:

" You're the Gestalt man!

We've been hearing about you for years. You've been visiting us in our weekly meditation sessions."

He was amused. He turned to me and asked:

" What's all this about? What have you been telling them about me? Why is this lady calling me the Gestalt man?"

Suddenly realising what the lady meant, I told him:

" During our visualisation process which leads into a meditation, I've been taking my clients on a journey to a beach.

When they arrive at this image of the beach, they notice a cave that's cut into the hillside.

Out of the cave steps a beautiful, long-bearded, wise elderly man. I tell my clients he has the answer to a very important question.

Before they leave the beach, the old man always gives them a miraculous gift that is symbolic of the answer to their question. She's right, I've been describing a man who looks just like you!" He laughed.

After this conversation, I began to think about this man who'd told me in Hobart, that he was my new Teacher.

I remembered my grandmother had told me I would have another Teacher after she'd left her body.

It was extraordinary that he was the same man I had seen in a vision as a small child.

Now I understood that I had always known who he was, and that I had apparently been preparing my clients for his coming.

All I knew was that he was my Teacher for the next stage of my spiritual journey.

After this seminar, he came to my house to discuss the possibility of my accompanying him, on a tour of New Zealand, during 1995.

My family and friends pledged their support. Everything miraculously arranged itself.

I was going to New Zealand!

CHAPTER 8

NEW ZEALAND

MY VISION OF NEW ZEALAND

As our 'plane prepared to land in Wellington, I had an interesting experience.

I began to yawn over and over again until I thought my jaw would crack.

My eyes watered and tears ran down my face.

I felt very sleepy and hot and dozed for a while.

I had an extraordinary vision of a small, plump brown-skinned Maori woman. She was standing on a hill with her arms outstretched to embrace the wide green land.

A leather-thong was tied around her forehead, which affixed a smooth blue-green stone to her brow. I felt that the stone was her badge of office.

This woman felt to be a leader or a shaman of some kind.

I saw and heard a ring of Maori people chanting a beautiful ancient song with her.

I felt as if I knew this powerful Maori woman from the past.

During the vision, I intuitively understood the language of their song.

I woke up with a start to see my Teacher looking at me curiously.

I told him I'd seen a vision of the past which concerned the ancient indigenous people of New Zealand.

He nodded and said:

"Very good.

You've seen truly, my dear.

You've been receiving reactions such as the yawning, because the Divine is using your sensitivity to open the hearts of the people of Wellington.

You're being used to take on their heaviness which is being transformed into love.

In your vision, you've seen the female leader of these people, from a long time ago.

This is a very good omen for our visit to this country."

THE MIDNIGHT VISITOR

During the meditation seminar, I was invited to stay for a few days with a warm and loving family who were eager to show me their beautiful city. I decided to accept their gracious hospitality.

During my stay with this family, it soon became apparent to me that there was something wrong in their house.

My host and hostess appeared to be troubled by something.

I noticed dark circles under their eyes and felt that no-one in this house slept very well at night. I discerned a spirit disturbing this family.

"Perhaps this is the reason they've asked me to stay," I thought. I waited for my new friends to tell me their troubles, as I found people usually did once they came to know me.

One morning, over a cup of coffee, my hostess told me a sad story, as I knew she would.

Apparently, the husband had been widowed a few years ago and the two little girls were his daughters.

My hostess told me she loved her new husband very much. However, she sensed that something inexplicable was getting in the way of their happy relationship with each other.

She knew about my gift of clairvoyance, so she asked for my help in uncovering the source of the disharmony in her house.

I soon found out.

That night, just on midnight, something woke me with a jolt.

I had goose-bumps all over and felt alert and aware.

I quietly got out of bed, opened my bedroom door, stepped out into the hallway and saw an incredible vision.

At the end of the hallway, where the two girls' bedroom was, I saw a dark shadow emerging from the ether.

I witnessed a ghostly visitation that I've seen, with variations, so many times in my life.

One child lay on her back with one arm flung out beside her. The other child lay on a trundle-bed beside her sister's bed, curled up on her side, deeply asleep.

As I watched, I saw a small, dark, white-faced ghost with long black hair, bend and softly, tenderly kiss each child and touch their hair.

This pathetic and lonely little ghost appeared to be pulling at the blankets covering the children as if trying to cover them against the night chill.

The ghostly mother stood for a long moment and leaned against the door frame of the children's room.

Then, she de-materialised, appearing to fade back into the shadows. During this entire spirit manifestation, I stood in the hallway shivering and frozen.

There was a feeling that was palpable, of deep sadness and loneliness, that had emanated from this lost creature of the spirit realm.

After checking on the girls and saying a prayer of protection for them, I returned to my room.

I sat down on my bed, feeling a little shaky as I often did after a sighting. What had impressed me most during this visitation, were the strong emotions I had felt.

The ghostly mother's emotions, even after death, were so strong and passionate that they had remained with her and had impressed themselves upon the atmosphere.

It was apparent to me that this ghost was the girls' mother and the first wife of my charming host.

I was upset that this ghostly mother was suffering so much and I knew I had to do something to set her free from her nightly ritual.

I knew that the pathetic wandering shade of the dead mother was unconscious of its previous personality and needed to be sent on to its next realm of existence.

Its sadness and heaviness had cast a pall, a depressing atmosphere on the home and family which needed to be exorcised. This was why I was here.

It was fortunate for them that this family believed in the power of prayer and surrendered meditation and were actually attending the seminar.

Accordingly, they were amenable to the suggestion that we dedicate a special, extended meditation session for the liberation of the soul of the deceased wife. Their co-operation made it easy for me. The result of this was, that after our meditation, the lonely ghost no longer continued with her night-time ritual.

I was happy to see peace, harmony and love blossom anew within the family and their now happy home.

TOUCHED BY AN ANGEL

While I was in Wellington, I had an experience of another ghost which was this time uplifting and inspiring.

This time, in contrast to the lonely mother, joy, love and healing were facilitated by a gentle angelic spirit.

A young man who'd attended the seminar, approached me during a tea-break to ask if he could talk to me about his recent bereavement.

The seminar participants knew about my special gift and I'd mentioned I was happy to talk to anyone who had a problem.

During my session with this young man, the soul of his lovely young wife manifested beside him.

The entire room where we sat, was suffused with warmth, with light and a searing charge of psychic energy.

The radiant spirit presence was so delighted I could see her, that she reached out to me, laughing!

To me, this spirit appeared to be an angelic being.

All I could see was almost blinding white light, which told me I was in the presence of an angel.

There was no negativity, heaviness or sadness associated with this apparition. The feelings during a session always alerted me to the status of a disembodied soul.

All I could sense about this one, was clarity, purity and goodness.

An exciting thing happened next.

This angelic being projected to my inner mind a series of vivid, flashing, highly coloured images. Through this means, she led me through her life, brief though it had been this lifetime. It was as if her memories became my memories, and I felt as if I'd known her.

To me, her spirit was like quicksilver, a butterfly, a sweet little hummingbird. I felt and experienced only pure love.

This spirit manifestation of pure love was unique in my experience at this time. The only disembodied beings who'd projected love towards me prior to this, had been my mother and my grandmother. The young husband sitting beside me, was totally unaware of what was happening, so I conveyed to him the information received as images that she was sharing with me.

As I spoke of their holiday in Bali, of the birth of their precious son, of the way she looked in the mornings, her favourite dress, he began to sob aloud. His crying continued for a long time.

As he cried, her beautiful form of light vibrated in what seemed to be compassion and love. She put her spirit arms around him and held him close to her shimmering light body.

I noticed with wonder that after she'd held him, he'd stopped crying, calmed and said:

"I can't explain what's going on here.

I didn't tell you anything about Annie. You've told me about our life together as if you were there. I can't doubt it.

I've got this incredible feeling that Annie's here, in this room, with me now!"

I was happy that he could feel Annie and that he seemed to be calmer.

I said: "My dear friend, I'm going to say something to you that you might find very strange. I want you to just accept that your darling Annie has somehow been permitted to visit you briefly, to assist me in healing the grief.

I believe that your Annie is here right now.

I feel that Annie and you need to be together, alone, for a little while.

Annie will convey energy and love to you.

Please be willing to let go of all your conditioning and belief systems around death of the physical body.

You've asked for my help, now trust me in this.

Allow yourself to receive love. The love you and Annie shared is beyond the death of her body. This is what Annie's come to teach you. Love can't die."

After saying this, with his permission, I left Annie and Peter alone together.

I stood in the kitchen, looking out the window for a few minutes, realising with wry amusement that I'd just left a man and the ghost of his wife to talk to each other!

When I went back to the room where Peter was sitting, I saw that his face was glowing with an inner radiance and calm.

I sat down, without speaking and Peter and I just looked at each other, smiling, for a few minutes.

He looked very happy. He had no more questions. He'd received all the answers he needed.

In the next moment, before she left, Annie manifested one more time. I saw her smile at Peter, then at me.

Before she left to continue her journey in spirit, this sweet and lovely radiant being of light reached out a slim white hand and touched my hair lightly.

I felt the touch of an angel's hand upon my head!

After this session, Peter was healed of his anger and grief, and Annie was free to ascend to a higher realm.

HEALING HANDS

In Wellington, I assisted in the presentation of the seminars. My own spiritual growth was progressing during this time too.

After the physical reactions I'd received in Hobart and the mental reactions I'd received in the advanced seminar in Melbourne, came the more subtle spiritual experiences in Wellington.

The changes I felt happening within me were so faint and so subtle, they were almost imperceptible.

One afternoon, during a meditation, a strange thing happened.

As the singing began to taper off, and I stood with eyes closed, a surge of intense heat ran through me.

On one level, I felt surprised as I'd thought the gross physical reactions would no longer occur for me.

On another level, I felt something telling me to let go of any thoughts around this experience and to go deeper in the meditation.

As I let go of the thoughts, a searing, prickling, burning pain began to manifest in the palms of my hands.

At first, I tried to let go of the pain, then when that didn't work, I tried to ignore the pain.

It really hurt!

I opened my eyes and saw what looked like brilliant sparklers streaming from the palms of my hands.

They looked like white, hot, fizzing lights. The intensity and the pain increased to an unbearable level.

Without thinking what it would look like, I dashed up to my Teacher, grabbed him by the arm in the middle of his meditation and silently showed him my hands.

By this stage, I was crying and whispered to him urgently:

"It hurts, it hurts. There's something happening to my hands."

Immediately, he took my two hands in his, closed my fingers tightly over into fists and held my hands firmly for a few moments.

It was only then that the burning pain and the white light stopped. He indicated for me to continue meditating.

Afterwards, I felt overawed by what I'd experienced.

So much was happening to me so fast.

That evening, he told me I'd been given the gift of healing and my hands had been empowered by the Divine.

When I asked him why all these things were happening, he said:

"Don't ask questions. All you need to know is that it's time for these things to happen. Trust in your Teacher as you trusted in your grandmother, and most of all, trust in God."

CHRISTCHURCH

Our seminar program took us to Christchurch.

When we arrived, it was a crisp, clean and clear day.

We both felt the oxygenated air in New Zealand was so clean you could taste it!

I loved New Zealand.

I spent my free time studying the lecture notes, as I was taking on a larger role in presenting the seminars by now.

During this time, I fought many battles with my ego and its dictates and expectations of how things ought to be.

I was rapidly learning to let go and let God.

He told me that so far, I was passing the tests he'd set for me.

"With any student, it's necessary to study hard in order to go to a higher grade," he told me.

On the first day in Christchurch, a reporter and cameraman from the Christchurch television station, took us to the Botanical Gardens to film a spot on the News Program.

While we sat on a bench being interviewed, the ducks in the nearby pond waddled out of the pond and sat at our feet. It looked beautiful. The ducks appeared to be meditating and were at complete peace.

We all laughed at this and it gave a nice feeling to the News Program.

My Teacher told me whenever he did meditation at anyone's house, the local dogs would bark and howl:

"They sense the subtle vibrations generated by the attunement to the frequency of Divine Love," he said.

TO THE HAIRDRESSER

One afternoon, I had some time to myself and decided to go and find a hairdresser, as I felt I could do with a colour and trim.

Not too far from my billet, I came across a neat fashionable looking little salon.

The young woman who seated me was the manager. While she washed my hair, we chatted easily, as women do in the hairdresser's.

When she stood behind me at the mirror, I began to see images forming around her.

I saw the image of an older woman standing in her auric field, quite close to her.

"She has a spirit around her," I realised.

Somehow, it seems, that whenever I meet anyone, if I just wait long enough, the topic invariably gets onto the supernatural or spiritual level.

Eventually, this woman told me her grandmother had recently passed away.

"So that's who it is," I thought to myself.

"We were very close," she went on.

"I find it hard to believe she's dead. I find it hard that I can't talk to her anymore.

She brought me up, so she was more like my mother than my grandmother.

I occasionally get these funny feelings that she's not really gone. Do you know what I mean?

Sometimes, I think it's just a bad dream and I'll wake up and she won't be dead anymore."

Her eyes filled with tears.

I said nothing.

After she'd washed my hair, I said gently:

"I feel it might be helpful to tell you I'm a clairvoyant and I can actually see your grandmother quite near you.

I've done this kind of thing all my life, so please don't be afraid.

My grandmother brought me up too and I know how sad I felt when she died.

Your grandmother has appeared here now so that I can see her and help her to communicate with you.

I have a feeling she wants to tell you something. Is it all right with you if I do this?"

She looked surprised and said eagerly:

"Yes. It's absolutely all right.

I had a feeling something funny was going to happen today. I woke up feeling funny. I had strange dreams all night.

When you walked in the door a little while ago, I sort of knew you were somehow connected with the way I felt.

It's been a strange kind of day. I even had to send two girls home at lunch-time today because most of my clients cancelled. Maybe you and I are supposed to be alone together this afternoon."

The hairdresser sat down in a chair beside me and looked at me expectantly.

I said a silent prayer and looked at the spirit of her grandmother, where she still stood silently, patiently waiting.

I felt the communication begin as a telepathic stream of consciousness, of images, from her grandmother to me. It was faint and distant at first.

It went like this:

"Remember my stories to you about doing what you think is right? I want you to remember, I brought you up to be a good girl. Don't trust men until you get to know them. You're too friendly and easy with men. I've told you about this. Keep yourself for the special ones.

So you'll know it's me and the lady's a good lady, remember my sewing-basket? You know the one you always loved, the one with all the lace pieces and coloured silks, it's yours now. I put a little note for you in the bottom, under everything. It gave me a lot of pleasure to write it, knowing you'd read it one day.

I love you, my girl.

Remember to be wise and canny with the money I left you.

Keep singing. You've got a lovely voice."

It may not sound like such an extraordinary message, but to the hairdresser it was. She was delighted.

She said in an animated and excited way:

"That's fantastic. Wonderful! Thank you, thank you. I'll look in Nanna's sewing-box as soon as I get home. I'm closing shop when I've done your hair.

Would you believe I'm a country and western singer? My two partners and I've got our first gig in Singapore at a pub in four weeks time. I think we're going to be big in Singapore. What do you think?"

"Yes," I told her. "I think you're going to be great."

She suggested we do a barter, and she did my hair in exchange for her impromptu reading.

She also loaded me up with gifts of shampoo to take with me. Before I left, I felt I'd made a new friend. We exchanged addresses and parted with hugs.

COFFEE! COFFEE! COFFEE!

I had just enough time for a coffee before the seminar.

I wondered if my Teacher had been looking for me.

We'd been having an ongoing disagreement about my coffee habit.

He felt it was not good for me to drink so much coffee and that I was addicted.

I got annoyed with him for going on about it.

When he asked me to test it, by saying:

"How will it be for me if I continue to take coffee to the same extent I am now taking it," in a meditation, I had sharp pains in my stomach, nausea and shaking.

He'd used my reactions to prove his point, but I still wasn't convinced.

It was a long-standing joke with my family and friends that I needed a few cups of coffee to get moving in the morning.

"Don't talk to Mum until she's had her second cup," my children would say. My oldest son gave me a mug for Mother's Day with that same inscription on it.

I'd been heard to moan and say in humour to friends:

"Let me just open a vein and put some caffeine in."

I was an expert on coffee, a seasoned and experienced connoisseur of the first rate!

Many of my friends gave me chocolate-coated coffee beans as gifts and little gold and black bags of delectable designer coffee for Christmas.

"My Teacher's on very shaky ground here, telling me to give up coffee," I muttered to myself that day in Christchurch.

I stood outside what looked like a great place to have a café latte. Cakes as well!

I put out my hand to open the door and as I did so, a deep, strong voice inside me said:

"No!" I tried again. I got the same 'no' again.

Whatever was going on? I was unable to open the door. I was totally powerless. I had to move aside to let other people go in and out, but I couldn't go in.

I gave up, puzzled and embarrassed and walked slowly, in deep thought, back to the house where I was staying.

I decided not to mention anything about this bizarre event to my Teacher because I knew what he'd say.

He'd say: "The Divine is trying to tell you something, my dear. Ignore it at your peril."

Each time we were with a meditation group and were teaching them discernment he would look at me and say:

"Shall we test coffee, dear lady?"

I'd moan and say:

"No, please don't test coffee," because I always got such unpleasant reactions from this test.

Just after the experience of trying to get into the café, I had a dream I was having surgery and the surgeon opened up my stomach. He pulled out what looked like a fine piece of lace shot through with holes and held it up for me to see.

He said:

"Look at this. This is your liver. It's shredded from drinking too much coffee."

I woke up feeling shocked after this dream, resolving to go 'cold turkey' for a few days.

When I told him about my dream, he resisted the urge to say "I told you so" and just nodded and said, "Very good."

A few months later, I met a young monk from India, who bemoaned with me the agonies of trying to cut down on coffee which was his favourite and apparently solitary vice.

He said to me:

" When I joined the ashram, I took the vows of poverty, celibacy and obedience.

Poverty easy for me. Celibacy easy too. Obedience not so easy. Giving up coffee impossible!"

We often enjoyed a coffee together, Swamiji and I.

A PICNIC AT THE HARE KRISHNA TEMPLE

We stayed in Christchurch for a week and after the seminar each day, I had free time.

One day I walked into the Hare Krishna Temple to give my Teacher's greetings to the monks and nuns, as he was an honorary life member of the Hare Krishna Society, and to give them details of the seminar dates for their interest.

I was curious about their ashram and temple, and a bit shy to be there by myself.

The women looked very young. They were all wearing colourful silk saris, and had their long hair covered. They were also New Zealanders, and I'd expected them to be Indian!

I wondered what had made them decide to leave the world and live like that.

"A bit like my wanting to live in a convent, I suppose," went through my mind.

They were all cheerful, smiling and happy, which impressed me.

A young man invited me to stay and share a meal with their small community and I accepted.

The meal was brought in on trays and it was obvious we were going to sit on the floor and have a sort of picnic.

I sat on my side, tucking my legs up under me, thinking:

"I'm not really dressed for this, I can understand why the girls wear long skirts."

We shared many delicious and new tastes and textures.

This was my first experience and taste of another culture and an Eastern Religion.

When I was leaving, the young people gave me a colourful copy of their scripture, called the Bhagavad Gita.

Later that evening I gave it to my Teacher, who laughed and said: "This is for you and for your education dear. Read it well and tell me what you think of it. You can begin your homework now."

QUEENSTOWN

In March 1995, we went to Queenstown.

What a beautiful place. I stayed in a large motel overlooking the lake, with an unprecedented view of the majestic mountains called 'The Remarkables,' because they seem to be forever changing colours as you gaze at them.

Queenstown opened its wide heart and embraced me.

Queenstown turned out to be another test for me, as it seemed that everyone was interested in my gift of clairvoyance.

"At least it's in New Zealand, not in Melbourne," I consoled myself.

"If anybody in Melbourne finds out I'm psychic, they'll think I've flipped my lid," I thought.

I'd known all my life I was what people called psychic or intuitive, and I'd even begun to accept it for myself. It was pretty hard to ignore.

However, I didn't usually let people know I saw things and sensed things they couldn't see or sense, for fear I wouldn't be taken seriously.

Even the doctors and other colleagues who referred patients to my practice, were unaware of my secret advantage over other psychologists.

SOURCE OF INSPIRATION

One night, my Teacher decided it was time to show me how to test the source of the information I was receiving.

I had never thought about questioning the source of the information I was picking up about other people. I didn't know that there were many possible sources of information from which an intuitive person could receive.

He showed me a chart which detailed several realms of inspiration and asked me to discern the realm from which I was receiving intuitive information.

My eyes led me to gaze at the top of the chart.

He agreed with me and said:

"My dear, you're most fortunate. I am in accordance with you.

You are indeed receiving your inspiration from a very high source."

He went on to explain:

"It's my experience that most psychics are receiving their information from the Earth Plane, which is within the Physical Universe.

Only a few of the most intuitive are able to receive information from the Angelic Plane. You are receiving from a much higher plane than this.

Unfortunately, many psychics are receiving their information from spirits on the Astral Plane. These spirits often claim to be Ascended Masters and delude the unsuspecting psychic.

Of course, this is not always the case. I mention it to you as a warning to always test the source of your inspiration and information received.

The psychic who gives her power to a spirit is very foolish.

The client who also gives her power to the psychic and the spirit is even more foolish.

Furthermore, many psychics become mediums, become unconscious vehicles or hosts for spirits to speak through, without knowing the danger in what they're doing.

In this way, the disembodied spirit is using the psychic's energy to live again, and will attempt to use any other person's energy to live."

He went on:

"Many well-meaning psychics also become ill as a result of receiving spirits into their auric field.

They don't know how to cleanse themselves on a deep level."

I was frightened when he spoke like this.

I began to understand why I'd always felt it was dangerous to use my psychic gifts.

I realised I needed training from someone who knew all about this subject.

Now I understood why this amazing man was my new Teacher. I wished that my beloved grandmother had known him.

THE CRYING MAN

A few people from Queenstown stand out in my mind as their stories were unusual and inspiring.

During the seminar, a young man cried pitifully.

Over two days, I observed this young man kneeling on the floor crying.

I felt like going to him and comforting him as his suffering was awful to watch. My Teacher stopped me from intervening and said:

"If you stop his suffering now, he'll just have to do it again later. Let him get it over with.

He's being cleansed of all the dirt he's picked up in his life so far.

He's got a good soul, but he's done some bad things. Remember my dear, dirt does not come out nicely.

Just let him be, let it all come out." Again, I found my Teacher was right.

The young man was transformed by the end of the seminar.

During our stay in New Zealand, the young man who no-longer cried, followed us everywhere we went and assisted us in any way he could.

ANNE BOLEYN

During my stay in Queenstown, a young lady came to see me after the seminar.

She was very disturbed by her relationship with her father. Her father had divorced her mother and the young lady was still living with her father in his house.

Her father was a wealthy and powerful man in the world of finance. She had a beautiful new sports car, expensive clothes and jewellery, but her father didn't allow her to have any friends or to go out of his sight. He was very jealous and possessive of her. She told me:

"I feel like I can't breathe around him, and I keep having panic attacks every time he comes near me.

I've been seeing a psychologist for months for the panic attacks and I don't seem to be getting any better.

I'm also seeing an osteopath for torticolis because my neck is stiff and painful."

While listening to this young lady's story, I began to see images of her most relevant past life.

I saw her in a setting that looked like medieval England, which showed me she had been called Anne Boleyn!

I received that her father this life-time had been her husband in that life-time, i.e. Henry the Eighth of England.

As I was considering sharing my vision with the young lady, she began to cry and hold her neck, saying:

"It hurts, it hurts so much."

We talked about the vision I'd seen, and she cried even more.

She didn't doubt my vision was genuine and gave me some information that left us both astonished.

She told me her father's name was Henry, and his friends called him Harry.

Her father had been married six times in this life-time, her mother had been his sixth wife.

The most miraculous outcome of our session was the young lady's realisation that she had been allowing her father to control her life for too long.

Several months later, I received a post card from her from France, saying she was wonderfully fit, healthy, in love, and had no more neck problems or panic attacks.

RICHARD THE LIONHEART

A young man who sat up the front from the first day of our Seminar and who had never taken his eyes from my face for a moment, asked to speak to me.

He was young, about twenty-six or so, tall, slender, with long blonde shoulder length hair.

He told me he'd been a teacher in Australia, was the only son of wealthy parents, had owned a red Ferrari and had dated a beautiful girlfriend.

Last year, he'd received a prompting from within himself that couldn't be ignored.

He'd left his job, his parents, the Ferrari, the girlfriend and his country to back-pack around New Zealand and was currently living in a tent in the forest around Queenstown.

He'd brought his savings with him and managed to live that way.

He felt he was guided to participate in the meditation seminar we were presenting.

He felt intuitively drawn to me, feeling that I could shed some light on the reasons why he'd left his former life of ease and comfort.

As soon as his reading began, I saw the young man sitting on a tall white horse.

He was dressed in beautiful shining armour and looked physically very much like he did now.

During my vision, he was being garlanded with roses and the people of the town were throwing rose-petals under his horse's feet where he rode.

I heard the people calling out his name over and over:

"God bless our Richard. God bless Richard, Coeur de Lion."

I looked at this young man and said aloud:

"I believe you are Richard the Lionheart of England!"

The young man was not surprised.

He said:

"I've had dreams in the forest that I was once a king.

I taught History when I was a school teacher, so when I had the dreams about England, I knew it was in the time of King Richard.

I think I've always known who I was. You've just given me the confirmation I needed.

I've never told anybody about my deep feelings and intuition that I was once Richard. I don't doubt your vision at all.

I feel I have an even more important mission this lifetime, another crusade. Can you tell me what you think it is?"

I felt his mission was only for himself this lifetime, not for thousands of others.

His crusade was now a personal one. His mission was to grow his soul, to find God within himself, to visit the Mecca within.

After I told him this, he was quiet and thoughtful for a few minutes.

"I understand everything now," he said.

Before he left the room, I was deeply touched to see him kneel in front of my Teacher who had witnessed this session.

I watched in wonder as the young man who had once been a great king, received a beautiful blessing.

After Queenstown, I flew back to Melbourne.

CHAPTER 9

MELBOURNE GHOSTBUSTING

HOME AGAIN

I was glad to be home again and enjoyed spending time with my family after having travelled to New Zealand.

Upon my return home, I'd asked a few of my friends and colleagues if they'd like to experience the surrendered, experiential system of meditation I'd learned.

Quite a few were enthusiastic, so I did a seminar for them.

MURDER MOST FOUL

A particularly frightening event occurred a few weeks later when a friend of mine moved house, and rang me to say she and her small son were unable to sleep.

I felt very uneasy during this 'phone call and sensed there was a malevolent spirit presence haunting her house.

She was a person who was open to the idea of spirit manifestation, and had actually attended my seminar.

I told her my feelings about her new house and she asked if I'd be able to cleanse it and exorcise the malevolent spirit.

Apparently, what had at first alerted her to a problem, had been the behaviour of her faithful old dog upon moving into the house. Her dog had refused to enter the house, becoming particularly upset near the kitchen.

When his food bowl was placed on the doorstep outside the back door leading to the kitchen, he would howl and shrink away, preferring to go hungry. This behaviour was totally out of character for her greedy old friend!

A few days later, I went to my friend's house.

As soon as I entered the house, I became aware of the depressive atmosphere.

It manifested as horripilation with all the hair on my body rising and goose-bumps prickling all over me.

I knew my friend and her child were in deep trouble here!

A heavy feeling attached itself to the back of my neck, to the heart area and my lower back.

I felt terror race through me. This was a big one! Was I ready for this?

I leaned against a wall, breathing heavily, trying to collect myself, praying rapidly.

I experienced a weighed-down, depressing and miserable sensation. I felt as if I were pushing through a barrier of sadness and despair.

I knew these were not my feelings. These feelings were alien to me, projected onto me by an Earth-bound, ancient entity.

My friend stood watching me in dismay, noting my pallor and pre-occupation with praying.

I was aware of the intense cold in the hallway, a feeling which was not apparent to anyone else.

I proceeded to check out the house in my usual way in these circumstances.

I slowly began to walk up the hallway, then walked from room to room, sensing cold or cool spots, being alert to odours and sensations.

Negativity manifested by Earth-bound entities has a particularly unpleasant smell.

It smells like country outdoor toilets, stagnant drains or something long dead.

When I entered the main bedroom, I couldn't bear to stay there for more than a few seconds, as the dread, heaviness and atmosphere was too thick.

I had the feeling that something terrible had once happened in this room. This was the room my friend had chosen for her bedroom and it was clear to me, even the most insensitive person would be unable to sleep in such an atmosphere.

When I came to the kitchen, my feet refused to carry me across the threshold! It was clear to me that something awful had happened in this room. I understood why the poor old dog had refused to enter it and decided to keep this information to myself.

I again circumnavigated the house, this time singing very loudly, being guided from within, spraying holy water all around the rooms, projecting the positive energies of prayer and Divine love into every corner.

My feet walked me into every room while my mind seemed to watch aghast from afar.

During this experience, I felt a conflict within me. A part of me that was very human and vulnerable was looking on feeling nervous and afraid.

The Divine part of myself was at the same time, very strong and doing what needed to be done without any fuss. It was interesting to observe these two parts of myself communicating with each other.

The malevolent entity followed me throughout the house!

I ignored it and continued to pray and sing very loudly, commanding any satanic influence to leave the Earth realm and to return to its source, in the name of the Divine and in the name of my Teacher.

I knew I'd been given the authority to command the spirits to leave, so it was with confidence that the Divine aspect of myself could do this difficult job.

It's my feeling that in order to do this job, a person needs unshakeable faith and belief in the Divine Creator. I certainly had that!

After the house-clearing was completed to my satisfaction, I could sense warmth and light returning.

I asked my friend to walk through the house with me to gauge her feelings.

My friend decided it was a good idea to use her poor old dog to check out the house, as she believed her dog was more sensitive than she was!

The old darling rushed into the kitchen the moment my friend opened the back door. He gulped two plates of food from the fridge, that was meant for the family's dinner, as his reward from his grateful owner!

Apparently, all was now well in my friend's house.

What a relief!

I rang my friend the next day and she told me that everyone had slept peacefully the night before. The dear old dog slept on the foot of her bed all night, and no-one sensed any disturbance.

It was my understanding that my friend's dog had been able to sense what the humans had not. Dogs are in Alpha in their brain-wave state, and already rely on subtle senses. The dog knew that the disturbing spirit had left the Earth realm.

I didn't tell my friend the whole story.

I usually don't tell people the whole story, unless I feel that it's entirely necessary for them to know the details.

During my walk through my friend's house, I'd received intuitive information that a very long time ago, in the previous history of this house, an elderly lady had been murdered in her bed by her unscrupulous son who'd become impatient for his inheritance.

The murdered lady had occupied the bedroom that my friend had been unable to sleep in!

The murdering son had later died prematurely, due to guilt and immoral living and had haunted the house alongside his grief-stricken mother.

Between them, these two dreadful spirits had driven many people out of the house. Their ghostly presence had contributed to misery and broken relationships as a result of the negative energies generated between them.

I received also that the son had attempted to hide his mother's body in the kitchen, in an enormous old stove in the corner, but he was eventually forced to remove it due to her noxious deterioration!

Now these troubling spirits were gone, my friend and her family could enjoy their home.

THE MYSTERY OF THE LITTLE GHOST

I remember another haunted house I was asked to assess for another friend about the same time.

My friend had been feeling more and more uneasy about the atmosphere pervading the beautifully restored terrace house he'd paid a small fortune for.

What was more worrying to my friend, however, was the bad luck that seemed to affect every venture he attempted. My friend had been a busy and successful psychotherapist with a large practice, prior to buying his new house.

After participating in my meditation seminar and hearing the conversations of other people who'd had their houses cleared of negative influences, he decided to approach me about assisting him with the clearing of his house.

Accordingly, I found myself standing outside my friend's front door.

Even outside this imposing house, the familiar gloom and doom began to descend upon me.

As I stepped inside, I found the air to be dense, heavy, cool and most oppressive.

I sensed age-old sorrow attempting to weigh down my spirit.

"How could you bear to live here? I bet you never get any sleep," I asked my friend.

During the months he'd been living in this house, he'd lost his sense of humour and didn't respond to my question, as once he would have.

My experienced eyes noted my friend's weary, heavy body and lack of energy. He'd also gained a few kilos.

I began to walk slowly down the hallway to investigate the ground floor.

It seemed that very little sunlight could penetrate this gloomy house.

I felt shivery and nauseous.

My friend and his partner travelled frequently overseas on business and I noticed a few curious souvenirs they'd collected.

I saw a rusted spear from Kenya mounted on a wall above a fire place. I observed a few drops of dark red blood dripping rhythmically from this spear onto the mantle-piece and running down into a large puddle on the carpet.

My friend, though a darling, was an insensitive sort of fellow and was unable to see what I was seeing as he was not clairvoyant.

I also noticed a small leather bag which looked to me like a medicine bag. I felt very uncomfortable about these two objects in particular.

In the next room, I was horrified to see, displayed in a glass-case, what seemed to me to be a macabre piece of art.

I asked my friend:

"What in heaven's name is that thing?"

"Oh that, it's a monkey's head. It's supposed to bring good luck." Shaking my head, I told him:

"Let me tell you my friend, that's not a monkey's head, that's a human baby's head that's been charmed to bring evil to its possessor."

He was very upset and believed me.

After investigating a person's house, I often ask people to remove from the house specific objects that I am guided to notice, because these objects emanate negative vibrations and are harmful to the house's inhabitants.

A few years ago, I was guided to tell a friend to dispose of a rusting Japanese bayonet that he was using as a barbecue tool, due to its potential danger to himself and his family, as the spirit of the Japanese soldier was haunting his family.

After looking at every room, I settled down to prepare myself for clearing the house by prayer and surrendered meditation.

I then walked around the house chanting loudly:

"Jesus, Ave Maria, Rest in Peace" and so on in a spontaneous manner. Before the chanting begins, I don't have any plan or idea about what to say, I am guided to chant particular words.

As I approached the stairs, I saw a pale-faced little girl ghost who was wearing a long, white ruffled nightgown and was crying piteously.

The pathetic child appeared to be floating down the stairs towards me.

The air was still and freezing.

I stood completely still.

The child came very close to me and gazed right into my face, still crying soundlessly.

Then, as I watched, she went up the stairs again still appearing to float just above the carpet.

She looked back at me as if she were making sure I saw her. She appeared to disappear into a wall to the left of the stairs.

The eerie spell was broken by her sudden disappearance. My friend saw nothing but felt extremely sad. As for me, I burst into tears. We could do no more at the time, except to say prayers together for the redemption of the small ghost's soul.

He and I later found out, from plans of the house and some research, that my friend's terrace house had apparently been one of two houses that were exactly alike and had been built about one hundred years ago.

At the spot where the girl had disappeared, there had once been a connecting doorway between the two houses that had been bricked up. Apparently the families used to come and go in each other's houses.

I later found out my friend and his partner sold the house, found they were happier without it and their good luck, prosperity and success returned in their new abode.

SABBATICAL IN MALAYSIA

In late March 1995, my Teacher called me and said:

"My dear lady, I've been thinking about the possibility

of your studying meditation with me in Malaysia. How do you feel about this?

You've shown great potential as a teacher of meditation, in New Zealand.

To study with me in Malaysia, can only enhance your career status in Australia later. Regard it as a sabbatical. It will mean a sacrifice on your part, I know. Discuss it with your family and let me know your decision as soon as possible, God be with you."

After some thought and family discussion, I realised it was too good an offer to refuse.

I was going to Malaysia!

CHAPTER 10

MALAYSIA

EN ROUTE TO MALAYSIA

In May 1995, my Teacher and I flew to Singapore en route to Malaysia.

One of my psychology students, had arranged for our flight to be upgraded all the way!

What a wonderful surprise and a very good omen for my first trip to South East Asia.

My Teacher told me the island nation of Singapore has earned a reputation as one of the most surprising islands on Earth, due to its friendly people, exotic points of interest, wonderful food, China town, little India, and the famous Raffles hotel.

CHANGI PRISON

While we waited at Singapore Airport for our connecting flight to Malaysia, my Teacher told me a story:

"Changi Airport holds many sad memories for me, dear.

During the War, what you now see as a busy, sophisticated airport, was the site of Changi Prison, a prisoner of war camp.

During the war, this was a dreadful God-forsaken place.

I was imprisoned there, after the fall of Singapore to the Japanese.

I had a way about me of fixing radios, so the Japanese let me tune their radios and work in the kitchens.

By working on their radios, I was able to listen to the BBC to get the War news on and off and I shared it with the other prisoners. This was punishable by death.

One of my most unhappy tasks was to count the dead who had died in their cells during the night.

Every morning, as I walked past the cells to do a head count, the poor living skeletons begged me for salt. Salt was what we all craved more than anything else. Our bodies were in such a sad state from malnutrition.

I used to put a handful of salt in my pocket when the Japanese guard in the kitchen turned his back, and as I passed the prisoners, I would give each a little salt. I was unable to steal any food.

They used to reach out their hands begging for food, so the soldiers didn't notice my giving them the salt, because I acted as if I were pushing their begging hands away.

I began to notice the prisoners I'd given the salt to were still alive the next morning.

I continued to give them the salt for a few weeks, until one day I was caught.

I was dragged before an officer who ordered that my head be cut off as an example to the other prisoners not to steal from the Japanese.

I bowed to the officer and asked permission to speak.

He barked at me: 'So speak!'

I said: 'Honourable sir, it is the custom of my people to pray to their God before death.

I beg you to allow me to prepare myself to meet my God.'

He agreed.

I knelt, face on the floor and prayed.

After my prayer, I bared my neck for the soldier who stood waiting to behead me, impatiently beating his sword on his leg.

As the soldier raised his sword, the officer yelled: 'Stop!'

The officer then said to me: 'Get up, you! Your courage is worthy of life.

Get out of here and don't ever let me catch you stealing again or nothing, not even your God, will save you.'

I thanked God for my deliverance and knew that my life was spared for a purpose.

I always remember how I felt that day when I visit Changi Airport."

He was quiet and thoughtful for a long time after he told me that story.

MALAYSIA BOLEH:
MY FIRST IMPRESSIONS OF KUALA LUMPUR

It was dark when we arrived.

My Teacher told me:

"There is no dusk or twilight here, you'll find. One minute it's day and then it's night. It's peculiarly Malaysian."

When we collected our luggage and stepped outside into the night, I was immediately assailed by a strong and heady scent that embraced me in the warm darkness.

The scent was made up of drains, flowers and ripening fruit all at once.

Malaysia has a distinctive odour and a flavour and I grew to love it over time.

There seemed to be people and noise everywhere.

Families were talking loudly, an elderly man was sleeping on a bench, children were running and squealing in play as children do everywhere, brown skinned babies slept peacefully in their prams. There was colour and vitality everywhere.

The women all appeared to be wearing long-sleeved dresses that went down to their feet with matching scarves and veils over their heads so that no hair could be seen.

I couldn't see one white face anywhere!

The women all looked like exotic flowers because their clothes were so colourful.

There was no Melbourne black in anyone's clothes here at all! Everyone looked as if they were dressed for a party, and no-one appeared to be in a hurry at all.

On their feet, most people were wearing strapless sandals that made hurrying impossible. I was told that Malaysians called them 'flip-flops' and they loved them.

We were met at the airport by several of my Teacher's Malaysian friends, who welcomed me in a most friendly manner.

As we were driven through the streets of Kuala Lumpur, affectionately called 'KL' by people who live there, I wondered what new adventures lay ahead of me.

In the car, everyone was speaking Malay Bahasa and I couldn't understand one word. I felt inadequate as I only had French and German and resolved to learn the language of Malaysia as soon as possible.

I found that most of the people I met in Malaysia spoke at least four languages, as well as English.

That night, I lay awake for a long time, in a strange bed, in a strange country, being almost carried off by a buzzing cloud of greedy mosquitoes, wondering if I'd been foolish in not having malaria shots before I left home!

There were strange noises and strange shadows all around me. It all seemed so different from home.

I drifted off to sleep praying and asking God to be with me.

I was woken at five O'clock in the morning by a loud and unfamiliar sound. It appeared to be a man's voice, calling out and singing. It was very loud!

I jumped out of bed frightened. What was it? It sounded like a loudspeaker!

What was he doing making such a racket at this unearthly hour? He'd wake everyone up. At this stage, I didn't know that the sound I heard was the Muslim call to prayer from a Mosque across the road! I couldn't go back to sleep and I needed a cup of coffee.

"Where on Earth is the kitchen? I hope nobody minds if I explore the place so early in the morning," I thought.

I dressed from clothes in my suitcase and tip-toed out of my room near the stairs.

My Teacher had given me a huge room with two double beds, huge built-in cupboards, fans on the ceiling, a cool tiled floor and a large mirror.

It was hot already!

I tip-toed around the ground floor, no-one was stirring. Eventually, I found the large kitchen. There were many windows in the house and I was fascinated to see the jungle right outside the kitchen.

I helped myself to a coffee and went back to my room and unpacked my suitcase.

MY FIRST MALAYSIAN BREAKFAST

My Teacher appeared about eight O'clock and said:

"Well, I bet you're looking forward to a coffee!

Come on, I'll take you out for your first Malaysian food."

He was very proud of his Malaysian Proton Saga, which was in his opinion 'the best car in the world'.

We pulled up in front of what looked like a temporary outdoor picnic area, that had a rather faded sign declaring it to be a 'restaurant'.

The tables and chairs were red plastic and the restaurant had a dirt floor, however, the Indian owner was warm and welcoming.

I learnt how to order a coffee in Malay Bahasa by asking for a 'kopi, sila'. This meant 'a coffee, please'.

My Teacher laughingly told me:

"This is your first Malay Bahasa lesson, my dear. I felt sure that 'kopi' would be the first word you'd want to know."

My coffee arrived in a plastic cup brought by a handsome Indian boy.

I looked into the cup:

"Interesting," I thought and took a sip. It was sickly sweet and I don't usually take sugar in my coffee.

Apparently, it's the custom to add sugar to everybody's drink or to include sweetened condensed milk. I learnt to enjoy hot sweet kopi.

Breakfast was a kind of pancake called 'roti canai', which was to be dipped into a chilli fish sauce. I'd never eaten chilli before, so that was an experience.

I was so hot.

My clothes seemed to all be very inappropriate for this sticky, hot, humid atmosphere. The perspiration kept running down my back, my legs and my face.

My carefully applied make-up had all run off, even my hair was wet. I wanted to have another shower and start all over again.

I asked my Teacher if the mosquitoes bothered him.

He said: "No, not at all. When you've done a lot of meditation as I have, the galvanic skin response is different and the insects can't penetrate the skin.

I'll get you some cream to rub on and an electronic device that will repel them."

He also said the mosquitoes were attracted to 'sweet' blood and it would be good for me to cut out white sugar and sweets from my diet.

"Vitamin B will also help you. The mosquitoes don't like skin when it exudes a vitamin B odour," he said.

TOUR OF KL

That first day he took me on a guided tour of the beautiful city of Kuala Lumpur.

I was surprised to see western-style department stores and luxury goods alongside food-stalls and open air markets. I saw blind beggars singing and playing guitars and electric key-boards for their living. We gave small coins to all the beggars we passed.

I saw more majestic and towering high-rise buildings in KL than I've ever seen in Australia.

There was an Eastern, Moorish flavour to everything that was so captivating. The KL Railway Station built in 1910, looked like a palace.

All through the city was music and colour, spicy-smelling food aromas and handsome, laughing, chattering people.

The Malaysian people seemed to be so full of life, vibrant, and alive. There was an energy about them even though they never hurried. I was impressed by this.

I was exhausted by the end of that first day in Malaysia and glad to go to bed. Thanks to my Teacher's kindness, I slept mosquito-free that night.

DOCTOR GURU

During my second week in Malaysia, I discovered that I had a very itchy problem, due to the tropical climate.

I had a scaly, hot rash on my bottom and my thighs which made me thoroughly miserable.

My Teacher advised me to attend his doctor for advice.

At the doctor's surgery, a movie-star handsome Indian doctor was waiting for me. When he saw my embarrassment, he explained:

"My Malay nurse is here to preserve your modesty, madam." After the doctor had examined me, he told me with a grin:

"It's only the typical fungal problem you people get in the tropics. It's not terminal!

You'll need some anti-fungal talcum-powder, I'll give you some. In Malaysia, you need to go about like the women here - no more lacy knickers, wear cotton loose ones or go without under a long skirt, and throw away your panti-hose. You can't wear those here." The doctor and I laughed together. I was very relieved that my embarrassing problem could be dealt with so easily.

I noticed that the doctor's name, which I could see on his name badge, was Doctor Guru!

I told Doctor Guru:

"It's awfully funny you know.

I flew to Malaysia with a real Guru, having no idea that I would need the services of a Doctor Guru."

Remembering Doctor Guru's advice, I asked a new Malaysian lady friend to take me shopping to buy some loose cotton dresses and cotton pants, which I discovered were cool and comfortable to wear. On the way home from our shopping adventure, she treated me to a western-style coffee-shop where we enjoyed a cappucino and tiramisu. While I sipped my coffee, I thought:

"Thank you, Lord. KL's exactly my kind of place."

GHOSTS IN THE HOUSE

Over the next few days, I began to adjust to the climate and to settle in a bit more.

I was becoming increasingly aware of some fleeting spirit presences on and off and decided to ask my Teacher about it one day.

He told me: "Yes, there are presences here. Many people, sensitives like you, tell me there is a spirit lion guarding my house and sometimes you can hear it growl and roar. Some visitors have even seen devas and nature-spirits in the garden.

There are benevolent spirits who remove the satanic influences people bring with them, and there are some saintly presences here also."

As I listened fascinated, he went on:

"There's been a lot of meditation done in this house over many years.

A lot of gurus, masters, mystics and saints have come to visit me and to stay in this house.

As a result, it has absorbed many energies and influences.

When a house has a lot of Light, it can also attract lost and wandering souls to itself, and so it is here. Be aware of this, but do not be frightened."

I had a chilling experience a few days later of what he meant.

A young man and I were in a room downstairs, wrapping and addressing last year's copies of a journal on meditation to send to various people who'd requested a copy.

We both looked up at the same time to see a tall dark shadow cross the room in front of us in broad daylight.

My hair immediately stood on end and my skin prickled all over. My young friend had never seen a ghost in his life and paled under his brown skin.

"Did you see that? Was it a ghost?" he asked me, eyes wide.

"Yes, I think it was," I replied.

'It' was still in the room.

The dark shadow which had no discernible features, stood in the corner of the room. I didn't like the look of it at all.

From the adjoining room where he was working, my Teacher called out:

"Are you two all right? Do you need me to cleanse the room?"

When I answered in the affirmative, most gratefully, the shadow immediately dissolved into smoke.

The young man went home early, somewhat shaken by his first experience of a ghost, which had been left by someone else.

THE YOUNG POLICEMAN

It wasn't long after my arrival in K.L. that a young policeman from Singapore came to ask for my help.

He had cancer in the testicles. He told me one testicle had already been removed surgically.

He was ill and anxious, in constant fear about the further progress of the disease.

This young man told me he was absolutely committed to life, so I felt something could be done for him.

He agreed to come and stay with me for a few days so that we could begin our therapy program. In my opinion, he needed a psychologist as well as a healer.

As well as the positive attitude he already possessed, he was in a loving relationship with a very supportive wife and two teenage children.

He had a strong faith in God and believed I could help him.

As an experienced professional, it was my feeling that all systems were go!

We embarked on a course of Positive Psychology using positive self-talk, assertion training and daily meditation.

He experienced many trauma releases and catharsis over the days we spent together.

He gained insight into the tragedy of losing his father at a young age and was able to move on in the grieving process. He let go of grief.

The young policeman was a joy to work with, as he was totally willing to let go of everything that weighed him down. He affirmed life and love with all his strength, which was considerable.

The outcome of our time together was a total miracle! The cancer went into remission, he was able to continue to experience loving his wife and he went back to work a healthy man.

During the chemotherapy and radiotherapy the doctors insisted on, he had no nausea at all and no hair-loss. This in itself was a miracle.

I'd explained to him that the negative auto-suggestions in the clinic brochures and the medical profession's negative affirmations about inevitable hair-loss and nausea, were fear-based concepts he could choose to let go of.

In place of these negative auto-suggestions, he wrote his own positive, life-giving, loving affirmations which then manifested. This young man understood the power of positive self-talk which he could use all his life.

A UNIVERSITY IN KL

In my first few weeks in Malaysia, I received several invitations to speak at various seminars and conferences as a visiting psychologist due to my professional permit.

My first introduction into the professional realm was as a guest at a university in KL for a psychology conference.

A driver dropped me off at the front entrance of the university.

I felt strange since I had no Malay Bahasa and wondered how I'd find the conference room by myself.

I carried a brochure on the conference in Malay and showed it to people who directed me to the conference room courteously and cheerfully. Everyone seemed to speak very good English and wanted to be as helpful as they could.

The conference room was enormous and was dominated by a huge oval table like the United Nations; each person's place had a microphone in front of it.

"They're very well organised" I thought.

I'd not prepared anything as I was a guest, and was not expecting to present a paper at the conference. I hoped there'd be a brochure available in English, as I wanted to be able to send a copy to my old supervisor in Melbourne for his interest.

During morning tea, I was introduced to the Professor of the teaching faculty for psychology.

As morning tea was being served, I noticed some delicious little Malaysian sweet cakes, which I was told were called 'quai'. The tea and coffee came in silver pots with generous amounts of milk and sugar already added.

"Malaysians really like sugar," I thought.

To my surprise, as the presentations began, all the guest speakers made their presentations in Malay Bahasa!

I didn't have a clue what was going on.

The overheads looked interesting, but again no English, so I didn't know what the topic was about.

Occasionally a word would jump out of a presentation that obviously couldn't be translated into Malay, such as 'classical conditioning' and 'stimulus response' which gave me a clue as to the paper's subject. I began to understand that we were talking about behavioural psychology.

I felt it would be impolite of me to ask the speakers to translate into English.

After the morning session was over, the Professor went to the podium and for the first time spoke in English:

"We have, as you all know, a visiting colleague here today as a special guest from Australia.

Dear madam, would you be kind enough to give us an overview of what's happening in Sports Psychology in Melbourne?"

I nearly fainted!

Sports Psychology! So that's what the morning's presentations were all about.

I knew absolutely nothing about Sports Psychology.

I thought:" Whatever am I going to say to these lovely people?" They all clapped to encourage me to my feet, apparently thinking I was shy and modest and looked at me so expectantly that I thought I'd better say something.

I said something about Pat Cash, our tennis hero, how he had a sports psychologist as an important member of his team to motivate and inspire him to win.

I began to warm to my subject as my audience looked so interested, and talked a bit about how Football was so important in Melbourne. I told them research shows that athletes who mentally rehearse their roles and visualise winning the game before the actual event, are more likely to win. I mentioned that visualisation equals success.

My Malaysian audience was kind to me, and clapped loudly once I was finished.

I was terribly embarrassed but I think they liked me. I later received a really nice note, from the Professor thanking me for my "interesting and informative address."

THE THREE MUSLIM GIRLS

After the morning's papers were presented, while I waited for my driver to appear, three young Malay girls came to meet me and to keep me company.

They were curious about me, about job prospects for psychologists in Australia and eager to talk.

They told me they were psychology students and they planned to complete their degree in Australia.

They hoped to be able to find supervision in Australia and possibly employment.

Just then, I heard the same singing that had awoken me each morning since I arrived in Malaysia.

The girls jumped up immediately and said:

"Prayers! It's the call to prayer. We must go to the prayer-room now. It was so nice to meet you."

One girl remained with me.

I said: "Please don't let me keep you from your prayers. I'll be all right here, my driver will be here soon."

She replied: "I'm having a period, so I'm not able to go to the prayer room during this time. If you don't mind, I'll wait with you."

I was curious to know about the prayers, so took the opportunity to ask this young lady some questions which she answered happily. Apparently, Muslims prayed five times a day and there were 'suraus' or prayer-rooms in most hospitals, businesses, universities, schools and public buildings.

The men and women prayed separately.

On Friday mornings, all business ceased and Muslims went to the Mosque to pray. The prayer was broadcast five times a day on TV, radio, and from every Mosque, so that Muslims everywhere would know it was time to pray.

I began to understand what was waking me up every morning at 5am and why it was repeated several times a day.

The young psychology student told me she had to wash her hands, feet and face before she prayed and there were always facilities for this in prayer-rooms and Mosques. This was all new to me.

I was curious about the way Muslim women dressed and asked her how she felt about being covered up from head to foot, especially in such heat.

She said she was proud to cover her body to keep her beauty a secret so that only her husband one day would see it.

She said she felt sorry for Western women who dressed immodestly, showing no respect for themselves. She felt that Western men must not respect their women at all, but treated them only as sex objects.

I was very impressed by the quiet way she said these things and privately I agreed with her.

MEDITATION IN KL: A FAMILY AFFAIR

Shortly after this, I met the members of the meditation group and found them to be warm and welcoming.

One Hindu lady told me she'd had a dream about me just before I came to Malaysia:

"I dreamt our Teacher brought us a white lady all dressed in white, sitting on a white horse as a gift to our country, you are the lady," she said.

It was interesting to do meditation in a large, open-sided hall in the middle of a housing complex. The hall seemed more like a marquee to me.

At first, I felt embarrassed by seeing curious children and passing strangers watching us meditate.

Some parents brought their small children and babies to meditation and it felt casual and informal, compared with the West.

It soon became quite comfortable for me to lead the meditation with a small baby in my arms and a toddler clutching at my dress.

My new friends had prepared a 'Pot Luck' welcoming meal, and I was requested to try a little bit of what everyone had prepared. There seemed to be such variety in the food Malaysia had to offer. I grew to love the food.

My favourite place to eat after a while, was the colourful and noisy night market.

The food was cheap and plentiful and tasted so good. I learnt that there were eleven varieties of bananas. Some were as small as my fingers and one was as long as my forearm!

It was a pleasure to be able to eat as many mangoes as I wanted to, because they were so expensive in Melbourne. I lost a lot of weight due to the heat and eating lots of fruit, fish and vegetables. I felt very healthy in Malaysia and quickly adjusted to the tropical conditions.

TEA-TIME TALK

I was asked to do a 'tea-time' talk for the Malaysian Institute of Management by a gentleman who'd attended my welcoming dinner.

When this gentleman invited me as a guest speaker, I told him I was a full member of the Australian Institute of Management in Melbourne.

He told me he felt it was a shame that Australians seemed to be reluctant to participate in an exchange program with organisations such as the Malaysian Institute of Management. He said that Malaysian members of his organisation were very keen to hear about management practices in the West.

When I arrived at the institute, I found an eager crowd of about forty people, men and women, waiting for me to speak.

An author of a new book on Malaysian management greeted me.

My presentation focused on 'Creative Management in The Twentieth Century' and was well received.

The emphasis of my presentation was on the need for management responsibility to bring the 'heart' i.e. love, back into the business world.

I said that in any company, people were the most important resource, we all have a responsibility to ourselves and to our staff to really love the work we do.

The focus of my tea-time talk was on love, as it was on everything I did.

I concluded the presentation with a short workshop on the power of positive affirmation and visualisation of goals and ambitions.

I really enjoyed the delicious tea-time delicacies that were offered after the presentation and resolved to write a letter to the Australian Institute of Management, telling them about the friendliness and warmth of my Malaysian colleagues, as soon as possible.

THE LOVE GURU

It wasn't long before I became affectionately known as the 'Love Guru' in KL!

Several organisations sought me out as a guest speaker and love seemed to be the topic they most wanted to hear about.

On this topic, a leading KL newspaper sent a reporter to interview me for their 'Women in Business' section.

When the reporter arrived, I immediately began to receive images around her of a recent bereavement of a very close family member. I tried very hard to focus on the questions she was asking me to answer, and tried to ignore the messages I was receiving from the spirit realm.

Taking courage, I trusted my inner guidance that could no longer be ignored and told the young woman:

"I'm receiving messages that you've just suffered a tragic bereavement and are very distressed and grieving at this moment. Please don't be sad, your dear one is in a very good place and loves you very much."

The young woman looked shocked, then burst into tears.

Somehow, with no more discussion of the bereavement or my comments, we both continued with the interview.

Apparently, upon returning to the newspaper's office, she told her colleagues what had happened during the interview.

Later that week, it was my very great pleasure to be treated to an enjoyable lunch, as a guest of the newspaper, at a delightful Indian restaurant.

This small, rather enlightened team of talented journalists soon became close friends.

My young reporter's article entitled 'Messenger of Love' attracted quite a bit of public interest when it was published and led to a journalist from another KL newspaper requesting an interview. Accordingly, one day in June, a reporter and a photographer arrived at my Teacher's house for an interview.

During the interview, I found it curious that the photographer to whom I'd not been introduced, was the one asking me all the questions! He intrigued me. There was something about his manner that eluded me.

I began to receive images about him and messages about his private life, that I felt I had to relay to him on his own, as their nature was so personal.

At the conclusion of the interview, I said to the photographer:

"It's really important that you stay behind for a few minutes. I've been receiving some intuitive messages that I must tell you about, which concern your personal safety."

During the interview, we'd already discussed my clairvoyant abilities at length.

The photographer paled noticeably and said:

"I've got a confession to make. I'm not a photographer. I took a passable photo of you but I'm really the Editor of the paper.

I do apologise for the deception which I felt was absolutely necessary.

I was curious about you after having heard a bit about your uncanny ability and wanted to check you out personally.

I've always been a bit of a sceptic where these things are concerned.

However, you've convinced me, madam. Okay. What have you got for me? I'm willing to hear it."

I told him what I'd received and after I'd finished, he became a believer.

The two newspaper articles had attracted a lot of attention in KL. The second newspaper article, written by the previously skeptical editor himself, generated so much interest that the newspaper office had to tell people to contact me personally, as the switch-board was jammed for hours.

AMERICAN ASSURANCE INTERNATIONAL

I was contacted by a representative of a group of insurance agents from American Assurance International, to be a guest speaker at a tea-time talk. The topic I was asked to speak on was 'Closing the Sale'.

When the group's representative arrived to collect me, to my surprise he presented me with a huge box of chocolates. This thoughtfulness was typical of the way I was treated by Malaysians during my whole stay in their country.

The evening was one of joy, humour, laughter and merriment.

I'd prepared brief notes for my one hour motivational Sales talk and found myself acting totally spontaneously during the whole time, needing no reference to my notes.

I decided to do my presentation in a very humorous manner and gave my audience two possible scenarios to consider.

One involved how to sell a comb to a bald man and the other involved selling a fur coat to an Arab.

My Malaysian audience rippled with laughter during the entire presentation.

American Assurance International agents in KL that night were treated to a very different way of closing a sale!

I sought audience participation which was challenging and confronting for these gentle, shy people initially. I found I had to spend a lot of time winning their trust and encouraging their confidence. After that, it was easy.

I asked them for suggestions as to how we could sell a comb to our bald customer in a humorous and creative manner.

To illustrate this, I did a role play with a gentle Malay man playing the role of my reluctant customer.

I convinced my customer it would be incredible machismo and a sign of his confidence as a man to carry a gold-plated tiny comb on his key ring signifying he had no need for hair to prove his manhood. After this comedy, selling a fur coat to an Arab was easy.

My role play with a Hindu man drew even more laughter.

I told my Arab customer he was quite above the dictates of climatic conditions in his country and was able to wear any garment he chose, even a fur coat!

I made my point that when you're a good salesman, you can sell anything and the most important lesson is to love yourself, love your work and love your customer. Love sells!

ROTARY CLUB KL

One night, I was asked to speak to the Rotary club in KL.

This was a great honour as there were no female members of Rotary and women were not generally invited as guest speakers.

I'd given a list of topics to the president a few days earlier and to my delight, he chose Love!

A delightful American millionaire drove me to the beautiful hotel where the Rotary club convened their meetings.

I'd been warned on my way to the hotel, not to be upset if my audience continued to eat their dinner during my thirty minute presentation, as it was their usual habit to dine during the guest speaker's address!

However, this night proved to be an exception.

As soon as I started my presentation, I noticed about forty male faces regarding me with interest. Dinners cooled on their plates, not a sound was heard, you could have heard a pin drop in that room. No one ate their dinner during this presentation.

I was aware of the fact that there were men of several races and religions present in the room that night and I was spontaneously guided to speak about the messages of love conveyed to Mankind by many Masters and Teachers.

I spoke about Divine Love, brotherly sisterly love, filial piety that children feel for their parents, about love for country and culture, and about the love of man for woman.

I quoted the words of many Masters on this topic, among them the words of Jesus, the Sikh Gurus, the Prophet, and the words of my own Malaysian Teacher about love.

I observed during the entire presentation, with absolute love in my heart, the look of wonderment that sat upon each man's uplifted face.

The presence of Divine Love permeated that room that night!

At the conclusion of the presentation, I told my audience:

"I'm going to give you gentlemen some homework to do tonight. When you go home tonight, I want you to go to your wife and tell her you love her."

There was general laughter from all the men in the room at this suggestion.

One young man put his hand up at the back of the room, with a big grin on his face, like a cheeky child in the classroom.

When I asked him why he'd put his hand up, he said:

"I've got a question to ask you.

Many of us here in this room, dear madam, have more than one wife. Which wife am I to say 'I love you' to?"

I understood their masculine amusement at my embarrassment as they knew well I was a new arrival to Malaysia and knew little of the Muslim way of life. I'd forgotten Muslim men may have up to four wives!

I said:

"I want you to say 'I love you' to all of your wives!"

Even more laughter at this suggestion and many amusing comments to each other in Malay Bahasa!

These delightful gentlemen, among them many titled gentlemen of rank and high office in KL, gave me an outstanding ovation that night, as well as flowers, an engraved plaque commemorating my talk and an instant photo which had been taken during the presentation. After my talk, more hot food arrived and I enjoyed a delicious meal in very amusing, chivalrous company.

CHAPTER 11

SINGAPORE

SINGAPORE

In mid 1995, my Teacher told me:

"I've been thinking my dear, it would be a good idea for you to travel to Singapore, teaching meditation and doing some counselling by yourself. I believe it's time for your solo flight."

I felt a little nervous about going on my own to stay in another strange country and being housed by people I didn't know, but I trusted his judgement.

He arranged for me to be billeted with some colleagues of his who lived in a high-rise apartment building, as most Singaporeans do, due to the lack of space on such a small island.

During my stay in Singapore, I taught meditation to friends and colleagues of my hosts and met several interesting people.

THE EVIL PRIEST

One morning, a woman came to ask for my advice.

She told me a dreadful tale of being seduced by her spiritual teacher.

When she'd first begun to study with him, she'd believed him to be a pure soul and a true spiritual teacher.

She soon discovered her teacher had actually sold his soul to the devil and was a devotée of the occult religion.

By the time she'd discovered his true intentions, she was powerless and unable to escape from his influence.

She told me his satanic power was so great that he knew her thoughts and her whereabouts and controlled most of her movements.

This woman told me in great distress, with a sense of abject despair, of the sexual practices she'd been forced to submit to under this man's influence.

I was very shocked to hear her sad tale.

As a psychologist, I felt that the young woman, given the extraordinary circumstances of her entrapment, was still sane and reasonably balanced. She appeared to be an intelligent, well-educated professional woman who'd been a genuine seeker after spiritual knowledge, when she drew the attention of this odious man whom she told me was revered as a saint.

As she was telling me her story, she drew her chair closer to me and reaching out, she began to stroke my knees and thighs!

I jumped away from her, intuitively protecting myself. I felt shocked and afraid.

The woman's eyes had glazed over, she appeared to be unaware of what she was doing and I felt the presence of a malevolent spirit. The woman's hands sought me out again and a sneer came across her face briefly.

When this happened, I stood up immediately, terminated the session, assuring her I would pray for her and her dreadful situation.

I felt worried and confused about what had happened during our brief session.

Before she left the room, the woman tearfully apologised for revealing her sordid story to me, saying that the Priest had told her if she ever revealed the story to anybody, he would deal with the person to whom she told it.

These words made me feel even more uneasy, especially since there had definitely been a masculine presence in the room during the 'touching' incident. I felt sure that the masculine, malevolent presence I'd felt overtaking the young woman when she attempted to touch my body, was in fact the projected spirit presence of the evil Priest who was possessing her.

After the woman left, I spent some quiet time in prayer and meditation.

I felt that there definitely was an evil presence around the woman, which was manipulating her and was now threatening me!

I felt that I would need to pray and guard myself during the coming evening.

Later that night, after my final meditation and prayers, I slipped into bed and turned off the light.

As soon as I did so, a dreadful thing happened.

I saw a face, a hideous, colourful and menacing face, come rushing at me out of the darkness, and I saw at the same time a pair of disembodied, large hands outstretched for my throat!

My physical reaction was instantaneous.

I was paralysed with fear. My heart was jumping in my chest.

I felt hot, then terribly cold.

My mouth went dry in absolute terror.

With a sense of horror, I knew this manifestation of evil was sent by the evil Priest.

This was REAL!

As I struggled helplessly against the cold, hard, unbelievably realistic hands that were around my throat choking me, I heard a beautiful, melodious strong male voice speaking in my ear:

"Recite the name of the Lord."

As I said "My God, my God," the horrible face and strangling hands were whisked away at great speed.

It was all over.

Only now could I move and I sobbed with relief.

I got out of bed on shaky legs and prayed for the rest of the night.

I later found out the occult power of this man was considerable.

No doubt he'd directed this woman to come to me to use her to entrap me, and then to use me as he was using her.

Apparently this man had a terrible lust for spiritual power and didn't mind how he got it.

The next day, I telephoned my Teacher to discuss with him my experiences of the previous evening.

We agreed that there was no point in my seeing the unfortunate woman again. We felt it was her karma to have submitted herself to such a vile man.

My Teacher told me:

"You are under the protection of the Divine, that's all you need to know."

I thanked him for his support, feeling that except for the grace of God, I could have been in the same situation as that young woman.

THE GHOST IN BLUE DENIM

A young woman rang me, referred by a friend who'd seen me for counselling concerning her relationship and who'd been impressed and touched by the experience.

The young woman and I made an appointment to meet the following day.

The next day, after asking me several questions about my background and experience, she paused, looked embarrassed and said:

"Could you do an intuitive reading for me now?

Would that be all right? I need some help with a personal matter and I feel that you'll be able to help me, as you helped my friend. If we don't do it now, I just know I won't get the courage to do it again.

Do I have to tell you anything or will you just know?"

I told the young woman to relax and that I would be guided to receive the information to help her resolve her problem, whatever it was.

After saying a prayer of protection and asking the Divine to be with me, I began to see, intuitively, vivid images forming around the young woman.

I saw a very handsome, charismatic Asian man wearing faded blue denim jeans with an ornate silver belt and a blue denim long-sleeved shirt.

As I described this man to the young woman, she cried out:

"That's my father you're talking about. Oh, my God" and she began to cry, sobs choking her.

I gave her some tissues and held her hand, while she collected herself and calmed down.

All the while, I could see the man in blue denim standing beside her, looking down at her and looking at me with tears in his eyes, as if he wanted very much to tell me something.

The young woman continued, when she could speak again.

"Dad killed himself last month. He shot himself. I don't understand. No-one can. I miss him so much. I feel it's all my fault. Why did he kill himself? Why didn't he tell me what was wrong? Why?"

She cried some more and I waited. Experience told me she needed to cry it all out.

The handsome 'blue denim' man communicated many images to my mind explaining to me the circumstances of his life and death.

I saw him after the tragic death of his young wife many years ago, in absolute despair, feeling totally alone. He had no religious faith to turn to.

He drank too much; he had several relationships but no love, and he grew to hate himself.

He kept his suffering and despair to himself and grew even more isolated from his former friends and colleagues.

He also felt guilty about letting his young daughter grow up in the care of relatives, as he felt he was not a fit person to look after a daughter. His self-esteem was very low, yet he still continued to work hard at his business.

Everything came to a head when he turned forty and realised he'd wasted his life, that it all amounted to nothing without love.

In grief and depression, he bought a gun and ended it all, alone and unloved, unloving of himself.

After his death, he realised, with guidance from angelic spirits, that the life he'd been leading had caused the depression, his very soul had become depressed and oppressed.

He realised he'd denied the expression of love within himself and had been untrue to himself.

Eventually, things had reached such a low point that a malevolent spirit had enticed him to suicide.

He conveyed to me telepathically, that he had good karma from previous lifetimes and had been a deeply God-centred Being several times.

The Divine had used the man's daughter to bring him to me so that his soul could have a chance to explain to his daughter the reasons for his suicide and to set her free from suffering and grief.

The soul of this man was desperately in need of help as he was trapped on the Earth plane by guilt, regret and concern for his child.

I communicated all this information to his daughter while she sat open-mouthed and incredulous.

"What can we do to help Dad? It sounds horrible," she asked me.

"We're going to meditate together and ask the Divine to send your father on to his next realm of existence, darling," I told her. Sometime after this was accomplished, I saw her father smile and kiss her cheek and then he bowed in an old-fashioned and courtly way to me, with a cheeky boyish-grin.

"How handsome he is," I thought, and then he turned and began to walk away. It was amusing to me that even out of body, this man could still attempt to woo a lady! How much potential this man once had for love and connection with others, I thought.

As he walked away from us in spirit, I saw a door open in front of him, then another door opened, then another.

As I watched in fascination, it seemed as if many doors opened, one after the other and he was walking down a very long corridor.

At the end of the corridor, only one door was left and as it opened, the most brilliant almost blinding white light burst from the opening.

He turned and waved at me and then just stepped into the Light! The entire room was warm and sweet-scented by our experience of Divine Love.

I told the young woman I'd seen her father's spirit being guided to the Light.

I held her for a long time as she soaked my blouse with her hot tears.

She rang me later to thank me again, and said:

"I'll never really understand what happened during our session today and I don't care. I just know I feel wonderful and I now understand my father's life and death a lot better. Thank you."

A BABY IS BORN

Several ladies came to me asking for help in conceiving a child. They seemed to have wealth, happy relationships and successful careers, but no baby, which was heart-breaking for them and their partners.

Sometimes, after a consultation with me, a child came for them and sometimes it didn't.

For those for whom a baby didn't come, I spent time helping them to find acceptance of God's Will.

A forty year old lady who owned a successful business had been to many world-famous doctors in many countries in her efforts to conceive a child, to no avail.

Apparently, she and her partner were fit and healthy, and there seemed to be no physical reasons for infertility. The medical experts were unable to explain why this couple could not achieve conception, despite their best efforts and considerable expense. This woman, her partner and I worked with hypnosis, surrendered meditation and Regression in an attempt to let go of any sub-conscious, deeply-held fears and traumas around parenthood.

It seemed to me we'd done everything possible, so the only avenue left to us was the impossible!

After discussion, we agreed to let go of the expectation of ever having a baby at all! I felt that this expectation and strong desire to conceive had set up a resistance to creative potential. We decided, after having agreed to truly let go of the idea and attachment to a child, to affirm a pure and honest intention to surrender to the Will of the Divine in our lives.

This man and his wife were an extraordinary couple and it was a great pleasure to work with them. Their love for each other, their absolute faith in me and their trust in God contributed to a miracle of love.

Their miraculous baby boy arrived twelve months later!

The child's mother rang me with the good news when I was visiting her country again and held the 'phone to the new baby's ear so he could hear my voice. This tiny baby, at three weeks of age laughed and gurgled when he heard my voice; we already knew each other well.

ANCIENT ICONS

A lady asked me to do a house clearing for her as she was feeling afraid to be alone in her beautiful penthouse.

As she told me about her feelings, I began to receive information that told me there were several ancient spirit presences disturbing her sleep and her peace of mind.

I asked the lady:

"Do you have in your possession any antique or ancient belongings such as jewellery, photographs or objets d'art?"

She answered:

"Yes, I do. I've travelled a lot on business and I've collected several beautiful Byzantine religious objects that are very dear and meaningful to me. Could these be the objects?"

After discussion, we decided it would be useful for me to visit her home to assess the situation.

As soon as I arrived in her home, I saw at once the objects that were the source of her problem.

They were obviously terribly rare and expensive items, collector's items which had once been held in churches and museums in Europe.

I told the lady I'd do my best to clear these objects of the negative energy they were emanating, but I had a feeling they might have to go to a museum or back to a church.

I felt that these ancient icons were not meant to be in her house. This lady was a deeply intuitive and sensitive person, with her own latent ability to be a gifted psychic, yet was totally unaware of the dangers inherent in keeping such objects in her possession. She was ignorant of prayer, meditation or spirituality and held no profession of faith or allegiance to any doctrine.

I received images of many of this lady's past lives and realised she'd been a nun, a priest and a monk in many lifetimes in Europe and still held deep attachments to these type of symbolic images of Eastern Orthodox Christianity, although in this lifetime she was not a Christian.

She was amenable to the idea of meditation together and as she was unable to consider prayer, I prayed for her on an inner level. During our meditation, I saw a black shadow which looked like a large black moth or a small bird, vacate the Madonna Icon and fly up through the ceiling and out of her apartment!

I felt the heaviness and negativity around this object which had been depressing this sensitive lady and had no doubt she would feel much lighter now this presence had gone.

With further meditation, the remaining negative energies also dissipated.

After the cleansing of her apartment, the lady later arranged for an auction of her excess designer clothing and antique estate jewellery collection. She began by cleaning out her apartment and her wardrobe and continued to clean out her life.

She began to understand, she later told me, that the negative energy projected upon her ancient icons by many sorrowing souls over time, had depressed her life and energy.

She now affirmed allowing more Light and love coming into her life.

I later heard that the lady changed her profession and focussed her considerable energy into showing others how to have more love in their lives.

THE MIRACLE OF THE TEN CENT COIN

A young Asian man came to see me to talk about his family business and his concerns about his older brother, who was apparently making financial decisions that were detrimental to the continuing viability of the family business.

During the course of our session together, he explained to me that his family's business had been long standing and solid since the early days of the colony.

Since his father had passed away and his older brother had inherited the managerial position, it seemed that ego and arrogance had overtaken his brother. The young man was very distressed at the breakdown of communication between his brother, himself and other family members.

He said to me:

" We've always been the kind of family where decisions are made in conference with each other. Our family emphasis has always been on harmony and discussion, with respect for each other's wisdom and experience."

I reflected quietly for a while upon this young man's concerns and began to receive how it felt to be a part of an ancient and wise Asian dynasty. It was as if I became intuitively Asian.

I said to the young man:

"It seems like you're asking me for a miracle, my friend. Is that what you're asking me?"

He looked surprised for a moment, then said:

"My dear lady, you've seen my intentions truly.

Several people have told me you've been able to effect miraculous solutions to their problems. Can you help me, can you guide me as to how I can get my brother to listen to me? We're all very worried about his gambling, his drinking and the new woman he's seeing."

I told him:

"You and I can meditate together on this problem and ask the Overlord of all to give us a solution, a miracle to our problem.

I feel guided to tell you from my heart, you'll see a symbol or an answer this very day that will tell you, you've been heard."

After our session, just before another person arrived asking for help, a telephone call came for me.

It was the young man who was calling me from his brother's car downstairs, outside the apartment where I was staying!

He said:

"I'd asked my secretary to send the car and driver to pick me up after our session today and to my total astonishment, my brother picked me up himself!

He's sitting here beside me as I speak to you. We've been having a long talk for the first time since our father died, and I think everything's going to be all right now.

When I opened the car door, the first thing I saw was a shiny new ten cent coin lying on the carpet glinting in the sun. I remembered what you said about the symbol of my miracle. It seemed to me that the little coin was a symbol of prosperity returning to my family. Thank you for giving back to me my faith and trust in the Creator."

For me, the true miracle in this situation was that the young man noticed the tiny silver coin as a symbol of his miracle.

THE MAN WITH A STROKE

A family brought their father to me because he'd had a stroke that had left him paralysed and without the power of speech.

Their father, they told me, appeared at times to be terribly distressed about something and they felt he wanted to communicate with them, but lacked the means to do so.

This was the first time I'd been asked to communicate with a person with this sort of handicap and it proved to be a fruitful experience on both sides.

I remembered how I'd felt when my mother had been unable to communicate with me anymore and how we were gifted to be able to speak to each other telepathically. Perhaps, I would be able to communicate with this poor man in much the same way my mother and I had communicated with each other.

I mentioned my personal experience with my mother to this family and they were amenable to the suggestion that the heart can communicate when the body cannot.

This was a most devout family and they asked me if I would pray for the healing of their beloved father. I was happy to do this.

The four adult children, the man's elderly wife, the man himself and I prayed together.

During our prayerful meditation, the man's eyes were communicating his agony to me.

I began to receive a telepathic stream of consciousness from the paralysed man. His heart was saying to me:

"So numb. My legs, legs gone, can't feel legs. Can't feel body at all.

It happened all at once. At least I can't feel the pain anymore; I'd rather have the numbness than the pain.

Help me, English lady, please. Your eyes are soft and kind. You can hear me, they can't.

My wife is so sad.

Why has this happened to me? Is it my karma? Will it improve or get worse?

I'm in a prison - my own body is a prison."

I told the man telepathically:

"Dear friend, your family has told me your faith in God is strong and constant. Nothing happens to us that is not from Divine Will. It must be God's Will that this suffering has come upon you. Our souls grow and mature through suffering; you have the opportunity to pay back any karma through this suffering and to become purified.

Trust in God, say your prayers in your mind ceaselessly, the same way you are now communicating with me. God hears your prayer which is coming from your heart.

Use your eyes to tell me you understand what it is I'm saying."

After having said this, I looked deeply into the man's dark eyes and saw a flicker of light which told me he'd understood everything I'd conveyed to him.

I spent the next few minutes radiating pure love and support to him and felt he'd received it. He fell asleep in his chair.

I told his family what had passed between us and they felt a sense of peace, believing their father's mental anguish had been removed. I prayed for the man often, but did not see him again.

WE ASK FOR LORD BUDDHA'S HELP

I was asked to visit a young man who'd been diagnosed with cancer of the liver, operated on and sent home to die. Apparently, the doctors felt there wasn't much more that could be done for this young man.

His family requested that I visit the young man at home as he was too ill to be brought to me.

When I arrived, I found all his relatives gathered at his house to meet me.

Upon seeing all these people, I felt a little shy, but felt they were even more shy than me, so I acted confident.

Everyone bowed at me respectfully, beaming friendly smiles.

As there were several small children and elderly ladies, the whole place seemed full of people and colour and noise.

At the bottom of the stairs, leading up to the bedroom where the young man lay, was a large altar as is common in Singapore households.

This altar was ablaze with candles and vivid flowers, surrounding a large colourful photo of an Indian Guru, to whom the young man's large and extended family had been praying for healing.

I bowed to the altar as I passed it, respecting the family's belief system.

A young lady, whom I found out was the young man's wife, led me upstairs.

In a simple bed, under a white sheet, lay a young Asian man, almost naked except for a pair of underpants and large white bandages around his abdomen.

Next to him lay a tiny newborn baby.

"This is our new son," his wife explained.

"He wants to spend as much time with the baby as he can," she said.

As soon as he saw me, the handsome, painfully thin and yellowing young man, tried very hard to get up out of his bed in respect for a lady who was a guest in his house. He was clearly very ill.

As he struggled to raise himself, my eyes filled with tears of compassion, I put out my hand and said:

"No, no. My friend, don't trouble yourself, please lie down, it's all right."

I felt helpless.

"What can I do for this poor man?" I thought.

"God help me to say, to do something. Show me the way, Lord. What is your Will here, Lord?"

The Divine, always merciful, came to my aid.

Inspired, I said to his wife:

"What Religion does your family follow?"

Her answer was:" We are followers of the Lord Buddha."

I thought for a moment and said:

"We'll pray for the help of our Lord Buddha, and then we'll pray for the help of Buddha's Lord, the Great Lord of all Mankind, the God of us all."

The young man, his wife, his new born son and I surrendered to the Divine in that hot little bedroom, and he went to sleep.

He slept a deep and peaceful sleep.

I touched the young man lightly on his silky hair and kissed the little baby, also asleep, before his wife and I tip-toed out of the bedroom.

Outside the bedroom, I held the young man's wife while she cried and thanked me for giving her suffering husband some comfort and peace.

LET GO AND LET GOD

A young man came to learn meditation privately.

He sat in his chair to begin, and after relaxing deeply, he began to twitch, to toss his head back and forth and to jerk his arms and legs about.

His rapid, uncoordinated movements became more violent, so I asked him to end the meditation session.

I was completely at a loss to understand why this young man had reacted to surrendered meditation in such a way.

The young man asked for another meditation session four days later and I asked him if he had been learning any other system of meditation.

He told me he'd been learning quite a popular technique for many years and had been curious to explore the surrendered meditation I'd been teaching. I decided, after hearing this, to give the young man a lot of space and get him to stand up.

When he stood up and surrendered, he jumped up and down vigorously and threw his arms around. I stayed well out of the way and after a while he calmed down.

He said later:

"I felt very active when I stood up. In fact, I'm feeling really good. All the pent-up anxiety is gone."

I explained to him that if you sit in a rigid, unnatural posture always for meditation, the energy that wants to free you up can't flow through you, so the muscles will pull the limbs and jerk the body to try to release the posture.

The young man had a learning experience about surrendered meditation that day.

The young man's experience reminded me of a girl who'd danced spontaneously like a ballerina in a meditation in KL.

When I'd asked my Teacher why she'd moved like this during meditation, he'd said:

"Many meditators who have been learning rigid posture techniques, once directed to stand, are made to dance by the Divine to free themselves up."

If you've come from a passive and quiet 'meditation as peace and serenity' mode, it can be disconcerting to be part of a group of people that cough, laugh, cry, sleep and dance spontaneously. I know I found it surprising at first.

But, to be able to let yourself be moved by the Divine is a very liberating experience and it soon effects other areas of your life.

I recalled that one of my Teacher's favourite expressions was:

"Let go and let God."

This surrendered, experiential system of meditation I was teaching, was an experience of free-flowing energy which led to responses and reactions as evidence of the awakening of latent soul energy. This was why people danced and experienced energetic reactions, like the girl in KL.

During my own experience, I'd discovered that the reactions were either coarse or subtle, depending upon the depth of surrender. There was also a cleansing element to this surrendered meditation, which could remove negative energy, potential for disease and karmic consequences.

My Teacher told me often:

"My dear child, always remember that whenever you feel less than love, whenever you feel depressed or troubled, realise you've fallen from your ideal state of Divine Love, surrender in meditation to the source of Love and ask to be cleansed."

THE SONG OF NEW ZEALAND

A man from New Zealand came to see me to learn meditation.

During our first session together, he asked me to use my psychic ability to look into the past, to uncover the reasons for his present personal dissatisfaction. This sensitive and intuitive man had been having a recurring dream that had troubled him for many years.

He told me:

"I always have a sense of a shadowy and ancient life in New Zealand that I lived prior to this life. In this dream that keeps coming, I feel that the past is somehow influencing my life today. Can you see anything that will help me to understand?"

At once, I began to receive vivid and colourful images concerning this man's past lives in antiquity.

I saw a tall, wise-looking man, with a cloak made of some bird's feathers around his shoulders, standing beside the man sitting in front of me.

This regal looking man in my vision appeared to be a guardian or an angel of some kind.

Then I saw an ancient island, surrounded by the clearest bluest waters I've ever seen.

As I watched, I saw a large crowd of people, led by a young man holding the hand of a beautiful woman with a small baby, make their way down to waiting bark canoes on the beach.

The young man and his small family led the way across the ocean to a new land for these people. He was guided by intuitive visions, birds, dreams and spirit Beings to take his people to a new land. All the while I was experiencing this vision, I heard a most beautiful and eerie singing in my inner ears.

As the beautiful voices sang to me the story of this ancient pilgrimage to a new land, I found myself singing along with the seductive voices in the language of their song.

My client looked at me startled.

As I sang, he began to cry.

His crying brought me back from the vision and when we'd discussed what I'd seen, he told me an incredible story.

Apparently, I'd told him a story he believed was the true story of the migration of his people to the new land called New Zealand a long time ago. He felt that the song I had been guided to sing was a Maori song from long ago and was somehow familiar to him.

The spirit Being who'd stood by his side during the vision had now faded.

The amazing thing that I remember most of all about this young man was that he cried for a whole week, night and day, after his visit to me.

I later heard that he'd resolved after the conclusion of his business venture, to go home and search for his roots and his lineage, to immerse himself in the history of his people in an effort to understand what it was to be Maori in a modern world.

The young man felt he may once have been that intrepid leader guided to explore a new land for his people.

A HOSPITAL VISIT

Just before I left Singapore, I was asked to visit a young man who'd suffered a near-fatal heart attack, who was being cared for in a large hospital in Singapore.

The young man was unaware that I'd been asked to visit him to pray for his recovery and was totally unprepared to open his eyes and see a strange Australian lady standing by his bed.

As I stood, gazing down at the wasted features of what was apparently a very sick man, I was made to pray for him in his own language, using his own prayers, which he'd forgotten since his childhood.

He told me later that when he'd opened his eyes and saw me, all in white, with white skin, reciting his prayers to him like a mother, he thought he'd died and gone to Heaven!

My new friend recovered almost miraculously from his premature brush with death.

After I left the hospital that day, the person who'd accompanied me was quite shocked to witness my being violently ill on the grass outside the hospital!

This sudden vomiting was caused by taking on the heaviness of the young man's illness and the negativity of the hospital situation, with all its attendant greedy ghosts.

JOHOR BAHRU (JB)

From Singapore, I caught a train to Johor Bahru, called 'JB' by the locals, which is a Malaysian city right on the border of Singapore and Malaysia.

It was an eye-opening experience to travel on the train from Singapore to JB. This was the first time I'd travelled by train and I found it to be cheap and very clean.

I noticed that a woman in a pink apron kept coming up and down the aisle to collect rubbish and she always seemed to be wiping surfaces down with disinfectant!

Each car had its own TV and I particularly enjoyed the advertisements as they exemplified the Asian culture and conditioning.

I was interested to see advertisements for skin cream that would 'whiten' and 'lighten' the complexion! I thought the women had marvellous complexions.

Milo and chocolate Horlicks were popular too as well as the ubiquitous Coca-cola.

I'd eaten in a few McDonald's restaurants in KL and had sent the tray-mats printed in Malay Bahasa, home for interest.

One day, when I'd been enjoying a Big Mac in KL, I'd felt that if I closed my eyes, I could just as well be eating in McDonalds in Melbourne, as the food tasted precisely the same everywhere.

When dining in KL on another occasion, I found that the food at Pizza Hut was almost the same too, just a little sweeter pizza dough to cater to the Malaysian taste.

At JB, my new hosts awaited me. Again, strangers soon became friends.

My hosts had a sweet Indonesian maid who called me Auntie and who was happy to bring me a cup of coffee anytime of the day or night. The maid didn't speak English and I didn't speak Indonesian Bahasa but we communicated with each other very well. She got cross if I made my bed or ironed my own clothes and would frown and 'tut-tut' at me in Indonesian.

I was given a suite for my own use and air-conditioned as well. I was thrilled about the 'air-con' as Malaysians call it, and slept deeply and well.

My hosts were good and loving people and I was not troubled by spirits at their house.

THE DEAF-MUTE GIRL WHO PRAYED

An interesting event happened during my stay at this house.

My hosts asked me to assist them in conducting an extended meditation session for the benefit of their family and close friends.

According to their faith, it was their custom to invite friends to pray and meditate with them, to state an intention at the beginning of the meditation and to direct the energy of prayer to their intention.

As we began our meditation, all the dogs in the neighbourhood began to howl and bark, sensing the vibrations.

The elder daughter of the family who had been affected by measles before her birth, had been born deaf and mute. She touched my arm and joined her hands together in a prayer symbol, pointing first to herself and then to the little altar where her mother meditated quietly.

I realised it was the girl's intention to sit behind the altar, to offer her prayer for the family's intention of well-being and prosperity.

I felt the girl's sweet and pure consciousness communicating with mine, through the heart, and went quietly to her mother and whispered:

"Your daughter wants to take her turn at praying and meditating also, as you are doing."

A little surprised, the mother moved aside to allow her daughter to take her place.

I watched as the deaf-mute girl prayed a silent and beautifully eloquent prayer. I could feel the purity of her heart-felt intention as she raised her face to Heaven, with a look of rapture on her face. As she raised her face, all the dogs in the neighbourhood went mad!

The vibrations of this girl's powerful prayer were evident to all assembled at that house.

I MEET A HINDU SAINT

My hostess in JB said to me one morning just before my departure:

"A friend of ours would really like to meet you while you're here. He's a very special Hindu man from a spiritual family, his younger sister was a saint.

We've been told he hasn't long to live and wants very much to meet you. I've told him about you, would you mind?"

Of course I agreed to meet the Hindu man, who was brought to the house by his wife.

It was obvious that he was very ill and I watched in compassion as he tried to make himself comfortable on a cushioned chair on the verandah. Our host offered him a beer and to break the ice I said I'd have one too, with lots of tonic-water. He smiled, surprised that an Australian lady whom he had been told was very holy, would have a beer with him!

I'd felt intuitively it would be easier for him to talk to me about his fears if we shared a drink together.

He told me that he and his sister had always been healers and he'd grieved for her when she'd died at a very young age. I told him that I'd also lost my little sister at a young age.

He also told me that many people considered his sister to be a true saint, in their tradition.

He'd written and published a beautiful book in memory of her and gave me a copy. His little book had many Christian and Hindu quotations on the Divine, which I found interesting.

As we sat on the verandah in the setting sun, having a beer together and looking into each other's eyes, we somehow felt at one with each other. It was a nice feeling.

Before he left, he leaned forward, his eyes dark with pain and said:

"Tell them! Tell all the healers and all the psychics you meet not to let this sickness happen to them. Make them listen!

Our dear hosts have told me about the meditation and the cleansing technique you've learnt from your Teacher.

Everyone needs to know these things. Promise me you'll tell them. If I'd known about such things sooner, I wouldn't be dying like this now."

His passion and the way he said this affected me.

After he left, I remembered how my dear mother had died so young, my sister also, and I particularly thought of my grandmother and her suffering.

I realised that my family was as sensitive, intuitive and spiritual as this poor man's family. I felt I could so easily have been in his place today if it hadn't been for my Teacher.

THE PHOBIC ENGINEER

On the short flight from JB to KL, I found myself seated next to a pale and trembling man.

He appeared to be quite ill and I asked him if I could help in any way, feeling that he was either air-sick or terribly afraid of something.

He turned to me and said:

"I'm in a very bad way.

It's part of my job as an engineer to commute daily between JB and KL.

I haven't told my employers, I've got what my psychiatrist calls phobic anxiety about flying.

Every time the 'plane starts to take off, I get into a sweat and I think I'm going to die. God help me, what am I going to do with myself? Sorry, lady, just don't take any notice of me. I'll pop a couple of pills and I'll take a nap until the attendant wakes me up on arrival at KL."

Inwardly, I smiled to myself and thought:

"Here's a job for a psychologist! Okay, Lord, let's have some mid-air psychotherapy and see what happens."

I said to the engineer:

"As luck would have it, I just happen to be a psychologist and I've got a lot of experience helping people to let go of phobias. I actually had quite a bit of success just before leaving home with a fellow just like yourself.

Are you willing to let me have a go at showing you how to deal with this phobia? No charge, I promise you and you'll never have to see me again. What have you got to lose, except fear?"

The engineer and I did surrendered meditation together up the back of the 'plane all the way to KL.

Upon the 'plane's descent, I promised him that he would let go of the fear once and for all and he believed me.

Upon arrival at the airport, I said goodbye and good luck to the engineer who was now smiling and relaxed.

As I was collecting my bag from the luggage carousel, I heard a voice calling my name loudly.

Somewhat surprised, I turned around to see quite a distance away, due to the crowd of people awaiting baggage, the engineer jumping up and down on the spot, waving his briefcase to attract my attention and calling out:

"Thank you, thank you, whoever, whatever you are!"

CHAPTER 12

MEETING WAYNE DYER & SWAMIJI

WAYNE DYER COMES TO KL.

In late 1995, Wayne Dyer came to KL as a special guest for a motivational conference of business and insurance salesmen.

When I was studying psychology, I'd read several of his books and had heard him speak in Melbourne in 1994 at a conference with the world's top motivators, Louise Hay, Stuart Wilde and Marianne Williamson.

My Teacher and I arranged to attend the insurance conference in KL.

The KL conference was well attended and very entertaining.

The 'Wizard From Oz' who was an Australian presenter, motivated the audience to do a little self-esteem magic every day; an Asian lady advised on personal presentation and professional business dress by reminding the Malaysian ladies in the audience:

"No sequins or sparkle in the office, please ladies!"

An Australian motivational presenter advised the audience to believe in themselves and their product.

Wayne Dyer as special guest, was last presenter for the day. No matter the topic or the subject he's asked to present, Wayne Dyer brings everything back to love, which is something I've always really liked about him and his books.

Before expanding on the topic he was asked to present, Wayne told the audience he always takes a few minutes backstage, to meditate before presenting and allows himself to be totally spontaneous in his presentation.

He told us he gave up making plans a long time ago and surrenders himself to each day.

As he spoke, I felt so in tune with what he was saying and feeling, that tears ran down my face. My Teacher who was sitting beside me, smiled at me and said quietly:

"This gentle person, Wayne Dyer, really knows about love."

After Wayne Dyer's presentation, the seminar concluded and my Teacher and I made our way to the exit.

As we were leaving the room, I glanced back and noticed a large crowd of eager Malaysians asking questions of Wayne and wanting to be near him. As he was quite tall, it was easy to see him above the crowd.

When I tried to leave the building, I found myself being turned around to face the way I'd just come!

I was being walked back into the room I'd just left!

"What's happening to me?" I thought.

I felt like a puppet being walked back to the spot I'd just vacated.

At that moment, Wayne Dyer looked up, saw me and started walking towards me, away from the crowd of admirers surrounding him.

We stood and stared at each other.

I said: "I tried to leave the room and the Divine brought me back. With your presentation today, I was so in tune with what you said about love and how you said it, that my heart opened. Thank you for the experience."

To my amazement, he said:

"It's my heart that opened. You opened mine."

At this, he put his arms around me on impulse and kissed my cheek warmly.

My Teacher's voice spoke from behind me:

"There you are, my child. I wondered what had happened to you." I introduced these two special gentlemen to each other and they talked for a few moments.

Wayne explained that unfortunately he had another speaking engagement overseas and a 'plane to catch.

Before we parted, he wrote his home address and private 'phone number on the corner of an insurance brochure, in case we ever visited America.

Wayne Dyer didn't forget us or our meeting. A few weeks later, we received an autographed copy of his favourite book called 'Gifts from Eykis'.

My Teacher told me it was his feeling that one day I would meet Wayne Dyer again.

I MEET SWAMIJI

My Teacher told me one day:

"Tomorrow we've got an old friend, a monk, coming to stay for a few days on his way to India. He stays here about once a year. He's an interesting person. We call him Swamiji."

We went to meet Swamiji at the KL airport the next morning.

He was a youthful looking man and could have been anywhere from thirty to fifty years of age.

He was short, thin and his head was shaven in the manner of Indian monks.

He was wearing a cotton, apricot-coloured skirt, with a toga-like robe over one shoulder which was called a 'dhoti' and he had leather sandals on his feet. He was brown-skinned, dark-eyed and shy to meet me.

When he saw us, he knelt down and touched my Teacher's feet.

My Teacher was quick to laugh and say:

"No, no! Swamiji, I've told you a hundred times, don't do that" and pulled him gently to his feet.

Swamiji surprised me then by kneeling to me and putting his head on my feet. He said:

"Dear Mataji, so happy to meet you."

This greeting was performed in the spirit of respect and tradition towards all women.

Swamiji and I became great friends. He loved his coffee as much as I did and this made a bond of warmth and camaraderie between us! Swamiji was asked to lead the group in meditation as a special guest and he did an interesting talk on the gifts that the Lord (he pronounced it 'Lard') had given us.

He asked us in his quiet and humble way to have our supper after meditation with our eyes closed to appreciate the gift of sight. We all did as he suggested, and there was a lot of bumping and giggling, as we ate our supper with our eyes closed, but we got the point.

That night, quite late, over a coffee in the kitchen, Swamiji told me about himself.

He told me he'd been a very bright little boy who grew up in a tiny village in India. He was fortunate enough to attend school and had the very good fortune to be sent to America to study.

Though he had a successful career and financial abundance, Swamiji found that something was missing from his life.

That something, he told me, was the Divine.

Eventually, he left the world of finance and comfort and joined an ashram as a monk.

Over the next few days, I overheard my Teacher and this gentle monk having many colourful conversations.

Apparently, their theme was like an ongoing chess-game they'd been playing for years.

Swamiji apparently disagreed with the translation of the word 'Naam' from the Scriptures, as being the 'Holy Life Force', believing that it more correctly meant the name of God.

I heard my Teacher say:

"In the Scriptures, it's clearly written Naam is the 'Holy Life Force', Swamiji.

I ask you my friend, how can the chanting of the name of God awaken one's soul? The chanting of a mantra, whether that name be God, Rama or Waheguru, keeps one trapped in the conscious mind.

The Divine resides in the Superconscious Mind of man.

I tell you Swamiji, that it's only by letting go of the 'name' of God, by stopping the chanting, that one can experience the 'Naam'. Naam is not Name!"

I went to bed at this point confused, and left them to it.

MY TEACHER TELLS ME A STORY

The next morning, my Teacher told me a story to illustrate his on-going discussion with Swamiji and many other students of Scripture:

"There was once a man who wanted to be enlightened during this lifetime.

He went to a Guru who told him:

' Chant this word - Rama, Rama ceaselessly.'

The man did his best to chant, but forgot the word and became tired and nodded off to sleep.

It was in the nodding off to sleep that he experienced the Divine gift of the awakening of his soul and he became enlightened.

It was in the letting go of the chanting of the Name of God that he was imbued with the Naam.

And then there was another man who asked the Guru for enlightenment and he gave him a name of God.

The second man was poor of hearing and repeated the word he thought the Guru gave him, for many years.

He too became weary of chanting the word and began to sleep after a while.

During his sleep, he also became enlightened!

When the second man also went back to thank the Guru for his word, the Guru said:

' You have been chanting the wrong word, you silly man! But, God has heard you and has given you the Gift because of your faith and trust, even though you forgot the word.'"

My Teacher continued:

"It doesn't always work this way, my child.

Enlightenment is a gift of the Divine. You can't demand a gift. It comes freely from the generous heart of the one who gives it, through no virtue of your own. So it is with the Divine.

You can be very polite, ask Him nicely, and then let go of the asking. He may give you the gift as He wills."

Each day Swamiji stayed, he gave me a small gift.

One day it was a wooden mala which was a bracelet of small beads for counting my prayers, much like a rosary.

The next day it was a little holy picture.

The next day it was some incense from the ashram.

Each night before Swamiji slept, he knelt down in front of everyone who was in the house and asked their forgiveness in case he'd said or done anything to hurt them. He was a most loving person.

MY DREAM OF LORD KRISHNA

I told Swamiji one day, I'd had a dream in New Zealand about a beautiful young Indian man with blue skin who sat on a cloud, cross-legged, playing a flute, with beautiful girls in brightly-coloured saris dancing around him.

Swamiji said: "You are very fortunate to dream of Lord Krishna. This shows you have Krishna consciousness and is a very good sign. You must tell your Teacher about this dream."

Every day I told my Teacher about the dreams I'd had during the night. He was able to take me much further in interpreting my dreams than my grandmother had.

It was warmly comforting to me, to once again sit down over breakfast with a caring person and tell my dreams, as I had as a small girl.

It wasn't long before I participated in a Dreams seminar and increased my understanding and experience in dream technology.

LIVING IN THE EAST

By this time, I was becoming more comfortable living in an eastern household and was fast adapting to Indian and Malaysian ways. I'd found it difficult at first to eat with my fingers, and was taken aback the first time I had banana-leaves instead of plates, laid on a table in front of me.

"No washing up," I thought to myself.

I still had a challenge eating rice and curry with my fingers as I managed to get into an awful mess, but I could manage roti which was a kind of bread and vegetables quite well with my fingers now.

I was getting used to sitting on the floor too, and found it more comfortable than sitting on chairs. I enjoyed the informality of sharing a meal as one of a family in a Malaysian household. It was the custom to share large bowls of meat, vegetables and curry. Another thing I noticed was that everyone in Malaysia removed their shoes before entering another person's home or their own home. I had a funny experience with this custom one night.

I visited some friends and following their custom, I left my shoes on the porch outside the door.

When it was time to go home, one of my shoes was missing. My host was terribly upset and insisted on looking for it with a torch. One of the dogs had chewed it up a bit and left it lying in the backyard!

I put my shoes up high after that experience when visiting Malaysian friends again.

There were several customs in the East I felt the West could well adopt.

I noticed that when a baby was born, the new mother would be very protected and made to feel special by her family and her husband's family.

Apparently, it was the custom to keep the new baby within the confines of the home until they were about three months of age. I was pleased to see that all the new babies I saw were breast fed by their mothers and kept close to them, in their infancy.

It seemed to me that Malaysians loved their children and made the family their focus. Even though some Malay men had more than one wife, I realised that they took equal care for each wife and each child. This was fascinating to me, as a psychologist and a sociologist.

SWAMIJI AND I COOK UP A STORM

Before Swamiji left to continue his journey to India, he said he'd like to prepare a meal in gratitude for the hospitality shown to him. I offered to help him as I'd heard he was an excellent cook and I was curious about the way food was cooked in an ashram. Swamiji was delighted with my offer and we put on aprons and banished my Teacher to the office, as we wanted to surprise him.

I chopped and sliced and stirred under direction, and it wasn't long before tantalising aromas began to waft from all the saucepans on the stove.

While we were cooking, Swamiji told me that the kitchen in the ashram was probably the happiest and holiest place you could be, as everyone prayed, thanked God and chanted and the food was made holy.

He sang me some of the prayers while we worked and they made me feel happy too. We sang and danced around the kitchen, in Divine bliss, while the dinner cooked:

"Hare Krishna, Hare Krishna, Krishna, Krishna, Hare, Hare...Hare Rama, Hare Rama, Rama, Rama, Hare, Hare," over and over until I was giddy and giggling.

It was a sumptuous meal we prepared with so much love.

No animal suffered and died for it, and we were the better for it. My Teacher loved it and blessed us both. Swamiji rang me from the airport the day he flew to India and thanked me for the coffee-chats and for being his friend.

ONE IN A MILLION

An editor from a new magazine had seen the article 'Psychic Woman' in a local paper and asked for an interview.

The magazine called 'Malaysian Woman Today' had a monthly interview with a woman who was extraordinary and who made a difference to other women's lives. I became the subject of an article entitled 'One in a Million'.

The editor and I met and related to each other instantly. As her father was unwell, she asked me for an impromptu reading and we said some prayers together for him and his recovery.

DREAMS

I also wrote a regular column for this magazine during my stay in Malaysia, where readers sent their dreams for interpretation. The Dreams column was innovative and very popular.

It was interesting for me to receive and interpret the dreams of people from another culture.

I knew the symbolic language of dreams was usually regarded as universal. However, one of the first things I noticed with my Malaysian readers, was that Hindus regarded snakes as a positive symbol of spiritual enlightenment and wisdom if seen in a dream. In my experience, Western dreamers viewed snakes as a threat or something negative to be feared.

It was interesting to me to discover that Malaysians were very aware that they dreamed. They remembered their dreams and knew intuitively that their dreams and the symbols they contained, meant something.

In my Melbourne practice, I was constantly surprised to hear my clients tell me they didn't dream. Over and over again, I would tell them they did indeed dream three to four times each night, with each dream being of at least twenty minutes duration, according to the latest research.

The great masters of psychology, Sigmund Freud and Carl Jung, felt dreams can be valuable tools for objective, practical guidance, as well as for subjective insights and spiritual, physical and mental directives. These gentlemen felt if we learn to interpret our dreams correctly and then apply what we've learned, they can be a powerful instrument for personal growth.

My Teacher and I felt it would be a good idea for me to present a Dream Seminar building on the success of my Dreams column in the magazine. This turned out to be a lot of fun and was well attended by people of several races. Even a black African Prince studying at a local university attended and managed to sleep right through it! He enjoyed it very much.

My dream seminar opened with a dear elderly gentleman singing spontaneously the old Everly Brothers' song 'Dream, Dream, Dream', which was warmly applauded. This impromptu performance was entirely his own idea and it set the tone for a warm and fun-filled seminar.

During the seminar, I showed the enthusiastic participants how to interpret their own dreams, with a workshop, small group approach. They learnt that there are more than fourteen categories of dreams with clearly identifiable and recognisable characteristics.

I reminded them of the ancient Chinese saying, "One picture is worth a thousand words."

The seminar was a total success and I made many more new friends.

LANGUAGE IS NO BARRIER

During the whole time I studied in Malaysia, I kept discovering language isn't a barrier at all when the heart is open.

Many times I was asked to help people who couldn't speak English and I couldn't speak their language! There were many times when an interpreter was not available. To overcome this semantic challenge, we smiled, we hugged, we spoke with our eyes and our hearts and love did the work.

Professionally, I noticed my counselling style changed and became enriched when working with these people.

I slowed down my speech and spoke more clearly. I became more aware of body language, eyes and facial expressions as well as subtle nuances of tone.

I became more physically expressive too, using gesture, facial expression, and non-verbal communication more than I ever had before.

I watched and listened more than I had in Australia also, which deepened my understanding of a person. At the same time, I began to sense and intuit more about people and what they were trying to communicate to me.

All this growth happened on an emotional and intellectual non-verbal level, without my having to access the psychic, or soul level of communication.

The Malaysians taught me that language and words are inadequate when it comes to communication and that feelings are far more eloquent.

MEDITATING MONKEYS?

I was putting my washing out on the clothes-line out the back of the house early one morning, when I noticed movements in the trees around the garden.

Curious, I looked hard and saw literally hundreds of monkeys playing and jumping around in the trees!

I'd never seen monkeys outside of a zoo in my life, so I watched them in wonder.

Many people told me the monkeys often came down out of the jungle looking for something to eat. Since the area around the house where I was staying was periodically cleared of jungle, the monkeys were always hungry. I soon became accustomed to seeing the monkeys.

I wrote a long letter to my little boy to tell him about the monkeys the first time I saw them.

They came down to the house sometimes when we were doing a meditation in the meditation room, and after making themselves comfortable in the trees, they would be very quiet and still until it was all over and would then disperse noiselessly.

It was a magnificent sight for me to observe them only a few feet away, watching us silently as if they were meditating too!

On another occasion, a large cobra came into the garden and almost into the kitchen when we were having a 'Pot

Luck' lunch! Everyone was quiet and still and afraid. I was frozen in terror. People had told me how dangerous these snakes were and I couldn't believe that I was actually so close to one of these venomous serpents.

To our amazement, my Teacher was cool and untroubled. He went outside, bent down and told it off sternly!

The cobra appeared to listen to him, turned and swished away soundlessly. Everyone was impressed.

THE GHOSTS IN THE FACTORY

After the cobra's visit, I asked my Teacher if he'd ever been psychic and if he'd had visions like I did.

He thought for a while and told me:

"Yes, when I was a young man, I did have visions and I saw clearly.

When I started 'ghost-busting', it was very frightening for me to see horrific creatures. I had no-one around to ask, like you had your grandmother and you have me. I had to be strong on my own. I learnt to trust in God and I learnt to trust in myself.

I lived in a house once where I would see naked and horrible creatures in the trees outside my house and all around. In order to cope, I had to ignore what I saw.

Once, I was asked to go to a factory where ghosts were scaring all the employees away. When I got there, it was almost dark and I was alone.

I saw hundreds of dead, demented lost souls rising up from the ground like mist and I asked God to help me, to veil my eyes from the awful sight so I would have the nerve to stand to do my job. It's necessary, vital, to eradicate all trace of fear from yourself in order to be a good exorcist.

God was kind to me, little one, I've not seen spirits again.

One day, as you evolve spiritually, you also may not see anymore. The 'seeing', the psychic vision, is a transition.

Now that I no longer see, I just discern. I just know without needing to see. Do you understand?"

I thought I knew what he was talking about. He'd given me a lot to think about.

SINGAPORE BOOK FAIR

We received a 'phone call from a journalist in Singapore to attend the Singapore Book Fair 1995 as her new book, with two chapters on me, was going to be launched at the fair.

She asked me to do five minute 'on the spot' readings to promote her book and to sign books as people bought them.

It proved to be a very busy affair, with many people requesting instant readings. I found it amusing that many Singaporeans wanted numbers for lotteries and gambling.

"Lucky numbers please," I was asked over and over again.

Once much later, when I was staying in a friend's apartment in KL, a man nagged me so much about numbers that in exasperation I gave him my friend's floor number, street number and apartment number!

To my surprise, he won a lot of money with those numbers and annoyed me even more! When I told my Teacher what I'd done, he laughed a lot and confessed:

"When I was very young, I intuited the numbers once and won a lot of money on horses. God took it off me the same day to teach me a lesson. My wallet was stolen. We don't use the gift for gambling."

BE A REAL PSYCHOLOGIST

One evening, on our way to visit some friends, my Teacher spoke to me about Psychology.

"My dear, I want you to be a real psychologist.

The word 'psychologist' comes from the Greek word 'psyche' meaning soul.

I want you to study the soul of man, not his behaviour, and to teach others how to develop and grow a healthy soul through attuning to Love and surrendering the ego.

The conscious mind of man, wherein resides the ego, is the barrier to enlightenment.

This is the reason why I've worked so hard to humble you, in order to access your soul. I had to break down your stubborn ego in order to effect a breakthrough into your Higher Mind, which is your soul.

Do you now understand the purpose in my demanding obedience from you?"

I nodded, very focussed on what he was saying. It was rare for him to engage in a conversation like this and I wished the journey would take longer.

"Freud was on the right track with Hypnosis and Jung was on the right track with understanding the symbolic language of dreams. But, it's my feeling that modern Psychology has lost its way."

My Teacher went on:

"Even Freud's message about the Mind has been mistranslated and misunderstood.

In my opinion, Freud understood the nature of the Mind. The term 'sub-conscious mind' is incorrect. Freud meant 'supra or super-conscious Mind'.

There is not a level lower than mind.

There is in fact, a level higher than man's consciousness. This is the over-mind or the Super-Conscious Mind of Man.

In consciousness, Man uses only seven to ten percent of his Mind's creative potential. The remaining ninety to ninety-three percent lies in the Higher Mind of Man. This is what I mean when I refer to one's potential to be a Superman!

You yourself are tapping into this potential when you 'read' people. You are reading the soul!"

This conversation was so amazing to me that I wished I could tape-record it. I remembered as much of it as I could and wrote it down as soon as we reached the home we were travelling to.

He continued:

"The responses and reactions received during surrendered meditation, dreams and visions, are proof of the existence of the Higher Mind. This is what Freud and Jung discovered and did their best to convey to the world.

The Divine is able to reach us through the Dream state.

In fact, it says in the ancient scriptures:

' I am a vibration.

I am known only as a vibrant feeling in man and woman.

When you sleep and dream, I am very close to you.'

Remember these words my dear. You don't need to sleep to receive images and visions; you are able to tap into the Higher Consciousness through surrender.

In order to reach enlightenment, you must let go of all attachments to an ego state.

Do this and you will one day be totally liberated from the shackles of ego, trust me in this. I know what I'm talking about.

Always do what I say and don't take any notice of what's said about you by others. Know that I am with you, always."

While he was saying these incredible words to me, I felt great love and respect for this simple and caring man.

We turned into the driveway of our destination and a group of children waved to us excitedly. I would always remember these words he spoke to me that night and often pondered their meaning.

LETTING THE CAT
OUT OF THE BAG AT A WEDDING

In late 1995, my Teacher was invited to attend a wedding.

He asked me to accompany him as his guest, since he felt it may interest me, to experience a wedding in Malaysia.

When we arrived, the congregation was seated on the floor. This was the first time I'd ever been in a church where everybody sat on the floor.

Curiously, I looked around me. Everyone was dressed in their best. The young women wore vivid jewel-colours of yellow, green, blue, hot-pink, violet, every colour imaginable, each trying to out-do her neighbour.

Indian women always wore all their wedding-gold to a wedding, my Teacher told me, and I saw a lot of it that day, around wrists, upper arms, hanging from ears, in noses and around foreheads! Malaysian and Indian gold, I saw, was cut differently from what we wore in the west. It caught the light and glinted with each movement and it seemed to be quite yellow and shiny.

The older women's garments were in soft pastel colours and grey and white. It seemed to me that they no longer needed to attract a young man's eyes with colourful clothing, as they no longer had marriage prospects in mind.

I'd almost made a social faux-pas by buying what I thought was an elegant outfit to wear to the wedding, all crisp white linen, only to be enlightened by my Teacher that white was only worn by widows! A lady in KL lent me an appropriate wedding outfit so for once I was appropriately dressed, though I was still conspicuous due to my white face and green eyes.

When my Teacher and I were in New Zealand and dining in a Hare Krishna Restaurant, he was asked by an elderly Indian lady:

"Where did your daughter go to school? Her English is so good." We chuckled about this one often!

While I was in Malaysia, some people thought I was an

Indian from Kashmir, some thought I was Persian and many Malays thought I was a Muslim from Serbia!

The bride wore red, I noticed with surprise.

Her wedding dress was a vivid red organza gown and long jacket, which had been heavily brocaded in India with gold thread.

Her long black hair was piled high on her head under her heavy red veil, which covered her face.

Heavily made-up kohl eyes peeped out like burnt holes in a blanket. She was weighed down with gold which was her dowry in the traditional way.

The modern Indian woman's dowry now includes a professional degree, so that she can bring her husband money. Once she could only bring her husband her precious gift of virginity and her beauty, as well as her parent's gold.

I noticed that the bride's palms and feet were covered in henna which is a brown paste. The henna made intricate and beautiful patterns which was also part of the traditional Indian decoration and regarded as adorning a bride's beauty.

The groom was beautifully dressed in a red and gold brocaded vest, with a long red shirt and trousers. His eyes also were rimmed with black kohl to enhance his masculine beauty.

The Priest stood at the front of the congregation, dressed in white and read from the Holy Book.

There were the traditional readings about marriage my Teacher told me about on the way to the wedding:

"A man and woman, once married, must regard every

man and every woman as a brother and sister, so that they may stay faithful to each other," he said, and continued:

"They'll walk around the Holy Book three times, with the bride being bound to her husband's hands by a sash, which she mustn't let go of. It's symbolic of their being joined as one during life; during the difficulties in front of them it's her duty to cling to him and follow him."

Before the ceremony concluded, my Teacher stepped up to the podium and spoke:

"I'm often asked to speak to young people at their weddings.

I've been doing this for more than twenty years and they always tell me later how my words remained with them and helped them. So, I'm confident to repeat the same words to you both today.

Marriage isn't a bed of roses, as people will tell you.

Marriage is a bed of thorns!

When two people live so closely together, their egos are going to impact upon each other every day.

For example, you'll want your belongings to be arranged in such a way, she'll want them another way and will move them when you're not looking.

She'll want everything in the house to be pink, you'll want everything to be blue.

Listen very clearly, remember these next words.

I want to let the CAT out of the bag now and tell you how to live in harmony with each other.

C is for Compromise.

A is for Adjustment.

T is for Tolerance.

You'll need this CAT in your new home.

Give in to each other, give up your ego. Compromise. Adjust to living with each other.

Each of you must let go of always having things the way you want them to be.

Tolerate the differences in each other.

Let each other be the way they need to be. Learn to appreciate each other's differences.

I see there are a few couples here who've heard me 'let the cat out of the bag' at their weddings once.

I want you to tell this new young couple today how you fared during your early years.

God be with you both, may God bless you with many children."

After this, there was a huge wedding feast, with singing and dancing. Everyone had a great time.

A GRIEVING GHOSTLY MOTHER IN KL

Sometime after the wedding, back in KL again, we were invited to dinner at a converted British mansion that was now owned by the Japanese and used as a tourist hotel.

It was dark as we were driven up the winding hill to the large glowing, spotlit white mansion.

As soon as I got out of the car, I felt as if I were stepping through a web of old cob-webs which clung to my face and in an effort to remove them, I brushed at the air. When my Teacher saw my agitated movements and obvious distress, he came around to my side of the car.

"What is it? What are you sensing? What's happening to you?" He asked me.

When I told him my experience and the feeling of fear that was arising within me, he said:

"There are no physical cobwebs around you, my child. It's my feeling that you've stepped into another dimension, into the spirit realm. Let's remain aware and observe what eventuates this evening. Have no fear."

I've often had this feeling of fine lace or cob-webs around my face during a spirit manifestation and I was glad to have what seemed to be an explanation of an unusual psychic phenomenon.

As we approached the building with its large verandah, I saw a spirit manifestation.

Even though I'd been warned in advance by my subtle senses, I still felt myself fall back a little in shock when I saw her.

My Teacher asked me to describe to him what I was seeing.

As I haltingly did so, our host listened with interest, realising he'd have a good story to tell his family and friends later.

As I watched, I saw a tragic scene played out before my eyes. I saw a ghostly woman, with fair hair hanging down her back, wearing what appeared to be a lace cream-coloured night-gown, wringing her hands, crying piteously and pacing back and forth along the verandah.

The woman's form was so weak as to be almost transparent in places. I noticed as she passed the windows of the mansion, the harsh electric light shone right through her.

I realised the woman was not at all aware of my presence or of this century.

I felt I was seeing an old and sad silent movie, that was playing over and over the same scene of tragedy and loss.

I intuitively realised that the woman's grief was due to her only child dying of a tropical fever a long time ago. The grieving mother had not been able to let go of the child's death even after her own death!

As a consequence, she was still trapped here, playing out mindlessly, a tired old drama of life and death.

It was sad and awful to watch and I felt miserable.

At that moment, my Teacher spoke in my ear:

"Wake up, child! Don't be fooled by the feelings passing through you. These emotions are not yours, you're sensing the emotions that the dead woman is emanating and projecting onto this area. This creature isn't a woman or a human any longer.

Don't attach emotion to what you are witnessing. We'll now tell this creature to go."

At his calm words, I came back to myself with a jolt. He was right.

There was a job to be done here.

We walked slowly up the steps to the verandah where she still paced back and forth, totally unaware of us or of anything else but her own silent, selfish grief.

I felt very grateful for my Teacher's presence at my side.

I sensed the cold, heavy, desolate feeling around the woman's ghost and did my best to avoid it. I felt sick at the thought of her walking through me!

As we went into the front reception area of the hotel, the unfortunate ghost floated up the stairs in front of us.

It was as if two realities, the past and the present, life and death, were happening in front of my eyes, at the same time.

She was existing in her time and we in ours, simultaneously!

To me she was dead, to her I didn't exist.

I knew intuitively that this scene, her crying and pacing the verandah for hours, mourning the child lying upstairs, and then going upstairs to cry over the child, had repeated itself for a hundred years, uninterrupted.

We followed the ghostly mother upstairs into a large open parlour that had once been the child's nursery.

There she stood, in the middle of the room, wailing over the still and ghostly form of a small dead child in a ghostly cradle.

My Teacher spoke to her:

"Listen to me! You are no longer living! Your unfortunate little child has long ago passed on to other realms of existence. This is all illusion.

It's no use carrying on with this haunting of human habitations and the Earth realm.

The Earth realm is for the living, you are deceased.

I command you to leave this realm now and forever!

There are those Beings who are instructed by the Divine to lead lost and wandering souls to their next dimension. This will be done for you. You will now obey me and let go!"

My Teacher spoke all these words with power and authority.

The ghost seemed to be unaware of his words and of our presence, yet I sensed intuitively she'd let go of her hold on that place.

As I watched intently, I saw her quivering form de-materialise little by little, until she was gone.

I knew she'd moved on because I felt warmth and light return to the room.

After the exorcism, over dinner, my Teacher told my host and I that it's necessary to be strong, positive and confident when dealing with disembodied entities.

His calm manner reminded me a little of Father Bon's faith and total confidence in God that I'd witnessed as a child, when Father Bon had exorcised our house.

GOING HOME

In December 1995, I decided that it was important for me to spend Christmas with my family.

I enjoyed a well-earned holiday in Australia, before attending a meditation retreat for advanced students and teachers in Sydney.

CHAPTER 13

I FOLLOW MY HEART

MEDITATION RETREAT 1996

January 1996 saw me in Sydney for the meditation retreat which was held in a country homestead, outside of Sydney.

Participants came from Malaysia, New Zealand and all over Australia.

During the retreat, one participant had a transformative event that stands out in my memory.

Apparently, she'd been about two years of age when Singapore fell to the Japanese. Her father, a British diplomat, had been sent to a prisoner of war camp for men.

She'd been sent to a women's camp with her mother and had witnessed terrible scenes of brutality and indignity.

The painful memories of incarceration had been suppressed by her subconscious mind, until the 1996 retreat.

During the first night of the retreat, her room-mate woke me and asked for my help as the lady was re-living the traumas she'd witnessed as a child with her mother and was in a pitiful state. When I entered the room, she was curled up in the corner, crying like a child and quite incoherent.

I sat on the floor with her, wrapped her in a blanket and held her while she cried all the pain out.

After her catharsis and release of trauma, she felt liberated.

Apparently, the intensive day of surrendered meditation had made it possible for this lady's sub-conscious mind to release the memories of pain and suffering, experienced by her two year old self. The positive atmosphere of love and camaraderie between the meditation participants had facilitated the release of the past.

We all felt happy to witness this lady's joy and peace over the next few days.

I FOLLOW MY HEART

After the retreat, there was a seminar in Sydney for the retreat participants and other advanced students and teachers of meditation.

During this seminar, a lady told my Teacher that she'd had a dream and sought his assistance and interpretation.

When he'd given her his interpretation, I felt uncomfortable because I felt there was another meaning to this dream, which he'd neglected to mention.

I said:

"With respect, I feel there's another meaning to this dream, that's even more important to this lady's life than the one you've mentioned.

I feel it's vital for her growth to understand the message her mind's trying to convey to her via this dream.

May I give my interpretation for consideration?"

He frowned, then nodded.

After I'd told the lady and the group my interpretation, to my surprise and embarrassment, my Teacher told me he felt I was mistaken.

When he said this, everyone turned around and stared at me.

I felt very silly and a little upset. I was sure I'd got it right. The lady herself felt my interpretation was right for her.

Undaunted, I tried again and said to him:

"Again, with respect, you've taught us all to test the meaning of dreams when there's a conflict of opinion. Could we, as a group, test which is the most useful interpretation of this lady's dream?" I felt nervous and uncomfortable at this stage. You could have heard a pin drop in the room, as everyone was looking at me, wondering why I had the audacity to disagree with our Teacher.

No one had ever disagreed with him before.

He agreed to the test.

We all tested by asking the Divine within each of us to give us an answer to the question:

"Is the second interpretation of the dream more appropriate and meaningful for this lady and her life?"

After we'd all received our individual inner answer, my Teacher said he still stood by his initial interpretation.

I disagreed. My answer was still the same.

When asked for the results of their test, unanimously, the group agreed with his interpretation.

Apparently, I was the sole dissenter! I felt so alone.

He spoke sternly to me:

"Are you prepared to accept my interpretation as the correct one, my dear?"

Regretfully, I said: "I can't accept it.

I believe what I've asked for from the Divine within myself and received is the correct answer in this situation."

He shook his head and I sat down in confusion.

Everyone avoided me that day.

That afternoon after the seminar, feeling troubled, I went to him to apologise for any disrespect I may have shown by questioning his authority and wisdom in front of the senior meditators.

As I tried to find the appropriate words, he interrupted me, to ask gently:

"Why did you oppose me, my dear?"

I replied sadly:

"Because I felt in my heart, and my test told me I was right, that the dream had more than one meaning. I felt that the second interpretation, my interpretation, was more useful to the lady. You have taught me that ultimately the dreamer herself is the one to understand the dream and its meaning for her life. She felt my interpretation was correct in her situation."

After a moment of thoughtful silence and a searching look into my eyes, he smiled broadly and said:

"Very good, very good, child" and walked away smiling.

I CAN SMELL AGAIN

A lady who'd participated in the January 1996 Seminar in Sydney, came back to the follow-up session with this story to tell:

"I'm seventy years of age and some time ago, I lost my sense of smell and taste.

I was quite distressed by this. When I consulted my family doctor, he advised me that loss of smell and taste is considered normal at my age and nothing could be done about it.

My son and daughter-in-law have done meditation for years and said it would help me to sleep better, so I enrolled for the Seminar. Nothing much happened for me, though I felt nice during the meditation. Everyone else had things happen for them and I felt a bit left out. I thought maybe I wasn't very good at meditation.

The last night of the seminar, I went home to my son's house where I was staying for the weekend.

When I opened the front gate, I smelt the roses in the garden. The sweet and heavy scent was something I've not smelt for several years.

I felt I'd already had an incredible miracle being able to smell again and was totally unprepared for the sweet smell of my little baby grand-daughter, whom I'd never smelt before.

When I tip-toed into the baby's room to look at her sleeping, and bent to kiss her little head, I realised I could smell the talcum powder on her body, and I could even smell her hair. This return of smell is a miracle for me and I thank God for it."

This lady's experience was proof of the awakening of the coarse sense of smell that in her case, prior to meditation, had completely disappeared.

As well as the five coarse senses of man, there are at least fourteen subtle senses that can be awakened through surrendered meditation.

People generally call clairvoyance the sixth sense. I feel it's more correct to say that clairvoyance is only one of the fourteen subtle senses that lie dormant and sleeping in most people.

After the meditation seminar, I presented a public talk on Healing, which attracted a good crowd.

WITH A SONG IN MY HEART

After the talk on Healing, a young man approached me during supper to tell me the following story:

"I'm a singer but I can't sing anymore, due to a bad car accident last year, which injured my throat and larynx. Since the accident, I haven't been able to sing.

When I try to do vocal exercises, my throat just freezes up. The doctors and specialists I've consulted say there's no damage now, and I should be able to sing.

My singing teacher's devastated, she feels I've got the potential to join the Sydney Opera and do very well.

All I've ever dreamed about is joining an Opera company and travelling the world, but now it seems that it's all over for my singing career.

Is there even the faintest chance that you can help me? I'm willing to give anything a try.

When I heard about this talk on Healing, I thought maybe you could do something."

My heart went out to this tall, dark-haired Spanish looking young man. He was earnest and so upset. He introduced me to his fiancée, who was waiting in the background.

I suggested the best thing he could do was to attend the next meditation seminar which was planned for the following week.

I felt meditation could help him to relax and to let go of fear around his voice and his future.

The first day of the seminar, he was there early with his fiancée. I'll always remember what happened that day, because we all witnessed a beautiful miracle of faith and love.

After lunch, when we were ready for our second meditation session, I went to the young man and said softly:

"My friend, this one's specifically for you and your throat. I'm asking God for healing for you."

He said:"Thank you, I'm asking too," and so we began.

Halfway through the meditation, some of the other participants began to sing spontaneously.

I went over to the young man where he stood with his eyes closed and said gently in his ear:

"Sing! Now, sing!" And he sang.

He sang an aria that grew in beauty, power, range and resonance so that everyone stopped meditating to stare in wonder at him and his voice.

Tears ran freely down his face at the end of his song and everyone present turned to embrace him.

He came over to where I stood, took my hands in his and said:

"I just had a vision while I was singing, that one day I'll be on the stage at La Scala in Milan, singing that aria.

When my dream comes true, I'll fly you from wherever you are so that you can hear me sing."

I laughed and said:

"I didn't do anything. God did it all and your faith made it possible."

I did hear my friend sing again, not at La Scala, but at the Sydney Opera House much later.

It was clear to everyone in the audience, that this was a brilliant new talent that was going to be too big for Sydney one day!

After his virtuoso performance, I was invited to supper with the cast, his teacher and his family and had a wonderful time.

I saw this young man once again on a later trip to Sydney.

He and his fiancée invited me out for dinner with a group of their friends, and he sang a beautiful song for me that had all the patrons of the restaurant on their feet applauding!

I look forward to hearing him sing at La Scala one day.

I told my young friend it's my intuitive feeling that he is the reincarnation of the great singer, Mario Lanza. He felt this could be true.

GRAVESTONES IN THE BACKYARD

While my Teacher and I were in Sydney, a lady asked for our help. She'd been feeling very nervous and unhappy in her new rental accommodation.

She told us that an elderly man had let the top floor of his huge house to her and she was happy living there at first, except for 'creepiness' and 'bad dreams' which troubled her from time to time. Recently, the negative feelings and troubling dreams had intensified.

At her request, we went to her house to take a look at it.

It wasn't absolutely necessary for us to be present in the house physically; we could have viewed it from a distance, but it was useful for people to learn how to cleanse a house for themselves by observing us.

Often on our way to a haunted house, my Teacher would realise that "the devils have already run away" and we'd just turn up anyway to teach the house's owners how to keep their house clean of negative influences.

This lady's house was on the bottom of a hill near a graveyard! She'd not apparently, given a lot of thought to the negative environment generated by the house's close proximity to a graveyard. Apart from the possibility of spirits on the loose, the emotions generated by thousands of mourners over many years also had an impact.

The landlord downstairs was bereaved, his wife of many years had died not too long before he'd rented out the top floor.

We found that his dead wife was still present on the Earth plane and not wanting to move on, so a cleansing meditation to send spirits on was called for.

We did this together and I went outside with a bottle of holy water to spray the perimeter of the house and to look around the garden.

I noticed a grey, stone barbecue in the back-yard and a few more grey stones lying around.

There seemed to be a tremendous amount of dense, negative energy emanating in the vicinity of these stones. As I examined them more closely, I reeled in shock.

I realised they were gravestones and tombstones! As evidence, they actually had the names and dates of deceased persons carved on them.

When I went inside to relate this information to my Teacher, he suggested strongly that these stones be removed and demolished as soon as possible, for the well-being of the house's inhabitants. Apparently, before letting the house, the elderly landlord had picked up these stones in the graveyard's rubbish tip, finding them useful for his barbecue!

THE SHOPPING MALL

Shopping malls and public spaces have always been a source of discomfort to me, due to the collective energy of so many people in one place, so I usually avoid them when I can.

While staying in Sydney, I went with some friends to a coffee shop in a mall. As we passed a particular shop, I found myself shivering uncontrollably and feeling ill.

Something was very wrong!

I stopped for a moment and looked around me to see if I could locate the source of the psychic disturbance.

I couldn't see anything psychically, but I felt fear all through me and around me, as well as sadness and a terrible heaviness. These feelings manifested as weight and aching pain in my chest area, neck, head and lower back. These were signs that I knew only too well.

Noting my sudden pallor and distress, my friends gathered around me, concerned.

They knew me well enough to know I had felt the presence of a lost and lonely Earth-bound spirit.

One of my friends told me that at this mall on this very spot, where I was standing, a young girl had died.

I wasn't surprised to hear this since it explained my feelings.

An amazing coincidence manifested.

One of my friends present, had a young daughter who'd been best friend to the girl who'd died! All of this told me we had to do something to liberate the lost spirit.

Accordingly, I showed my friends how to do a cleansing and a prayer for the spirit to be released from this place.

We did this on the spot, quietly and unobtrusively and left.

To remove any remnants of the girl's spirit, we went back to my friend's home and did a longer prayer and further cleansing.

The next day I went back to the mall alone to sense if the spirit had gone and found that all was well.

For some time afterwards, I dedicated several meditations for the elevation of this young girl's soul. No doubt that was why God took me to this particular mall to send the lost and wandering spirit on her way.

CHAPTER 14

HEALING WITH LOVE

BACK TO MALAYSIA

After the Sydney Retreat and seminars, I went home to my family to spend some time with them, before completing my sabbatical in Malaysia.

In early April 1996, I flew to Malaysia.

I had a curious sense of homecoming when I saw the Malaysian flag at the KL airport and remembered how strange I'd felt the first time I arrived in KL. How familiar it all was to me now!

I was greeted at the airport by many people who were now friends and who were glad to see me come back to them.

For the remaining four months of my sabbatical, I was offered the use of an apartment by a Hindu couple who'd befriended me.

I was planning to write a book during my time in KL so the prospect of living alone appealed to me.

My friends' apartment was on the twelfth floor and I soon saw that it was the perfect place to continue my spiritual journey.

As I stood out on the balcony of my apartment, I saw that I was literally surrounded by spirituality of every faith. I saw beneath me a Buddhist monastery and Temple, to my right was a Catholic Church and behind that a Hindu guru's ashram, to my left was a Muslim Mosque where the prayers were broadcast to the faithful five times a day and in the hills straight ahead, I could see a Temple dedicated to Kuan Yin, the feminine Goddess of mercy and compassion.

As soon as I was settled, my Malaysian friends brought 'apartment warming' gifts and food.

My generous Hindu friends had already bought new furniture for their apartment, after the previous tenant took all the furniture with her, so I was very fortunate. The Malaysians spoiled me the whole time I was there!

Not a day went by without someone bringing a hot delicious breakfast on their way to work of roti and dahl or roti canai from the local Indian restaurant, or bringing afternoon tea from a temporary stall set up by the highway.

I saw many of these make-shift stalls run by women trying to augment the family's income. A card table, a gas bottle and burner, a shady umbrella and there you have it - a restaurant!

They would be moved on by the Police, but would be back later a little further down. Their cooking was delicious, hot, clean and cheap. Many times I had little spicy dainties with pickles for my afternoon tea from one of these stalls.

I found it was possible to live very cheaply in KL and to eat well. I learnt to eat where the locals did, and the locals were delighted to have a white lady as their guest.

THE AMERICAN MAN

One day, an American man of mature years came to learn meditation with me.

After our first session, I suggested I take him to lunch at my favourite restaurant.

I was very comfortable with the staff, the location and the food by now, but had completely forgotten my initial reactions as a newcomer to Malaysia.

Apparently, the American gentleman who was wealthy and sophisticated, hadn't been in this area of KL prior to this invitation. The area where I was staying was quite off the tourist track!

As our lunch was ladled out of a bucket and placed on a banana leaf in front of us by a beautiful old Tamil man, my friend paled and said:

"I can't eat here. There are flies all over the place and it doesn't look too clean. Look at the state of the floor. What is that stuff in the bucket?"

I laughed, seeing myself in his reaction, just a few short months ago.

"The stuff in the bucket is fish-head curry and believe me, you'll love it, it's delicious. All the food here is fresh and hot. I've never been ill in Malaysia yet. This is how the real people eat," I told him.

He gave in at my laughing suggestion and thoroughly enjoyed the spicy food as I'd told him he would.

During my stay in Malaysia, I'd found restaurant staff to be very clean and fastidious wherever I'd dined.

I'd seen them pouring boiling water from a steaming kettle over the cutlery before anyone used it, and I'd seen every diner washing their hands before and after they'd eaten, not something you see in western restaurants.

Every now and then, I'd be invited to a hotel for a European-style meal by a well-meaning Malaysian lady but I must admit I enjoyed the local food-stalls, markets and 'restorans' much more due to the variety of food provided.

LIVING WITH THE LOCALS

Elderly fellows pedalled their bikes around my apartment block several times a day, tooting loud horns, offering all sorts of goods that a housewife may need, from sweets and papers to bread. I found this handy at times and would patronise these portable supermarkets.

I'd thought that living in a high-rise apartment building in KL would be awfully noisy, but was pleased to note how courteous and peaceable my neighbours were. We all had 'air-con', as Malaysians call it, so that masked much of the human sounds at night. I only heard the normal sounds of families with babies and children the whole time I was there.

I never heard a radio or TV turned up too loud, and I never heard an argument. It seemed to me that everyone had an awareness about living in harmony with others.

As time went on, I found I was an object of some curiosity to my neighbours, being the only white lady in the area, and I was guarded fiercely in a most chivalrous manner from unwanted masculine attentions, by the apartment security guards.

During my entire time in Malaysia, I only had one uncomfortable experience. One late afternoon, as I was walking home with some groceries, a couple of teenage boys of the cheeky variety were lounging near a bus-stop.

One of the bolder boys, showing off to his friends, approached me and called out:

"Hey, lady! Where you go without your man? You got no man to protect you?"

As I'd been told to do by a wise lady, in the event of something like this happening, I turned and faced him and said firmly:

"Young man, my husband was a Haji and died on his way back from Mecca, now Allah is my protector."

They all looked very uncomfortable and silly, and apologised, eyes downcast.

After thinking about this later, I realised it was probably wiser to reach home earlier in the day, as unaccompanied ladies didn't walk around the streets on their own as a rule.

HEALING WITH LOVE

One evening after meditation, someone produced a brochure advertising Doctor Leonard Laskow's 'Healing With Love' Malaysian Tour.

I'd read Dr. Laskow's book in 1992, so I was keen to meet him and hear him speak.

After meditation that night during a dinner that we shared with some meditation group members, my Teacher and I discussed attending the seminar and decided we'd go.

The introductory night was held at a large KL hospital and we were rather late due to heavy rain and poor visibility. We sat up the back and listened intently to this gentle American man tell his story:

"While on a retreat, during a deep meditation, I felt a burst of light within and an inner voice spoke to me with awesome clarity and authority. It said, 'Your work is to heal with love.' As soon as I heard this, I knew it to be so. 'Oh, so I am worthy?' I then said. The voice replied, 'You are no more or less worthy than anyone else. Your work is to heal with love.'"

Had he had the same experience as I had? I thought.

Leonard said he received guidance that he'd be leaving his specialist practice and researching vibrational healing, writing a book about his findings, and teaching it to others.

He left his practice, spent ten years researching energy and love and was now travelling the world to share with others what he had learned.

Leonard showed us some slides illustrating how energy forms cohesive patterns in nature. From my memory, his point that evening, was that there is a universal intelligence at work behind everything. My Teacher called this intelligence God or The Divine.

After his lecture, as Leonard was packing up to go back to his hotel, we approached him and introduced ourselves.

Leonard said: "Come to my hotel, have supper with me and we can talk a little more."

He was a most courteous man.

At the hotel, we sat down to supper with a group of people who were Leonard's supporters and staff.

I was aware of a gentle angelic presence around Dr. Leonard Laskow and found myself warming to him.

The next day, Leonard showed us his method of discernment, calling it 'dowsing' by using copper rods to elicit a response to a question or a feeling from within.

He showed the seminar participants how to raise the vibrations of water and food by projecting love into it. He believed that love was the force that healed people. We agreed with him.

I MEET A STAR

On the Sunday, a new couple arrived from Singapore to meet Leonard. During a lunch break in the hospital cafeteria, we had just finished lunch when they came and sat down at our table. The lady was an attractive Australian and her husband was a Professor of Reproductive Medicine, I later learned.

As the couple sat down, I was struck by the image of a bright, silver star radiating around and above the lady's head. The impulse to tell her about the star was overpowering.

I leaned over and spoke quietly to her:

"This might sound funny, but I see a beautiful silver star just over your head and it radiates light all around you."

She was delighted and smiled at me, saying:

"Thank you for telling me. My name means 'star' in Greek. I'm Australian with Greek parents. Who are you?"

An enduring friendship of like-minded souls began.

During the day, Leonard asked for a volunteer for a demonstration of Healing with Love.

He chose a lady intuitively and we were all privileged to observe the healing that eventuated.

After the healing, we had a break and my Teacher took me around the corner to do a cleansing. Apparently, I had attracted a spirit from someone in the room around me and we sent it on!

After the seminar was over, Leonard had an intuitive reading with me, and a meditation session with my Teacher and I.

I thought that was the first and last time I'd see Dr. Leonard Laskow, but we were destined to meet again in Singapore in 1997.

I VISIT A PALACE IN BRUNEI

I received a 'phone call from a lady in Brunei who invited me to be her house-guest. She was a dear friend of a lady I'd met in Singapore.

She was an American, married to one of the Royal Family's Physicians. She thought I might like to visit Brunei while I was in Malaysia. I was delighted at her generous and warm-hearted invitation and looked forward to the prospect of seeing another new place I'd only read about in magazines and newspapers.

The staff of Malaysian Airlines omitted to tell me I needed a Visa to enter Brunei, so when I arrived in Brunei and was informed that I couldn't stay without a Visa, I was at a bit of a loss to know what to do next. It appeared as if I'd have to get on the next 'plane back to KL.

At that moment, I saw a tall thin blonde woman waving at me from outside the glass doors of the terminal.

"That must be my hostess," I thought.

I tried to communicate to her I wasn't allowed to come any further. She talked to an official near the door and apparently conveyed to him that I was her guest. I was relieved to finally be permitted to meet her.

She was lovely. Warm, bubbly and I felt as if I'd known her all my life.

I found out later, I was very lucky to be permitted to stay in Brunei, because apparently Australians were not held in high regard at the time.

As we drove to my new friend's home, I felt, as I so often did since leaving Australia, that I was stepping into a dream.

Her home was like a palace. It had originally been the Indonesian Embassy, she told me and I was awed by its beauty. Tall gates were opened for us by a security guard with fierce looking dogs straining at their leashes.

I was curious about all the white shrouded vehicles in the front yard. My friend explained:

"Those are cars, gifts to my husband from the Sultan. He's so warm and generous to my husband that he gives him a new car and forgets he's already given him so many!

For his last birthday, he gave him a Lear jet for his own use!" This was like a Hollywood fantasy.

The house was huge, white and luxurious. She lived there with her husband, (who was with the Sultan in Mecca) her small child (who was in Egypt with relatives of her husband) and a small band of servants.

After morning tea, she showed me to my room and introduced me to a maid who was to wash my clothes and serve me in any way I needed. My hostess had taken great pains to provide every possible luxury for my comfort, for example, there was a silk kimono ready for me to slip into after a hot bath. There were expensive French skin care and beauty products.

As well as all this thoughtfulness, she'd placed several inspirational books beside my enormous bed. In addition to this luxury and care, she'd provided a fragrant candle that was burning a welcome, on a side-table.

That night, we dined in solitary splendour in a huge dining-room, from Sevres porcelain commissioned just for her in France. I was nervous handling her beautiful crystal and delicate porcelain. It seemed to me that no expense had been spared in this incredible house.

She told me she flew to Paris for her seasonal wardrobe and she had almost everything any woman could want.

She had a devoted, loving though busy husband, a beautiful little girl, the best parents (in the States), comfort and financial security. She had a warm circle of friends in Brunei, American and British personnel who worked for the Sultan, but what she wanted most of all was another baby.

I began to understand this was the reason why my charming hostess had asked me to stay with her.

She told me she'd just had a miscarriage, was very sad about it and hoped I might be able to help her.

I was happy to show her how to meditate and she was glad to be able to relax and let go of all the stress and anxiety that had troubled her. During our time together in that beautiful palace, she was also able to release the grief for the lost baby.

During our meditation, I became aware that her home was oppressed by negative energy. Later that evening, after my private prayer and meditation, with her permission, I walked around the entire building and cleansed it of all heaviness and disembodied presences.

At my hostess's request, I also did an intuitive reading of her situation, in order to ascertain the cause of the miscarriage.

It immediately became apparent that she'd dismissed a servant at some stage for stealing and this servant had cursed her! The curse involved the servant's visit to a local bomoh (commonly known as a shaman in the West) to project infertility and miscarriage upon her former employer.

This curse and the heaviness it carried with it had oppressed my friend and had indeed contributed to her miscarriage, even though she'd been unaware of her servant's malicious action.

(In mid 1997, I heard that my lovely friend had just given birth to a little boy. Her prayers had been answered at last.)

The following day, my friend drove me around magical Brunei.

As I stood outside the fabulous new Mosque the present Sultan had built for his people, I marvelled at the Mosque his father had built before him, both glowing like pearls in the sun.

I found Brunei to be a quiet and peaceful place, where everyone seemed to take their time.

It was a place of startling contrasts. On the one hand, it could be seen as a peaceful, natural, timeless village. On the other hand, it had a modern cosmopolitan flavour, with an international style hotel for visitors, with all the latest amenities including a five-star restaurant.

In the evening, to my delight, my friend took me to see the Disneyland-type playground, built on several acres, that the Sultan had provided for the children of Brunei. I wished my little son could see it with me.

The playground at dusk, was lit up like a Christmas tree with neon signs and flashing lights as far as the eye could see. It was a child's paradise where all the rides for the children of Brunei were free! My friend told me the Sultan loved his people and they loved him.

As a further treat, my friend took me as her special guest, to the Sultan's Polo Club which was opposite his polo field, for a magnificent dinner.

The men and women in the restaurant were dressed in formal evening-wear. I gasped at seeing jewels on the women that flashed and sparkled in the light from the chandeliers.

Seeing all these elegantly clad people, I felt a bit self-conscious in my simple suit.

I was introduced to many wealthy, famous and beautiful people that magical night in fairyland Brunei, among them the Sultan's little niece, who was enjoying her seventh birthday party.

She was a sweet, plump, dark-eyed beauty who was wearing a king's ransom in jewellery around her throat as her birthday gift from her doting uncle!

Her mother looked like a pocket-sized Jackie Onassis with her pageboy haircut and Chanel evening dress.

The meal was buffet style luxury. Anything under the sun was available to eat that night and I couldn't eat anything. The opulence paradoxically took my appetite away. I just couldn't choose from so much choice. I wished I could have a 'doggy-bag'!

As if that weren't enough, my friend told me:

"Elton John and Tina Turner were here recently, in fact you just missed them. The Sultan flew them in for a private concert at enormous expense. Of all the Sultan's special guests, our favourite was Michael Jackson."

I could only imagine how it must feel to live in this enchanted country every day. I'd had only a taste of Brunei, and found it sweet and tender.

Before I left the next day, my lovely hostess gave me a parting gift of a small silk bag she'd made herself, which contained several samples of expensive French cosmetics for my personal use. I also took with me the memory of friendship, courtesy, warmth and an overnight stay in a palace.

COMMUNION IN A CATHOLIC CHURCH

One of my new friends told me one day, there was a lovely Priest at the local Catholic Church who'd be delighted to meet me.

One early Sunday morning, I made my way to the little church I was able to see from the balcony of my apartment building. I was curious to experience a Catholic service in Malaysia with Tamil Indian parishioners.

When I entered the church, mine seemed to be the only white face in the congregation.

It wasn't long before I realised the service was being conducted in the Tamil language and I couldn't understand a word. Fortunately, I remembered enough about my early Catholic years to understand what was going on, even in another language. So, in a curious way, I felt at home and yet alien at the same time.

Curious and friendly eyes looked at me openly and I smiled and nodded to the people around me, who smiled back.

It'd been many years since I'd attended Mass in a Catholic Church, though I'd managed to sit quietly in the back of many churches wherever I lived or visited, just to pray alone. Even in New Zealand with my Teacher, I'd often slip off to a local church and sit awhile.

I remembered a story the nuns had told me when I was a small child, about an old tramp who used to sit in the back of a Church hour after hour, looking intently at the altar. When one of the nuns asked him what he was doing, he replied:

"I just looks at Him and He looks at me."

The congregation in this little church was noisy and vibrant with families and babies all enjoying the service. The church was open-sided so the breezes could come through and there were fans on the ceilings. There were also cold thermoses of water at the front door, as this was a tropical climate. I thought this was extremely courteous and caring of the Priest to provide water for thirsty parishioners.

The Priest came onto the altar from a side door followed by two small black altar-boys, swinging incense-censers just as they used to when I was a child.

When it came time for Holy Communion, I felt a powerful urge to go forward with the others, but thought:

"I haven't been to confession for many years.

I haven't been to Mass for twenty years at least. I'm married to a non-Catholic.

I'm not allowed to go to the altar to receive the blessing of the faithful, because I'm not considered to be one of the faithful." Yet something inside of me wanted to go to the waiting Priest. That something became too strong to resist.

I remembered my Teacher had taught me to test everything, so I now tested my worthiness to go to the altar by asking my inner wisdom: " Can I go to Holy Communion just as I am, Lord?"

My full to bursting heart told me "yes" so I queued up with hundreds of Indian Tamil families and knelt down before a smiling Indian Priest, who noticed the tears running from my overflowing eyes when he placed the tiny white wafer of bread on my tongue.

It was very nice to take Communion again, somehow. I felt as if I'd come full circle. I was back where I'd started as a child.

After taking Holy Communion, I returned to my pew on shaky legs and cried quietly for a while.

After the service, the nice Priest came up the aisle greeting everyone, stopped when he saw me and said:

"Welcome back, dear child. I have a feeling it's been a long time for you. Do feel free to visit us often. You're so welcome."

I smiled and nodded at him, very grateful for his warmth and gentleness.

I met with this Priest another day on my way out of the Church. Over a cup of tea in his office, I told him about my Teacher and my spiritual journey in Malaysia. He was warm and supportive and gave me a beautiful blessing.

THE SPIRIT OF A CHILD

A young man came to see me, wanting very much to know what path he would follow in his future.

I explained to him there were many potential futures for each person.

I advised him that each path has its own challenges and rewards. I told him it's not my right to advise people which path they are to follow, as it's my understanding the Divine wisdom inside of each person will guide that person in the right direction.

For this young man, I could intuitively see there were at least three paths he could take, the choice was entirely up to him. It's my feeling that predicting the future bears a karmic consequence. For example, if a psychic tells a woman she and her husband will part, the woman will go home and treat her husband in an altered manner. She will act differently and he will react to her actions. The psychic's predictions may bring about the unfortunate result.

As I looked at this young man who sat before me, I noticed there was a small girl in spirit, in his auric field. She had long black plaits and was wearing a blue, checked dress. Unknowingly, he seemed to be haunted by this child.

When I described the child to him, he was shocked.

After a few moments of silence, he said:

"It must be my niece who passed away recently overseas. Her mother's in a dreadful state and grieving badly."

I told him: "We need to help the little one to go on. She can't stay with you. She needs to go on to the next stage of her soul growth and development. Because you're such a God-centered man, she's come to you for elevation of her soul so that she may have the impetus, the energy she needs, to go higher."

As I spoke these words, the little dark-eyed, dark-haired ghost was reaching out her thin little arms to me, crying and begging for my help.

As I've observed before, the benevolent spirits are usually very relieved when their hosts come to me, because at last someone can see them and hear them and help them. This was the case with this dear little thing.

I was reminded briefly, of the lovely angel I'd encountered in New Zealand.

Her uncle explained that she'd contracted a debilitating disease and had succumbed rapidly, despite all the heroic medical efforts taken on her behalf. The young man said he felt very angry that such a disease could take the life of a healthy child.

He spoke at length and with passion on the subject, venting all his unexpressed feelings of grief.

We talked about the child's mother, and I began to get a sense of her, reading her from her brother's presence. I communicated with her in the energy of Love, though she lived in another country. It's been my experience that people always feel and sense the energy of pure Divine Love, even when they don't consciously know it's being projected towards them.

As I focussed on the grieving mother, I saw her crying and mourning her child. The young man agreed to take on the family responsibility for letting go of the child, and to send her soul on with my guidance and assistance.

We prayed together and then surrendered and allowed the Divine to use our combined soul energy, to speed the little girl on her way to the realm that was appropriate for her. I don't know which realm of existence is appropriate, only the Divine knows.

During this process, the child didn't fight us, she was so grateful.

I asked the Divine to "send the Beings whose duty it is to convey souls to the next realm of their existence," and saw two glorious Lights take each hand of the little girl and in a moment of dazzling, buzzing Light, she was gone! My heart was warm and soft and open. The presence of pure Love filled the room.

The young man opened his eyes and with tears spilling down his radiant face, said:

"I felt it! I felt it all! She's gone, isn't she? I think I've just experienced a miracle. Thank you."

This beautiful, miraculous event happens again and again in my experience and I never cease wondering at the love and the joy present.

It's like being present at a birth, however humble.

The miracle always takes your breath away and you bounce and walk on air all day!

LANGKAWI ISLAND:
THE PRINCESS IS RELEASED

Mid 1996, we were invited to conduct a management seminar for executives and professionals, in the tropical paradise of Langkawi. Upon arrival at the local airport, we were greeted by a handsome and charming relative of a Sultan, who was interested in meeting us.

During our drive to our hotel on Kuah, he told me about Langkawi's fabled and historic past.

Pulau Langkawi is the largest of over one hundred

islands in the northern tip of Peninsula Malaysia close to the Thai border.

He told me that Langkawi was an island of magical myths and intriguing legends.

Our hotel was situated near a beautiful beach of clear water and pure white sand. This was indeed a tropical paradise.

Though my stay on enchanted Kuah was brief, it lives in my memory due to a miracle I was privileged to witness.

A JOURNALIST CRIES

Our two day seminar was well attended by several executives living and working on the nearby islands.

One highlight of my visit was in being interviewed by a journalist from a Malay newspaper. It was interesting for me to see the interview later and to see my name and details of my professional experience in Malay Bahasa.

During the interview, I asked the young man about his family, in a friendly attempt to obtain rapport. To my surprise, tears filled his eyes and he was unable to speak for a few moments.

Our interview became a sharing and tender expression between the two of us of loneliness and missing our families and children. In order to gain experience and further his career, the young man had left his young family in KL and missed them dreadfully. I told him that I also missed my family, especially my little boy.

At the termination of our interview, we felt we both knew each other very well and parted with warm han shakes and blessings.

MAKAM MASHURI

Before we left Langkawi, we were driven to a beautiful shrine in a village about twelve kilometres from Kuah.

As soon as we approached the glowing white mausoleum in the hot sun, I began to feel shivers and trembling. I had the same experience of walking through clinging cobwebs as I'd experienced in KL at the white mansion.

My Teacher noticed my trembling and weakness and held my arm tightly as we approached the shrine.

Our guide told us the shrine is preserved in honour of a maiden who lived on Pulau Langkawi more than two hundred years ago.

Before he could go on, I began to receive images about this maiden and told him and my Teacher the scene that was now happening in front of my eyes.

In my vision, as if it were still happening, I saw a young and sweet faced, brown skinned girl, who looked to be about fourteen years of age, being accused of immorality by an older woman. The girl was crying and protesting vigorously. It would have been apparent to anyone witnessing this scene that the child was telling the truth.

A young man approached, also crying as he was told about the girl's apparent sins.

It was obvious to me the two young people loved each other and he was stricken to hear the accusations being hurled at the girl by the older woman.

In another vision, I saw the girl being stabbed to death!

It was very distressing for me to see this happening and to be helpless to intervene.

I felt very sad seeing this lovely girl die in such a dreadful way.

At this moment, I became aware that the girl's spirit still resided within the tomb!

This tragic drama had been replaying itself for over two hundred years and had cast its unhappy pall over the entire surrounding area, depressing and oppressing all its human inhabitants.

I realised the beautiful princess didn't know she was dead and was continuing to live again and again her last fateful day of life and death. I had to do something!

When my Teacher heard all of this, he said:

"We'll now pray, meditate and ask the Divine to send the soul of this poor child to the next realm. How fortunate she is, my dear, that we've come to set her free. She has good karma with you, my child."

In the searing heat, beside the glowing white tomb of the maiden, my Teacher, our guide and I, in front of a small group of curious tourists, sent on the soul of a princess who'd been trapped in this place for far too long.

When our prayer was completed, I was guided to walk around her tomb several times. I laid my hand upon the white stone that was warm to the touch under the sun and felt a sigh pass through me, which electrified me.

I saw a wispy, white shape rise from the stone and ascend into the sunlight as the princess left this realm!

As this happened, we all saw every white blossom on a small tree near the tomb, fall one by one to the ground as her spirit ascended.

One or two of the fragile petals drifted onto the now empty tomb. I cried.

I had a very strong feeling that the young girl and the young man were re-united, in some other dimension and I was glad.

CHAPTER 15

THE MISSING GIRL AND A HAUNTED HOUSE

THE MISSING GIRL

After my visit to Langkawi, I spent a few weeks in KL writing. One morning, my Teacher rang me to say he'd been contacted by the family of a missing girl, who'd requested him to seek my assistance.

So, he asked me to meet with him to do an intuitive reading on the whereabouts of a missing girl.

Apparently, as well as myself, her family had also requested the assistance of a saint in India as well as a Malay and Thai Bomoh. Several other psychics and seers had also been consulted in an effort to uncover information leading to the girl's discovery. According to her parents, she left home for school one day and never came back.

Later that day, after quiet meditation with my Teacher, I had a vision of the girl.

She appeared to me in the centre of a circle of golden-green light, alive and well though distressed about leaving her family home so abruptly and without communication of her desire to leave.

At the same time, I saw a large lake or pond, trees, a small village and several people where she was living. Intuitively, I felt all would be well, in time.

My Teacher looked troubled when I told him what I'd received about the girl and my vision of the village near a large body of water where she was living.

Upon relating my vision, it was with some surprise that I realised he didn't share my optimism. He felt the girl was dead and was the victim of foul play. This was the first time he'd ever disagreed with a vision I'd received.

A strange gulf opened between us.

Shortly after this, he informed me he'd be doing a seminar in West Malaysia and would like me to accompany him. He also told me it was his intention for the both of us to meet with the lost girl's family, at their request.

We were invited to be the guests of a family in the local area.

He said: "The family's in a bit of trouble with some hauntings and I want you there for this one."

I thought:"A haunting! West Malaysia? It's a long way to go, this is going to be interesting. A seminar, a lost girl and a house clearing!"

I had a strong feeling this trip would involve my biggest test so far. As it later turned out, my intuition was right.

THE HAUNTED HOUSE

The house we were staying in was large and comfortable and our hosts were like most of the Malaysians I'd met, caring, gracious and unpretentious. My hostess took me under her wing immediately. I was introduced to her sons, one newly married with his blushing bride living in the house, and the other son still at primary school.

As soon as I entered the house, I was aware of that old familiar dread upon entering a haunted place. In spite of the humidity and heat, I felt a chill and nausea. My hostess was most intuitive and noticed my shivering. She had no English at all, yet I sensed a heart-to-heart communication with her.

It was apparent to me she'd been very frightened for a long time. Her dark-ringed eyes and sallow tired skin told a familiar story. The little boy appeared to be unaware of any troubles. I sensed that the newly married couple knew what was going on in this home, and the husband looked as if he'd suffered many sleepless nights.

"How long has this been going on?" I thought.

I began to suspect this would probably be the worst haunted house I'd ever see as the oppression of the atmosphere was overpowering.

My Teacher was chatting cheerfully with the family, keeping an eye on me, noticing my face and communicating 'calm' to me silently.

We were each given huge bedrooms upstairs. One belonged to the newly married couple who were going to sleep on the floor of the parent's room, and the other bedroom belonged to another married son and his wife who visited occasionally.

We went to the kitchen, which as in most homes was the hub of the house, to have some afternoon tea.

When I sat down, I saw a quick, dark shape flit into the open door of a large pantry and immediately got up from my chair to take a look.

"What was it?" I thought.

As this happened, everyone else seemed to look somewhere else at the same time and the chatting stopped. The scene appeared to freeze. My Teacher calmly gestured for me to sit down and be quiet.

The feeling in the kitchen was one of dread, misery and darkness. I knew everyone had seen and felt the darkness flit by them, but they were too shell-shocked to comment any more.

There was nothing to be seen in the pantry, yet I felt 'it' looking at me. What was it?

We all managed to have our afternoon tea without discussing the dark thing in the other room. I wondered why the family didn't talk about it since we were apparently here to help them.

That afternoon, we did our first meditation with the family upstairs in their large prayer-room. They appeared to be somewhat relaxed and relieved after this.

After our meditation, I asked my Teacher privately:

"Did you see it? Why didn't anyone say anything? Do they see it? I know we all felt it. What do you receive?

I'm going to have a horrible time staying in this house, I just know it. They're really lovely people but there's something horrible here."

He said gently:

"Slow down, dear, let me get a word in. Calm yourself," I waited.

He went on:"Yes, I felt it. It's strong and we're stronger. We'll show them how to meditate and cleanse their house of the negative influences while we're here, that's about all we can do.

All will be revealed to you in good time. Don't worry yourself. Keep chanting all the time and trust in God."

I didn't see any more manifestations that day, but that night I got a real scare.

We'd all enjoyed a traditional meal which had been attended by various people who were interested in the seminar we were presenting the next day, so it was quite a late night.

LOCKED OUT BY AN ENTITY

My hostess hugged me warmly before she went to bed and kissed me on the cheek. She was a lovely woman and my heart warmed to her.

I felt very hot and stressed and thought I'd wait 'til everyone else had bathed and gone to bed, before I had a quick shower, which was about my fourth shower that day.

There was no air-con and it was very hot.

As there were seven people in the house and only one bathroom upstairs, I waited a while.

I dropped off to sleep and when I woke up, there was silence all around.

In spite of the heat, I shivered, feeling suddenly very uneasy. I'd left all the lights on in my room for comfort and now I wished I could be anywhere else but here. I was very homesick and I'd had enough of this kind of business, I thought crossly.

I quietly opened my bedroom door and peeked out.

Every other bedroom door was shut, only the door to the prayer-room stood open. No crack of light showed beneath my Teacher's door.

I picked up a clean towel from a table in my room and stepped into the still space outside, which felt very strange and foreboding. As I stepped into the hallway, my bedroom door slammed without a sound behind me! No breeze, no sound, just slammed!

"What happened?" I thought.

I turned the door-knob, it wouldn't open. I tried again. It seemed to be locked. I couldn't get back in!

"Whatever will I do, now?" I thought.

I decided to have a quick shower anyway and realised I'd have to wake my hostess to unlock my bedroom door and let me in.

After the shower, I knocked gently on my hostess's door.

Nothing happened, not a sound, not a movement.

I knocked louder. Still nothing.

I opened the door gently, feeling worried and embarrassed about waking everyone up.

In the silvery moonlight, I saw my host and hostess lying in a big bed on top of the covers, with their little son lying between them.

I saw the young married couple lying on pillows on the floor, snuggled up to each other despite the intense heat. Electric fans clicked and whirred gently.

I whispered from the doorway:

"Hello, sorry, excuse me, please wake up."

No-one stirred. I tried louder. Still nothing.

"My goodness, they're heavy sleepers. They must be so tired," I thought.

I went over to the bed and gently shook my hostess's shoulder, hoping I wouldn't scare her out of her wits, by waking her up and seeing me standing in her bedroom in the middle of the night. She wouldn't wake up!

I shook her more strongly, still nothing.

Something was very wrong here.

I felt as if I might be having a nightmare. I was the only one awake in an enchanted house!

I tried very hard in a futile attempt to wake everyone up in that room.

I even turned the overhead light on in desperation, nothing worked! A bomb could have gone off in the room and no-one would have heard it. It was the strangest thing I've ever experienced.

Eventually, I gave up and sat outside the room on a small couch near the prayer-room, feeling very scared and alone, thinking:

"I hope that black thing I saw today doesn't come up the stairs or come anywhere near me!"

After a prayer of protection, I decided I'd better look for a key to get into my room, as I couldn't bear to just sit there in the hallway all night.

Tentatively and nervously, I went downstairs, turning all the lights on as I went, carefully looking around me.

I couldn't feel any dark thing hiding, so felt a bit better, though I didn't dare go near the kitchen out the back, where I'd experienced that malevolent presence earlier that day.

My flesh crawled.

In the lounge-room on a table, I saw a large key-ring that was bulging with keys of all shapes and sizes and thought maybe one would open my door.

When I went upstairs again, I tried all the keys one by one and was relieved to find one key fitted the lock perfectly and opened my door without any trouble. I'd found the spare keys!

I took the precaution of wedging a chair in the doorway, before running down and replacing the key-ring, then gratefully closed my door on the dark night.

I fell into a sleep as deep as my hosts.

At breakfast, when my Teacher asked me how I'd slept, I told him about my unusual experience.

He translated my story of the previous evening to my hostess.

When he told her I'd had the good fortune to locate a spare key to my room, she looked startled and spoke rapidly in her own language.

He turned to me and said:

"Apparently, my dear, there is no key in this house to fit that door. The keys you saw lying on the table and used, are the car keys and their office keys. It seems to me the Divine saved you from a most uncomfortable night."

I asked him why I'd been unable to wake anyone last night. He thought for a while and said:

"I've heard of this before. It would appear that this unfortunate household is under an enchantment, a spell of some kind, meant to trouble and bedevil them. This is the reason why they've sought our assistance. You'll have the opportunity to learn many new lessons and gain valuable experience during your stay in this house."

The next day our seminar began and we had a good crowd.

The new young husband had an interesting experience during his first meditation.

He said later:

"I felt like there was a big hand pushing me down, pushing my head down until I was on my knees, on my face, with my nose in the carpet.

I think God is pushing me down to humble me. I've bashed a few men up in my time, now God is bashing me up!"

When he related this experience to the group, my Teacher laughingly agreed with him.

Many people have experienced this feeling of being forced to their knees during a meditation. I've seen proud and haughty men and women of all races and creeds, myself included, fall to their knees and cry.

MANIFESTATION OF MALICIOUS ENTITY

That night proved to be a most interesting one.

After dinner, for no reason, the security-alarms persisted in going off at regular intervals, necessitating trips to the front door and outside gates.

Each time our host returned from inspecting the property, he remarked:

"There's no-one there.

This has been happening for weeks and it's really worrying me. If it's not the security-alarm, it's the front door-bell ringing with no-one there. It's really scaring my wife."

I remembered the story my grandmother had told me about the spirit manifestation around our house when I was a new born baby.

At some stage during the evening, I attempted to pray in the prayer room and found that each time I approached the door, it slowly and deliberately closed before my very eyes.

As I watched this happening, I felt sick.

I went downstairs to tell my Teacher, who told me that the disturbing spirit was very strongly fighting back, sensing in our presence a real threat to its continuing existence.

He decided we'd increase our prayer, meditation and vigilance.

That night, I slept badly.

I had shadowy nightmares and fleeting impressions of being troubled by some nameless presence. When I tried to wake myself up, it was impossible to do so.

Eventually, during a dream, my Teacher appeared and prayed with me. Only then, could I wake up.

When I woke up, I found myself alone.

I sat up in bed, dazed, looking around me in the early morning light, suddenly painfully aware of a burning sensation on my lower back.

I stood in front of the mirror, wondering why I felt pain and tenderness on my back. Twisting around, I pulled my night-dress away from my skin and cried out. To my horror, I saw dried blood on my night-dress.

"What's happened to me? I've been hurt! There's blood all over me!"

Gently, I explored with my fingers, what appeared to be broken skin.

I dressed shakily, resolving to tell my Teacher at the earliest possible moment and went downstairs to make a coffee.

Later that morning, I told him that a malevolent and malicious spirit entity had manifested during the night to scratch me and to drive me out of the house. This had frightened me very much. Fortunately, however, I'd experienced being attacked by poltergeists and malicious entities before, so I knew I would see this one out.

EFFECTIVE PARENTING

During my visit to West Malaysia, I was invited to appear as a special guest psychologist, at a public lecture organised by a Professor from a local University, to talk about Effective Parenting.

This topic promoted lively debate within the local community.

I've found that parents all around the world have the same worries, fears, hopes and ambitions where their children are concerned. These parents were no exception.

My audience that evening, was made up of Indians, Chinese and Malays.

The Chinese parents in particular, were worried about the stress and high levels of anxiety their children were experiencing at such a young age because school was so competitive.

Many Asian parents were working long hours at two jobs, mother and father both, to save so their children could study in Singapore or Australia, they told me.

These parents wanted the best possible education for their children, as they believed this would ensure freedom for them. They also told me the places at Universities were only for the financially successful and education was costly.

The parents I'd met in Malaysia and Singapore employed tutors for their children after hours, which meant their children studied long hours. As well as having home tutors, Indian children went to language school on Saturdays and Temple on Sundays, so they didn't have the luxury of free time.

In Singapore, schools operated two shifts so it wasn't unusual for an older child to return home in the early evening. I found that, as in any country, the children in a family followed their parents' hard working example.

During my talk, an Indian parent stood up and expressed her fears that her children would not gain a place at University at all, because so many places were reserved for the Malays (called Bumi-putras) who are the bulk of the population in Malaysia. She said Indian parents virtually had to sell their house in order to gain a place at University for their children.

Studying in India was exorbitant too, and many unscrupulous Registrars 'lost' the money or misappropriated it, she said. Her comments about Malays had caused a bit of an uproar within the Malay section of the audience and people began to get heated and upset.

At this stage, a Malay woman asked permission to speak.

As there was a bit of noise, I asked everyone to be calm and loving. I said:

"It feels to me as if a whole lot of fears and traumas are being expressed here, now. Let's all treat each other with love and respect and listen to each other. The common thread that unites parents all over the world, is love. "

They listened while I prayed quietly.

Feeling the energy of love all around her, the Malay woman said:

"Malays get places at University, financial loans and low cost housing because we need it.

We've been enslaved under the British for so long and lacked even the basic necessities of life, let alone any access to education to improve ourselves or our children's chances.

We need help in order to grow up. Our children deserve a chance. It's only been forty years since Merdeka, when we gained our independence and freedom from the British.

It'll take a long time for us to catch up with the rest of the world. Please be aware of this when you criticise."

She sat down, shaking. She'd been so brave and so dignified in her speech that I loved her for saying the words she said.

Privately, I felt that the indigenous people in my home country also deserved a chance to catch up, as the Malay woman had put it. I wondered what a difference it would make to Australia's indigenous people, if Australia had laws that ensured equal access to University places and education for native Australians.

I felt distressed that Australia had the highest infant mortality rate of any developed country in the world.

In Australia, unlike Malaysia, the indigenous people are in the minority. I wondered how different things would be if they were in the majority. It gave me something to think about.

THE EVIL IS EXPOSED VIA A DREAM

During our stay in our host's house, the malevolent feeling was still growing.

After my experience with the manifestation, we decided we'd show our hosts how to conduct a twenty-four hour meditative prayer. This involved calling friends, family and neighbours to assist with a special intention to cleanse and protect the house and the family, due to the conditions in this house.

We all slept in the prayer-room on and off over the next twenty-four hours, and only left the room when necessary.

We ensured that someone was always present for surrendered prayer and meditation in the room. I felt much safer during these prayer and meditation sessions.

During this long vigil, I remember lying on the bare wooden floor of the prayer-room and feeling it was the softest, sweetest bed I'd ever slept on.

I slept a deep and troubled sleep.

While I slept, I dreamt a dream about the dark shape that haunted this house.

I dreamt that a woman once loved the husband desperately and wanted him for her own. He wasn't aware of her passion and treated her as a sister, as he did all women. She wasn't a good woman and nurtured an affinity for the dark side. She was passionate, selfish and determined to get her way.

When the man married a sweet and gentle lady he'd long admired, the other lady went absolutely raving mad with jealousy.

She planted 'charms' (various innocuous looking objects recognised only by those who know, imbued with spells and negative intentions to harm) in the garden of the new home and focussed all her jealousy and revenge on the new bride, who began feeling tired and unwell.

The evil woman preferred to put her considerable psychic energy into destruction. This was the energy haunting the house and its inhabitants. By this haunting, she hoped to destroy the marriage.

When I woke up from the dream, I took my Teacher aside, told him about the dream and conferred with him as to its interpretation. He'd taught me that dreams and visions need to be interpreted carefully, according to at least fourteen possible categories. He agreed with me that there was indeed a person who was responsible for the distress and unhappiness in this house.

He went on to say:

"All we can do for this family is to try to convince them of the power of constant prayer and meditation. They must focus on the Divine and pray all their lives."

He told the family an edited version of my dream, not wanting to frighten them any more than necessary.

He said they must pray, continue to do extended meditations regularly and to stay in touch with him at all costs.

He stressed that he would pray for them, but it was up to them to have faith and to endure their suffering, in this way paying back karma from previous lifetimes. He reminded them their souls could only grow through suffering.

I saw a similar example of this kind of feminine malice and jealousy in Australia later, and realised why some people get very ill after a divorce when feelings run high on one side and the 'jilted' partner is not God-centred. The rapid rise of interest in witchcraft and spells in the Western world is troubling to me, after my experiences in the East. To me, there is a very real and clear danger in the occult; it's not a game and not something to be trifled with by curious amateurs.

I've learnt that the projection of anger and hatred towards another person does have an energetic impact on both parties. It incurs karma for the evil-doer and can trap the soul in eternal earth-bound misery after death of the physical body.

The only protection is to live a God-centred life, to meditate and to follow a spiritual practice.

The only answer to any questions on this subject is Love.

MY VISION OF THE LOST GIRL
Before we left, we met with the distraught parents of the lost girl.

They told us their sixteen year old daughter had disappeared from their home one day and they feared she was dead.

"We've contacted a saint in India, a Malay and a Thai bomoh and an Indonesian dukun for information and assistance on our girl. We both feel confident that you can help us," the girl's father said.

They handed me a photograph of their daughter and a blouse that belonged to her, for me to receive information.

On an inner level, I knew I was undergoing another test my Teacher had set me, by bringing me to West Malaysia with him and by introducing me to the lost girl's parents.

I thought:

"My sabbatical in Malaysia is almost over.

My Thesis, my book is almost done.

My Teacher's giving me a final exam.

I'm going to receive my Master's degree if I get this one right!"

MY TEACHER DISAGREES

As I held the girl's photograph and pink blouse in my hand, I saw the girl's face in my mind encircled by a green and golden light again.

"She's alive and she's all right!" I thought, not for the first time.

I felt so positive about this that I exclaimed aloud:

"She's alive! I know she's alive."

My Teacher said:

"I fear you are very much mistaken, my dear. I disagree with your findings."

I knew I was right! How could I be right and my Teacher be wrong? It didn't make any sense to me.

My mind in turmoil, my face hot with embarrassment and humiliation, I got up and left the room, leaving my Teacher to make some sort of explanation to the girl's poor parents.

Over the next few days, I could think of nothing else.

Somehow, I managed to keep my feelings to myself. My Teacher was quiet and distant.

During the night, I kept having vivid dreams of the young girl whose face I knew so well by now, calling to me and saying:

"I'm all right, tell Daddy I'm all right. Ask him to forgive me, I love him and Mummy too."

As I'd been taught to do, I kept testing the source of my information and my vision.

To me, the information and the vision I was receiving appeared to come from a very high source.

I felt sure about this.

Why then, did my Teacher disagree with me and say I was mistaken?

Tossing and turning in sleep, I had another dream, where I saw a forest of trees and what looked like a large dam near a little village.

I saw what I knew to be a bomoh, watching me.

I saw an old lady watching some chickens scratching in the dirt around a house on stilts.

I saw a baby in a nappy running around the yard, and always I saw and heard the girl calling to me.

In my dreams and in my visions, the lost girl was very much alive and living a new life in another place.

Shortly after this, the girl's father asked me if I would meet with the Malay bomoh to discuss my visions and dreams.

I felt apprehensive and a little excited about the prospect of meeting a real live bomoh.

THE MALAY BOMOH

The man who came to the door next morning was quite a lot younger than I'd expected, and ordinary-looking, apart from his piercing eyes.

He wore Malay dress, a long white shirt over a white sarong, and a white conical cap which told me he was a 'Haji' i.e. he'd done his religious pilgrimage to Mecca as a Muslim.

He smiled warmly, bowed deeply and sat down opposite me.

His eyes were almost hypnotic in their intensity.

We had a cup of coffee together and regarded each other curiously and shyly.

He spoke no English and as I had little Malay, my Teacher agreed to translate for us.

The young bomoh asked:

"Please ask her, how does she see?"

I replied:

"I have visions, I see pictures in my mind and I have dreams that tell me things. I've seen things since I was a child."

In reply, he said through my Teacher:

"I also see pictures in my mind."

He then asked:

"What religion does she follow?"

My Teacher told him I was a Christian.

The bomoh said:

"Does she pray? Tell her I am a Muslim. Tell her I pray five times a day and I look at my Holy Book, the Holy Koran and I see visions that help me to find missing people and to locate bodies.

I never do bad things, I only do love spells for people.

Tell the lady there are many others who do bad things for money. I cannot and will not do bad things for money.

Ask her, does she do spells?"

At this point, my Teacher laughed and told the young man I didn't do spells under any circumstances.

I was fascinated by the whole conversation and asked my Teacher to tell the young man:

"I'm glad to know you don't do bad things, neither do I.

I read the Holy Bible of the Christians. I've recently begun reading your Holy Koran.

As my Teacher has told you, it's not possible for me to do any spells at all, I pray for people."

His animated face and manner told me he was as interested in my words as I was in his. We just sat and smiled at each other for a while.

After a few minutes, he rose to his feet, bowed and said:

"I will pray now before I can see about the girl. It may take some time, please wait for me."

He picked up a prayer mat he'd brought with him and asked:

"Where is the bathroom? I must wash and prepare myself to pray."

When our hostess took him out of the room to wash and pray, we waited silently, my Teacher, the girl's father and I.

My Teacher looked at me thoughtfully and I wondered, not for the first time, what he was thinking. Was he angry with me and disappointed? How had I gone wrong? Had I gone wrong? Was I being stubborn? Why didn't we get the same answer?

I wondered why I couldn't just say:

"I got it wrong, you're right as you always are."

I couldn't do it! I wanted to, but I couldn't.

THE BOMOH'S VISION

After about twenty minutes, the bomoh returned.

He spoke quietly to my Teacher, looking at me every now and again. My Teacher translated:

"He says he's seen the girl alive, as you did. He believes she's alive. He says he also saw a large body of water and trees where she's living. He says he recognises the place, it's near here. He's asked me to check his vision out with you."

The young man looked at me expectantly.

I felt faint. I thought:

"Thank God, the bomoh's a famous man and he thinks she's alive. Maybe I'm right!"

I excitedly reminded my Teacher of my first vision of the girl in KL and asked him to tell the bomoh what I'd seen.

When he did this, the bomoh nodded his head excitedly and said:

"Yes, she is right. It is a dam and I know where it is! Let's go now and we'll look. I know where to look now."

As we all rose to leave, my Teacher said to me:

"No, not you, my dear. You're not coming, I want you to stay here and wait for us."

I was disappointed and upset at being asked to stay behind since I'd been looking forward to finding the girl and I'd felt a lot better since the bomoh agreed with my vision. However, I obeyed. My Teacher told me later he felt the bomoh was 'charming' me and that it wasn't a good idea to have anything further to do with a bomoh at this stage of my spiritual development.

While they were away, I felt very confused and upset.

My Teacher was still saying my test was wrong and he seemed to disagree with the bomoh, too.

Before he'd left, he'd reminded me of how I'd once, at the beginning of my association with him, done a reading on a friend of his who'd been dead for thirty years and had not been able to tell if he were alive or dead, at the time of the reading.

At the time, he was agreeably surprised that I was able to read a person who had been dead for thirty years, just as easily as if he were still alive. He said:

"I've never met anyone else who could do this. You can read the dead."

He said to me:

"How do you know this time, that what you're receiving is correct and that the girl is still alive?"

I thought for a while and replied:

"Because this time, I tested the source of my information the way you've taught me to do. The source is very high.

I also asked the Divine within me for the correct answer, a yes or a no, is she alive or dead, and I believe with all my heart that I've received the right answer. The girl is alive."

He stared at me intently, then walked away to join the others.

The men returned much later. Led by the bomoh, they'd found the dam, the trees which were part of a rubber plantation and the village, all as I'd described it. However, they'd been unable to find a trace of the girl.

The bomoh had even stopped at all the Mosques along the way and spoken to all the Imams who knew nothing. No good. We were all disappointed.

The bomoh and I said a shy good-bye to each other.

BACK IN KL

After my return from West Malaysia, I sat in my apartment alone, not wanting to talk to anyone about my experiences.

It had taken enormous faith and courage to stand against my Teacher in this instance, to speak my truth, to stand by the results of my test that said the girl was alive. I felt the same way as I had in Sydney earlier that year, when we'd disagreed in our interpretation of a lady's dream.

I felt as if my heart was breaking.

Apparently, the senior members of the meditation group in KL agreed with my Teacher and felt I was in error.

Furthermore, I learnt that other intuitive people under my Teacher's guidance in several other countries, also believed I was in error and ego.

I felt truly alone.

CHAPTER 16

GOODBYE

I'M GOING HOME!

It was now time for me to leave Malaysia and my Teacher and fly home.

My twelve months of intensive study, personal and spiritual growth, meditation and work experience was now over.

On the morning of my departure, I said a sad goodbye to my Teacher. After our disagreement over the lost girl, I'd felt unable to talk to him the way I used to.

Before I left he told me gently:

"Don't let your heart be troubled. Everything that's happened to you is God's Will, my dear.

Don't say goodbye to me.

Who knows, perhaps we shall see each other again.

May God be with you, my dear child."

As always, he didn't appear to be at all troubled, just calm, serene and detached.

As a friend drove me to the airport I thought:

"I'll never see Malaysia again. How sad it is to leave in this way."

Despite how I felt, I was extremely grateful to have had the opportunity to study in Malaysia, yet was very glad to be going home.

Once in the departure lounge of the Terminal, an old, tired looking Indian gentleman in old, tired looking clothes attracted my attention. He seemed to stand out from the well dressed crowd in his faded clothes and dignified manner.

BROTHER INDIA

On the 'plane, once seated, I closed my eyes and pretended to be asleep, not wanting to talk to anyone as I was completely pre-occupied with my own thoughts and feelings.

When the flight attendant arrived with a dinner tray, I decided to eat.

When I'd opened my eyes, I'd been surprised to see the elderly, Indian gentleman from the departure lounge, sitting beside me.

He was struggling with the plastic wrapper on his orange juice container, without success.

I watched him for a while, then leaned over and said:

"Here, do allow me to assist you."

He smiled at me gratefully and said:

"What a wonderful little cup this is. It's made of plastic, isn't it? I've not seen plastic before, though I have heard about it. You remind me so much of my dear wife, Christine, who was always doing little things for me I couldn't do for myself.

She just died recently you know," and he began to cry.

I thought:"Oh, dear! Poor man," and put my hand over his brown, leathery old hand.

During the long night flight, my new friend and I talked and listened to each others troubles while the other passengers slept and snored all around us.

It's my feeling the Divine put an angel, in the seat next to me that night to comfort, inspire and support me.

He told me he was a Christian and lived in a little village in India. His flight from India to KL was his first ever and I was the first white lady he'd ever spoken to.

His English was flowery, old-fashioned, courteous and very good.

He went on:"After my wife died, I received a letter from a Christian group in Tasmania who'd heard about my Bible classes for poor Indian children.

These good people sent me the money for clothes and an airline ticket to Australia to talk about my work and my village."

He added:"As a child, I was brought up by Christian missionaries who taught me to love Jesus with a passion. Jesus is my guru.

My wife and I were desperately poor all our lives. This didn't trouble us at all, because we believed that God would always provide our daily bread.

We only had one little boy and when he was weaned from his mother, we prayed daily for milk for our child and through God's grace, it always came."

I forgot my own troubles while I listened to his life story of faith, hardship and poverty.

I told him my story too and he marvelled at all the things that had happened to me, since I was a child.

When I told him about the way I'd learned to pray for the elevation of our departed loved one's souls, we prayed for his wife together. We didn't sleep at all during the long night flying over the sea to Australia.

When morning came, we shared an early breakfast and when the plane landed, as I prepared to leave, he took my hand and said:

"I feel you'll see your Teacher again this lifetime. I also feel it will be all right between you two, again.

Trust in God, remember to keep your eyes on Jesus and the lonely path He walked, dear sister, and you'll never lose your way."

As we parted, I thanked my new friend and pressed a one hundred dollar note into his hand to buy something in Australia. He was very grateful.

MY DARK NIGHT OF THE SOUL

After arriving home in Melbourne, I had a long rest and a peaceful time with my family.

I did a lot of quiet prayer and surrendered meditation on my own. I needed to be alone.

I found I didn't want to be with others, as I really needed time to internalise everything that had happened to me in Malaysia.

I found it difficult to find words to express my feelings and relate my experiences to anyone else.

I knew I'd changed so much during my time away and sensed that everyone else had stayed the same.

I suffered terribly with the thought that my Teacher and I had parted from each other in a sad way, due to our disagreement over the lost girl.

No matter how hard I thought about it, I couldn't change my conviction of having received the correct information.

The greatest part of the suffering came from the feeling of alienation, of being alone and not being supported by others who loved and respected him. I felt rejected by everyone.

The only comfort I found was in meditation, where I felt strongly a Divine and loving presence upholding and strengthening me.

During this time of loneliness and suffering, only one thing remained constant, the same thing that had remained constant all my life.

My guiding star, the light in my darkness, was the Divine voice inside my heart saying:

"Don't be afraid, I am at your back. You can't fall when I'm holding you up, my beloved one."

So, I stood firm, believing in myself and following the inner guidance that told me God loved me, and I was all right.

I realised I had to let go of what everyone else thought, said and believed about me.

I even had to let go of what my beloved Teacher thought about me.

I began to understand that when the Divine is awakened within you, you're not alone anymore.

Everywhere I went it seemed, I heard that popular song: "You are not alone, I am here with you," and I knew those words were for me from my Beloved, the Divine! He was all around me.

I realised He'd never left me alone, not once, not for a moment in my entire life.

For as long as I could remember, He'd been sending guardians, angels and Teachers to inspire and motivate me until my soul had enough Light and enough energy to stand alone.

This was the time.

I knew this was the test of my soul, to believe in myself, to follow my own truth.

During this time, my grandmother's words spoke in my heart often:

"To thine own Self be true, my darling," and now I finally understood.

I understood that I'd always been looking outside of myself for love, acceptance and approval.

I'd sought the friendship and love of others.

Now I knew that no-one and nothing else could give me the love that I needed.

I knew that the love I had been searching for was now awakened within myself. Knowing this, I could let go of everything.

This realisation liberated me totally, once and for all.

I knew we are all born alone, and we all die alone.

We each have our own unique mission and purpose.

I knew the only reason for living was to love myself, to be guided by the Divine within myself.

I remembered how my Teacher used to say to me: "Love is God and God is Love."

I knew without a doubt, I loved God and God loved me.

I was soon to discover that once I'd let go of my Teacher's love and approval forever, I would gain the love and approval from him, I'd been seeking.

I SEE MY TEACHER AGAIN

In late December, a friend from Sydney rang to tell me my Teacher was attending the January Retreat in Australia and had requested that I attend.

After prayer and meditation, I felt it was God's Will for us to meet one more time.

So, I went.

I hadn't seen him for five months.

When he came into the room, he was dressed in the same snowy white suit he'd been wearing when we first met this lifetime in late November 1994.

It felt as if a hundred years had passed since then.

So much had happened to me in such a short space of time that I was no longer the same person.

He walked towards me, smiling, as if we'd only parted yesterday.

As he greeted me, he held out his hands to take mine and said:

"How I've looked forward to seeing you again, my dear.

I've thought of you often, since we parted. You've been in my prayers every day.

Do you remember I told you the last time we were together, to stop saying goodbye to me? Well, here we are again.

How are you, my child? Are you well? You look a bit tired."

I told him I'd had a lovely time being back home again, I was well and I'd made peace with myself. He understood what I was saying.

He was pleased.

He said:"We need to talk to each other privately. Let's meet after the lectures finish tonight. Would you eat with me this evening and we can talk afterwards?"

I agreed willingly.

That night, we ate at the same table and chatted to the people who'd attended the retreat from all over Australia.

It was a good way to have all the committed meditators in one place. Such an energy radiated from everyone at such times that we were all uplifted and motivated and basked in pure love.

It was a wonderful experience for the Australians to have our Teacher leading meditation again, as everyone had missed his warmth and humour. We ate in a real party atmosphere and everyone was warm and friendly to me.

After dinner, we excused ourselves and sat in a little parlour to talk. I wondered why he wanted to talk to me privately.

He began:

"I want you to know, dear child, you were right all along about the lost girl.

I knew you were right.

The girl and her new husband have contacted her family and all are reunited.

It's just as you said. The girl and the young man ran away to marry, feeling that her family would not accept him, and his family would not accept her.

After the Malay bomoh's enquiries, the girl and her young husband realised that her family needed to know she was alive and well in her new life. All is well.

You'll be glad to know Love has had its way."

During this extraordinary conversation, I stared at him, open-mouthed.

He went on:

"I set you your highest test in West Malaysia, my dear. It was time to see if you could go your way without me.

I felt you had enough courage, enough love for yourself and enough faith in the Divine's messages to stand against even me, your Teacher.

I knew all along the girl was all right. I knew your visions and your dreams were indeed coming from a high source.

It's my feeling you have the potential to go very far, as I've always told you.

Your final test was to let go of me, to let go of my approval and love for you, to cling to your belief in what you receive.

Your faith in God was tested to the utmost.

All that matters for you now, is to know that the Divine communicates with you and you communicate with it."

I was speechless!

My heart was bursting.

I felt hot all over, totally enveloped in his energy and love, just as I had when I'd first met him.

All I could think was:

"I got it right! He's pleased with me!"

Just when I'd finally let go forever of his love and approval, I had it!

He continued:

"You passed all the tests I set for you all along the way.

I saw your struggle, I saw your suffering and I felt for you, as my Teacher once felt for me.

Do you remember the dream you had when we first met?"

MY DREAM

I'd once had a dream where I took my Teacher to my old Primary School, to the room I'd studied in as a child.

In the dream, I took out a tiny knife and accidentally cut him with it on his chest. I was terribly upset at what I'd done, but he'd put his hand on the little cut, laughed and it was healed.

I'd found this dream extraordinary at the time and when I'd told him about it, he'd explained:

" The dream means you're a child in spirituality, you're the student and I'm your Teacher.

For your growth, you'll wound me in little ways that the Divine in me will heal.

For all the hurts you may give me, remember I've forgiven you already.

This is a very good dream, my dear."

After we'd discussed the dream, he'd told me he'd loved his Teacher very much, and when the Divine decided he was ready to leave his Teacher and go out on his own, the other students didn't understand.

He'd told me he'd been criticised and judged by the ones who stayed.

I said: "I remember the dream very well and your interpretation. I also remember how you told me you were criticised by your Teacher's other students for leaving."

My Teacher then told me he'd once had a very similar conversation with his Teacher to the one we were having now.

He also told me he understood very well how I would be judged by his other students for leaving him.

I was grateful he spoke to me that way that night.

I cherished his words and remembered them. I remember them still.

'GOOD-BYE'

My Teacher and I said 'goodbye' to each other at a friend's house a little later and he blessed me.

His parting words to me were:

"Be brave, be strong, be positive, be confident! Have no fear. You'll be faced with many challenges and you'll meet them all. This is only the beginning of your new life.

Wherever you go, whatever you do, I want you to know my hand is always at your back, guiding and supporting you.

May God be with you always, my beloved child."

I knelt down and touched his feet.

He raised me up, smiled at me and walked away, smiling.

SURRENDERED MEDITATION

THE WAY TO THE DIVINE

Many books have been written about Meditation and its myriad benefits to health, emotional balance, mental acuity, peace of mind and harmonious relationships.

The **primary** purpose of Meditation is to establish a tangible link with the **Divine** energy that created us.

It's only through a spontaneous and submissive technique of Meditation that we can connect with the **Divine** energy. It's impossible for us to reach the **Divine** through the limitation, the physical barrier of the Conscious Mind. It's a gross illusion to believe that the **Divine** can be contacted via a Beta brain-wave frequency, i.e. the Conscious State. While we are in a Beta brain-wave frequency Conscious State, we stay in the material, physical realm.

When we chant a mantra, imagine, visualise, or focus on a particular area of the physical body, we're totally deluding ourselves. We're actually prisoners of our own Conscious Minds. When we can totally submit and surrender our Consciousness, we are able to reach the Alpha brain wave Frequency State, which is where the **Divine** is to be found. This is the *beginning* of Meditation.

Mankind has been functioning at a gross physical level on a dense physical vibration for centuries, using barely 7 to 10 percent of his **Divine** potential. Through a system of gentle, Surrendered Meditation, you are awakened to a higher level of Consciousness, where you are able to access and use the 90 to 93 percent of your **Superconscious Divine Potential** in miraculous and extraordinary ways.

FOR EXAMPLE:

Dreams and visions will guide you every moment of your life.

You'll be able to tap into Divine intuition and become clairvoyant.

You'll develop the precious gift of Discernment, i.e. the ability to test persons, situations and circumstances in all areas of your life to your great advantage.

You'll have the potential to enjoy vibrant health and well being of Body, Mind and Spirit.

You have the potential to become a Self-Realised person, i.e. to realise your authentic, **Divine** nature. This is the primary purpose of your existence, to connect with the **Divine Creator** Who made you.

Surrendered Meditation Is:
- ♥ **Simple**
- ♥ **Natural**
- ♥ **Easy**
- ♥ **Effortless**
- ♥ **Spontaneous**
- ♥ **Gentle**

♥ **Vibrant**
♥ **Active**
♥ **Responsive**
♥ **Dynamic, leading to a change of state**

TO BEGIN THE MEDITATION

Relax, sit in a comfortable position, uncross your arms and legs, and allow yourself to be guided from within to stand or to lie down, then say these simple words to begin the Meditation:

> "If it be Thy Will, may we be attuned to pure Divine Love from the Highest Source.
> May everything that is not Divine Love now leave us.
> Through this attunement to Divine Love, may we be blessed, cleansed and healed, balanced and integrated, made truly whole and well in all aspects of Body, Mind and Spirit.
> If it be Thy Will may this now happen."

After having said these words, just let go as deeply as possible and allow yourself to relax. During the period of quiet contemplation, thoughts may come and go. Just observe their coming and going. It is natural for the Mind to express itself through thoughts. These thoughts gradually become less and less important as the surrender becomes deeper and deeper.

This gentle Surrendered Meditation is **responsive** in nature. It's a two-way interactive process between you and the **Divine**.

After relaxing and letting go, you'll receive evidence, proof of your attunement to the **Divine.** This proof comes as a response, a movement, a feeling. You'll have an **experience.**

Evidence of this Attunement:
- ♥ **Yawning, which signifies a change of state.**
- ♥ **Coughing or a tickling in the throat.**
- ♥ **Watering of the eyes, crying.**
- ♥ **Emotion, which can be peaceful, or its opposite, disturbed feelings.**
- ♥ **Burping, sighing.**
- ♥ **Twitches in muscles.**
- ♥ **Tingling, burning vibrations.**
- ♥ **Change of temperature, feeling hot or feeling cold.**
- ♥ **A feeling of heaviness, or of lightness and floating.**
- ♥ **Stiffness in the nape of the neck.**
- ♥ **A headache.**
- ♥ **Upset stomach, rumbling.**
- ♥ **Visions, seeing images and colours.**
- ♥ **Hearing sounds like music.**
- ♥ **Changes in ear pressure.**
- ♥ **Goose bumps or skin prickling.**

Some of these responses or reactions may be extremely subtle and almost imperceptible in some people and extremely gross and noticeable in other people.

The important thing to note is that however slight, there will definitely be a change of state. This **change**

of state sets the technique of Surrendered Meditation apart from any other technique.

Time and practice will perfect the technique.

Please note that the best results come from practising with a partner or with a group of people who have already been attuned to the frequency of **Divine Love**.

This technique has the potential to heal Body, Mind and Spirit. It also offers the potential for Spiritual development and ultimately Enlightenment, in total adherence with the teachings of the entire world's Masters.

All the Scriptures of the World emphasise surrender, death and re-birth as the way to liberation of the Soul. Through surrendering to **Divine Love**, you have the potential to be re-born to a higher level of consciousness.

PRAYER FOR DECEASED PERSONS

"Dear Lord God, if it be Thy Will, may we now be attuned to the Highest and the Purest Source of Pure Divine Love."

Now address the soul of the disembodied spirit or deceased loved one:

"You are now deceased. Your life on Earth is now over. The Earth realm is only for living human beings. You are now commanded to leave the Earth realm. Go to the next realm of your existence with those Beings whose duty it is to guide you. No longer will you haunt humans, human homes, human possessions or inhabit the Earth in this form. Go now by order of the Divine, the Sublime. If you refuse to leave, you are condemned. Go now. If it be Thy Will, dear Lord God, may this now happen."

After having said these words, wait for a few minutes, then do the following cleansing meditation.

"Dear Lord God, if it be Thy Will, if we may have taken on any heaviness, or any energies not from Divine Love, may it now be totally removed from us and sent back to its source. May we be cleansed and healed, made whole and well in Body, Mind and Spirit. If it be Thy Will, may this now happen."

Let go and receive the cleansing.